Accession no.
36124562

D1759781

WITHDRAW

WITHDRAWN

Spirit Possession and Trance

Continuum Advances in Religious Studies
Series Editors:
James Cox and Peggy Morgan

Spirit Possession and Trance

New Interdisciplinary Perspectives

Edited by

Bettina E. Schmidt and Lucy Huskinson

LIS LIBRARY

Date	Fund
21/7/10	r

Order No
2130609

University of Chester

continuum

Continuum International Publishing Group
The Tower Building   80 Maiden Lane, Suite 704
11 York Road   New York
London SE1 7NX   NY10038

www.continuumbooks.com

Copyright © Bettina E. Schmidt, Lucy Huskinson and Contributors,
2010

All rights reserved. No part of this publication may be reproduced or
transmitted in any form or by any means, electronic or mechanical,
including photocopying, recording or any information
storage or retrieval system, without prior permission
in writing from the publishers.

British Library Cataloguing-in-Publication Data
A catalogue record for this book is available from the British Library

ISBN: HB: 978-0-8264-3574-3

Library of Congress Cataloging-in-Publication Data
Spirit possession and trance : new interdisciplinary perspectives /
edited by Bettina Schmidt and Lucy Huskinson.
    p. cm.
  ISBN-13: 978-0-8264-3574-3 (HB)
  ISBN-10: 0-8264-3574-2 (HB)
1. Spirit possession.   2. Trance.   3. Altered states of
consciousness.   I. Schmidt, Bettina E.   II. Huskinson, Lucy, 1976–
  BL482.S63 2010
  204′.2—dc22   2009035017

Typeset by RefineCatch Limited, Bungay, Suffolk
Printed in Great Britain by the MPG Books Group, Bodmin and King's Lynn

Contributors

Crystal Addey (Bristol University)

Saër Maty Bâ (University of St Andrews)

Louise Child (Cardiff University)

Andrew Dawson (Lancaster University)

Sarah Goldingay (Exeter University)

David Gordon Wilson (University of Edinburgh)

Kim Groop (Åbo Akademi University)

Graham Harvey (The Open University)

Lucy Huskinson (Bangor University)

Geoffrey Samuel (Cardiff University)

Bettina E. Schmidt (Bangor University)

Marja Tiilikainen (University of Helsinki)

Contents

Acknowledgements

The editors are especially grateful to Linda Jones for her assistance; to Kirsty Schaper and Tom Crick at Continuum for their support throughout the various stages of the book's production; and also to Peggy Morgan, James Cox and Greg Allen as editors of the *Advances in Religious Studies* series. The editors also wish to thank the participants of the *New Interpretations of Spirit Possession* conference (May 2008, Bangor University, UK), whose lively debates are captured within this volume; and the School of Theology and Religious Studies at Bangor University for enabling it to happen.

Chapter 1

Introduction

Lucy Huskinson and Bettina E. Schmidt

As this multidisciplinary volume testifies, spirit possession and trance incite curiosity and debate across academic fields and subject areas. The fascination with such phenomena has seen numerous works published on them, all of which have inevitably recast spirit possession and trance according to their own disciplinary bias. Collectively these works have been guided by a variety of presumptions to arrive at a multitude of conclusions. The range of – often competing – perspectives on the subject matter has made the phenomena of spirit possession and trance as elusive as ever, and subsequently, the debate over its nature and role continues to be rich, varied and heated. Tensions persist between the different viewpoints, and satisfactory compromise is hard to come by. How might we, for instance, begin to reconcile the tendency in anthropology and religious studies to regard spirit possession and trance positively as honourable customs that facilitate community, with the more negative tendency of Western psychiatry to pathologize such phenomena as disorders of the individual mind? Likewise, how can we resolve the apparent contradiction within anthropological portrayals of women, which, on the one hand, often regards spirit possession and trance as a mechanism of social empowerment for women, and on the other, tends to perceive possessed women as 'mad, bad and sad'?[1] Furthermore, if there is no phenomenological difference between possession by the Holy Spirit and possession by African deities, on what impartial basis can we distinguish between the two?

Before we can begin to enter into such debates that surround spirit possession and trance, we must attempt to clarify what we mean by these terms and determine the kinds of experience to which they refer. However, straightforward questioning such as this tends to yield as many more questions as it does a myriad of competing answers. For instance, as soon as we attempt to define experiences of spirit possession or trance, we are led immediately to a series of questions that question the very premise of our task. Thus, what exactly do we mean by 'spirit'? To what extent should we differentiate between spirit possession and trance? Furthermore, can we even speak of possession and trance as *experiences* per se, if they are thought to preclude conscious awareness in the one who is possessed or *loses himself* or *herself* in trance? There are no definitive answers to these questions, and consequently there is no ultimate account or interpretation of spirit possession and trance. The possibility of arriving at a convincing and coherent interpretation of possession and trance is fraught with difficulty from the outset. So where do we begin and how does this volume contribute to our understanding of these elusive phenomena?

Early Interpretations of Spirit Possession and Trance

A good place to start is with the early anthropological interpretations of spirit possession and trance, for it is upon the interpretations of such pioneers in the field as James Frazer and Mircea Eliade that schools of thought on the subject have been established. Likewise, it is in contrast to these interpretations that our long-held prejudices and assumptions about spirit possession and trance can be exposed and overcome: thereby paving the way for new interpretations, such as those within this volume.

James G. Frazer, arguably the father of modern anthropological studies in comparative religion, argues for the universality of spirit possession in his famous work *The Golden Bough* (1890). After noting that 'the belief in temporary incarnation or inspiration is worldwide', he describes what may be considered a *typical* anthropological interpretation of possession experience:

> Certain persons are supposed to be possessed from time to time by a spirit or deity; while the possession lasts, their own personality lies in abeyance; the presence of the spirit is revealed by convulsive shiverings and shakings of the man's whole body, by wild gestures and excited looks, all of which are referred, not to the man himself, but to the spirit. (Frazer 1911 [1890], p. 93)

Although anthropological study of spirit possession and trance has developed considerably since Frazer's conclusion that all spirit possessions are faked – consciously or unconsciously (in order to draw attention to the socially disadvantaged person who is 'possessed') – his description above (when ignoring its gender prejudice) can be regarded as a conventional account of spirit possession. Indeed, while Frazer himself is thought to be an 'armchair' anthropologist, having conducted little – if any – practical fieldwork to support his research (and is unlikely to have observed anybody undergoing the possession experience he describes), his description is corroborated by the fieldwork of other anthropologists. Take for example the description by Alfred Métraux, who in stark contrast to Frazer was particularly renowned for his excellent ethnographic skills:

> People possessed start by giving an impression of having lost control of their motor system. Shaken by spasmodic convulsions, they pitch forward, as though projected by a spring, turn frantically round and round, stiffen and stay still with body bent forward, sway, stagger, save themselves, again lose balance, only to fall finally in a state of semi-consciousness. Sometimes such attacks are sudden, sometimes they are heralded by preliminary signs: a vacant or anguished expression, mild trembling, panting breath or drops of sweat on the brow; the face becomes tense or suffering. (Métraux 1958, pp. 120–1)

Although Métraux's description is of a particular Haitian Vodou possession that he himself observed, it comprises characteristics of behaviour that we might presume to find in any apparent case of spirit possession.

Two decades after Frazer wrote of the 'worldwide belief' in spirit possession, T. K. Oesterreich – in what was the first cross-cultural study of possession (1921, in German) – argued for the 'constant nature' of spirit possession throughout time and across cultures. He did so through the comparative analysis of descriptions of possession from the New Testament with accounts from other historical, ethnographic, cultural and religious contexts. One description that he cites from a sixteenth-century case of possession is a particularly striking elaboration of the characteristic behaviour of the possessed person described by Frazer (and Métraux) above:

> The latter (a girl) was possessed by the demon who often threw her to the ground as if she had the falling sickness. Soon the demon began to speak with her mouth and said things inhuman and marvellous which may not be repeated. . . . The girl had always shown herself patient, she had often prayed to God. But when she had called upon the name of Jesus to deliver her, the evil spirit manifested himself anew, he had taken possession of her eyes which he made start out her head, had twisted her tongue and pulled it more than eight inches out of her mouth, and turned her face towards her back with an expression so pitiful that it would have

melted a stone. All the priests of the place and from round about came and spoke to her, but the devil replied to them with a contempt which exceeded all bounds, and when he was questioned about Jesus he made a reply of such derision that it cannot be set down. (Oesterreich 1930, p. 9)

Early accounts of spirit possession, such as we find in Frazer and Oesterreich, describe those characteristics that we have come to associate with such phenomena – the exaggerated bodily motions, the contorted facial expressions and sudden intrusion of an unfamiliar personality. Oesterreich provides extensive cross-cultural evidence to substantiate what we may now regard as a typical presentation of possession. From his analysis of their common presentation he postulated three principal external ways in which spirit possession manifests itself: where the physiognomy of the person changes (such as the distorted feature of the face or body); where the person's voice changes (for instance, when 'the feminine voice is transformed into a bass one', 1930, p. 20); and where the person adopts an ego-personality that is 'opposed' to the 'normal' one so that the person speaks with the voice of the possessing spirit and not from his or her own (1930, p. 21).

Oesterreich writes with conviction and his interpretation of possession is compelling, and yet, even at this early stage of scholarship on spirit possession, his views, although influential, were not regarded as conclusive. A common consensus or definition of spirit possession has eluded scholars from the beginning of its academic study. To this day the parameters of a workable definition of spirit possession are wide-ranging and difficult to formulate. As Vincent Crapanzano in his definition of 'spirit possession' in *Encyclopedia of Religion* (2005) writes:

Spirit possession may be broadly defined as any altered or unusual state of consciousness and allied behaviour that is indigenously understood in terms of the influence of an alien spirit, demon, or deity.[2] (2005, p. 8687)

Despite his appeal to a broad definition of spirit possession, Crapanzano continues in his definition to note that it does not encompass trance. Crapanzano differentiates between possession and trance, claiming for their distinct nature on the grounds that they comprise different states of altered consciousness. In doing so, Crapanzano adopts a division of terms that can be traced back to Mircea Eliade, to whom we now turn.

Distinguishing between possession and trance

In *Shamanism: Archaic Technique of Ecstasy* (1951, original French), Eliade distinguishes between shaman and possession priest based on an etic categorization of the ecstatic experience; that is to say, on the basis of whether the person sends a spirit on a journey (shaman) or whether he or she receives a spirit within his or her body (possession priest). From his extensive survey of then-existing studies of shamanism and possession Eliade claims:

> We were able to find that the specific element of shamanism is not the embodiment of 'spirits' by the shaman, but the ecstasy induced by his ascent to the sky or descent to the underworld; incarnating spirits and being 'possessed' by spirits are universally disseminated phenomena, but they do not necessarily belong to shamanism in the strict sense. (Eliade 1989 [1964], pp. 499–500)

However, I. M. Lewis, in his influential work *Ecstatic Religion: A Study of Shamanism and Spirit Possession* (1971), firmly rejects Eliade's dichotomy on the basis that Eliade has apparently misread the relevant primary sources (Lewis 2003 [1971], p. xiii). Contrary to Eliade's claim, Lewis insists that shamans – like Eliade's 'possession priest' – can also become possessed. However, instead of dissolving fully the dichotomy of shaman and possession priest, Lewis proffers his own distinction between them, a distinction that is determined by the degree of control the practitioner has over the spirit. Thus, according to Lewis, while possession priests have little or no control during the possession, shamans are in command of the spirits.

At approximately the same time as Lewis was making these claims, the anthropologist Erika Bourguignon began to analyse her own observations on possession and trance and deduced from these her own criteria for their dissimilarity. Bourguignon regarded the difference in very general terms, by associating trance with 'psychobiological' *behaviour* (1973, p. 11; specifically, 'alterations or discontinuity in consciousness, awareness, personality, or other aspects of psychological functioning'; 1976, p. 8), and possession with cultural *belief* ('when the people in question hold that a given person is changed in some way through the presence in or on him of a spirit entity or power, other than his own personality, soul, self or the like'; 1976, p. 8). Bourguignon's distinction has been heavily criticized. Michael Lambek, for instance, maintains that her separation of possession and trance is heuristic and somewhat arbitrary (1989, p. 37, see also Lambek 1980). In refutation of Bourguignon's classification, Lambek argues that if trance is to carry any meaning, it must be 'shaped by culture' (1989, p. 40); it must therefore share similar construction to possession as Bourguignon conceived it. In contradistinction to Bourguignon, Lambek maintains that trance and possession cannot be distinguished and regarded in isolation. With reference to Clifford Geertz, he asserts:

> [T]rance is not prior to spirit possession in either a logical or causal sense, and possession cannot be viewed as a 'model of' trance unless it is also well understood that it is equally a 'model for' trance . . . (1989, p. 40)

Despite his many critics, the legacy of Eliade continues to influence debates surrounding the dichotomy of spirit possession and trance. A variety of systems that classify the apparent difference between the terms have been – and continue to be – proposed with varying success in their academic reception. Such division of terms can be found within the pages of this book, and, indeed, the very title of this work – *Spirit Possession and Trance: New Interdisciplinary Perspectives* – presupposes their dichotomy. And yet, in offering *new* interpretations of spirit possession and trance we have opened, and have actively encouraged, a revaluation of such dichotomy and the overcoming of presumption. It is, as we continue to claim, within the dialogue and tension of competing perspectives that creative and fertile interpretations of spirit possession and trance can develop.

New Approaches to Trance and Spirit Possession

Definitions of spirit possession and trance according to their stark contrast and stringent separation can lead to misleading and superficial interpretations as various case studies demonstrate. When confronted with the ethnographic reality such dichotomy cannot be sustained. Experiences of supposed possession and trance phenomena are often too diverse and complex to lend themselves to adequate categorization. For instance, religious experience in the Americas was divided for a long time according to the dichotomy of shamanism versus possession. Thus, while Amerindian religious experience was categorized as shamanistic, Afro-American – as with African – religious experience was identified as possession. However, the Garifuna – formerly labelled Black Caribs – do not fit either side of the dichotomy, but encompass both. Thus, the anthropologist Paul Christopher Johnson notes, that the *buyei* (shaman/priest) 'exhibit features of both entasy and ecstasy: they alternatively are controlled by spirits who arrive to possess them (enstasy) and control spirits as they travel "out" to meet them (ecstasy)' (Johnson 2007, pp. 104–5). Consequently, Johnson claims it is inappropriate to label the *buyei* as either shaman or priest. Johnson's study is merely one of several that collectively reveal the prevalence of indigenous stories about religious specialists who engage in both possession and ecstasy. These studies reveal the fragile ground upon which the dichotomy of terms such as possession and trance are built. Indeed, in his chapter within this book, Graham Harvey confidently rebukes the academic labelling of religious experiences, and describes the terms 'possession' and 'shaman' as 'Humpty Dumpty words', thereby willing their fall from the wall that academia has built around itself.

Ethnographic studies often expose the difficulty in creating a definitive, cross-cultural theory about a religious practice that has so many permutations. This is particularly well documented in studies of spirit possession and trance, which support well Lambek's definition of spirit possession as 'a complex, subtle and supple phenomenon' (1989, p. 37). Rather than attempt one universal interpretation for – what Frazer and Eliade among others contend to be – universal cultural phenomena, we would do well to interpret spirit possession and trance according to the specific cultural contexts in which they are found. Indeed, Lambek argues that spirit possession is more appropriately defined in terms of a system or function of cultural communication. This is because 'the behaviour of spirits provides the substance of the public discourse on Otherness that is an essential interpretative function of possession' (Lambek 1989, p. 44). Monothetic and decontextualized categories inevitably fail to engage with the beliefs and practices attributed to spirit possession and trance by the particular individual or community concerned. Consequently, a useful universal account of spirit possession or trance is not possible, as there will always be cases that do not conform to the proposed typologies. Indeed, as Lambek notes (with reference to spirit possession in Mayotte, an island in the Mozambique Channel), possession comprises beliefs and practices that are often full of surprises, and – in stark contrast to what we might regard as a more conventional interpretation of spirit possession – of creativity and comedy (Lambek 1989, p. 53).

Lambek's allusion to the creative and humorous aspects of spirit possession exemplifies the atypical character of spirit possession as it is commonly conceived, and thereby highlights the limitation of our conception. More often than not Western interpretations of spirit possession have focused on those instances that imply pain and torment (such as we found with

Métraux's assertion that the face of the possessed expresses 'anguish' and 'suffering', and Oesterreich's allusion to the face of the possessed girl, which had 'an expression so pitiful that it would have melted a stone'), and not on those instances that imply joy and healing, or – as Lambek notes – of creativity and comedy. This focus has no doubt encouraged the negative associations that are still prevalent in academic studies of possession phenomena (such as we find in psychiatric discourse). The basis for this one-sided perspective can be attributed, at least in part, to the tendency of early scholars in the field to interpret the possessing agency as 'evil'.

From a Judaeo–Christian viewpoint – a viewpoint typically adopted by early scholars in the field – 'evil' is associated with human suffering and the privation of good. Thus, if an evil spirit possesses a person then it will use that person as a vehicle for pain, suffering, and generally 'blasphemous' behaviour. But the Judaeo–Christian understanding of evil is itself merely one interpretation among many. In other traditions evil is required along-side the good to form a duality that is necessary for the harmonious balance and creativity that enables life (see Parkin 1985). Although suffering may occur in some cases of spirit possession, there is by no means an inherent correlation between the two – even if one maintains that the possessing spirit is of 'evil' persuasion.

Clearly not everybody regards the possessing agency as malevolent. In her chapter in this book, Lucy Huskinson argues for the potential healing property of possession and explains – from a position of analytical psychology – how possession facilitates healthy development of the personality. Likewise, Louise Child in her chapter describes the relationship between the possessed person and the possessing agency as a 'seduction' that empowers both the person and his or her culture. Possessing agencies may be powerful goddesses, teasing tricksters and all-too-human heroes, as often as they are evil and malevolent demons. And they may not be per-sonified at all. Possession can even refer to 'divine inspiration' itself, as Crystal Addey explains in her chapter.

As was mentioned earlier, it is commonly thought that the possessed person behaves in accordance with the characteristics – or personality, if the possessing agent is personified – of that which possesses him or her. Thus, if a person is possessed by a trickster figure, we may assume that the spirit of the trickster will use the person to tease and taunt those around him, creating a jovial atmosphere. Such an experience may be cathartic for the possessed person, making him or her feel relieved and relaxed, rather than pained or tortured. The variety of ways in which spirit possession and trance present themselves is considerable. In parallel with Rudolf Otto's interpretation of numinous experiences (1917), possession and trance phenomena seem to manifest themselves across a vast phenomenological spectrum, from reported experiences of welcome calm and bliss to frenzied and often dangerous attacks.

Becoming less prejudiced in our interpretation

The difficulties and problems identified above are just a few examples of how acceptance of the prejudicial views of early anthropological studies on spirit possession and trance has led to their widely distorted interpretation. Indeed, although we cannot arrive at a definitive and accurate explanation of spirit possession and trance, we can expose errors in previous interpretations by bringing to light observations that both contradict and help to reformulate our understanding. We must always adopt a flexible, working hypothesis of the nature and role of spirit possession and trance to enable the assimilation of new insights and to hold contradictory evidence in creative tension. Adopting this stance in practice is, however, notoriously difficult. Indeed, it requires us to maintain objectivity in our judgement and to think outside the confines not only of our individual disciplinary expertise, but of all those prejudices we have all inevitably developed in our individual and cultural upbringing. Arguably, this is an impossible task, and yet it is the perennial barrier that prevents us from engaging accurately with phenomena that surpass cultural and disciplinary boundaries. This barrier is particularly apparent in anthropological research in general, where traditionally the principal aim was to *explain* 'alien' customs, and to translate foreign cultures into more familiar terms and concepts of the anthropologist's own.

Research within the anthropology of religion tends to rely heavily on participant observation. Anthropologists live for a period of time in the village they want to study and try to learn as much as possible from the villagers. The aim is to get a full understanding of their culture and their religion so that, upon his or her return home, the anthropologist can explain to his or her own people the foreign customs and practices he or she has experienced. The ethnographic data are therefore contextualized within the cultural, social, political and historical settings. Religion is seen in relationship to other social institutions or constructs, and never as a phenomenon in its own right. However, its interpretation is inevitably coloured by the anthropologist's own cultural and social upbringing. Accordingly, Godfrey Lienhardt, an anthropologist prominent in the 1950s, writes:

When we live with savages and speak their language, learning to represent their experience to ourselves in their way, we come as near to thinking like them as we can without ceasing to be ourselves. Eventually, we try
to represent their conceptions systematically in the logical constructs we
have been brought up to use; and we hope, at best, thus to reconcile what
can be expressed in their language, with what can be expressed in ours.
We mediate between their habits of thought, which we have acquired
with them, and those of our own society; in that we are exploring, but the
further potentialities of our thought and language. (Lienhardt 1963
[1954], pp. 96–7)

We might think of the anthropologist's task itself as a process of possession
and 'depossession': of letting go of the familiar, prejudicial orientation – or
familiar personality – in order to allow an empathic merger of the self with
the unfamiliar other, before returning to the familiar personality where the
experience is reflected upon and interpreted. The process of translating
alien or unfamiliar concepts into our own categories of understanding is
particularly difficult in the field of religious studies because the concepts we
tend to investigate are either abstract ideas or highly personal beliefs and
practices.

Unless one is able to 'go native' and interpret spirit possession and
trance from an insider's perspective, one is forced to rely on observable
data – such as body movements and perceived changes in personality – and
on subjective accounts of those who were possessed or in trance. Both
sources of information are unreliable and highly speculative. Body movements tell us little about the internal processes of the possession and
inform us of the likely physiological effects of the experience, and subjective accounts are often tainted by personal agenda. Moreover, accounts
from those who were possessed or in a trance are especially unreliable
if one accepts the proposition that possession and trance entail a loss
of conscious control, as the noted anthropologist Melville J. Herskovits
testifies:

[A possessed person] often exhibits a complete transformation in his
personality . . . and the character of his utterances are startlingly different
from what they were when he is 'himself'. (1948, p. 67)

If Herskovits is right, how can people who have been possessed describe
what had happened if they were dissociated from themselves at the time, or
if their familiar personality had been completely transformed or overtaken

by one that is very different? Are possessed people then reliable witnesses to the event?

We cannot adopt a wholly neutral and objective approach, and to rely on observable data and subjective – yet dubiously authoritative – accounts is a gamble. Certainly, when one surveys the history of research into spirit possession and trance it would seem that insider accounts are generally deemed too risky. For we often find interpretations that explicitly contradict the 'insider's' narrative, and yet these interpretations are themselves untrustworthy in their colonial prejudice.

Traditional prejudices within studies of spirit possession and trance

A brief survey of the history of anthropological research reveals that the process of translation from the 'alien' to the 'familiar' was often tainted by the anthropologist's colonial attitude. This attitude sparked extensive postcolonial criticism of 'translation', regarding it as an uneffective methodology for anthropological research. For instance, as Talal Asad maintains, the 'translator' needs to be aware that

> [T]he problem of determining the relevant kind of context in each case is solved by skill in the use of languages concerned, not by the a priori attitude of . . . intolerance or tolerance . . . And skill is something that is learned. (Asad 1993, p. 183)

Asad argues that it is not possible to value anthropological research without looking at the power relationship of the parties involved. We therefore have to acknowledge 'inequality in the power of languages', which, for Asad, includes the social dimension. He states:

> Cultural translation must accommodate itself to a different language, not only in the sense of English as opposed to Dinka, or English opposed to Kabbashi Arabic, but also in the sense of a British, middle-class, academic game as opposed to the modes of life of the nomadic, tribal Sudan. (1993, p. 193)

Richard King goes a step further and criticizes the myth of homogeneity as it is used to describe foreign religions. He vehemently argues against applying globalized, highly abstract and univocal systems of thought to religious experience because this can only arrive at overly homogenized conceptions of cultural diversity and religious tradition (King 1999, p. 98).

Arguably, the problem of interpretation is most visible in studies of spirit possession and trance. Spirit possession is a key practice in religions world-wide, and yet it is a practice that is – perhaps inevitably – misunderstood. This misunderstanding can have disastrous consequences, leading to possible vilification of such experiences (where, for instance, those who 'experience' possession or trance are demonized or regarded as mentally unstable). More often than not, the common negative reaction experienced by ignorant and uninformed people is the direct result of a lack of understanding of the role and meaning of spirit possession within the religion or culture concerned. Ironically, rather than expose these misunderstandings, academic scholar-ship has inadvertently sustained them. This is particularly apparent in the academy's blind endorsement of unwarranted dichotomies: such as the pro-longed employment of Eliade's division between possession and trance, the division of gender roles within ecstatic practices generally (a troublesome dichotomy taken up by Bettina Schmidt in her chapter within this book), and the fundamental Western paradigm of mind–body dualism.[3]

Beyond our preconceived dichotomies and towards a new paradigm for interpreting spirit possession and trance

It would seem that it is timely for us to broaden our perspectives and to overcome those conceptual limitations that have tainted our interpret-ations of spirit possession and trance, and indeed, of religious experience in general. The key is to be more receptive to that which is unfamiliar or in apparent opposition to our preconceived ideas: to open up dialogues with unfamiliar disciplines that may offer important insights into our own. To this end we might do well to consider in our approach to possession and trance the philosophical view of 'perspectivism' developed in the nineteenth century by Friedrich Nietzsche, and adopted by many, includ-ing the Brazilian anthropologist Eduardo Viveiros de Castro in his studies on Amazon cosmology (1992). Simply put, perspectivism is the idea that there are many possible conceptual schemes or perspectives that determine any possible judgement or value that we may make. The implication is that there is no one definitive way in which to interpret the world, but this does not mean that all perspectives are equally valid at all times, and that we are free to conceive the world in any way. In his studies on Amazon cosmology, Viveiros de Castro argues that each of us – along with other humans, ani-mals and other conceivable entities such as spirits, gods and the dead – interprets the world through a unique perspective (so that it could be said that animals experience human beings differently to the way humans experience animals; likewise, spirits, gods and shaman all view each other and the world around them according to an exclusive perspective). Perspectivism reveals how no one perspective or interpretation is inherently more valuable or accurate than another, and neither can one perspective be understood by another's terms. We can never escape our unique perspective and enter into another. What is called for and what is within our grasp is a general greater awareness of, and empathy with, the presence of other, equally valid perspectives. It is through such awareness that our individual perspectives can become enriched and can enter more easily and effectively into creative dialogue with others.

* * *

The idea for this volume developed out of a conference of the *British Association for the Study of Religions* in Edinburgh (September 2007), where Bettina Schmidt organized a panel on the interpretation of spirit possession, which led to a conference at Bangor University (May 2008) on the phenomena of possession and trance. The conference brought together scholars of a variety of disciplines and religious (and non-religious) interests and approaches. The aim of this meeting was to break through methodological barriers that separate interpretations of trance and ecstasy, shamanism and possession, and of perceived differences between ecstatic experiences of Indian and African religions, and Islamic and European traditions. This volume has developed out of a selection of papers that were presented at the conference.

Each chapter contains either an ethnographic or a theoretical case study that exposes a particular methodological approach to possession and trance. Collectively they comprise a polyphonic understanding of possession that combines interpretations of the individual, collective and social functions of possession within an understanding of its ethnographic context. By bringing together different approaches to possession and trance from a variety of academic disciplines and perspectives – such as psychology, anthropology, philosophy, sociology, phenomenology and performative arts – this volume provides an overview of new theoretical developments of such phenomena, and also demonstrates a breakthrough and overcoming of previous limitations in interpretation within the field of religious studies generally.

In this volume, we attempt to begin to dismantle the presumptions that surround spirit possession and trance and to break through the now outdated descriptions of spirit possession and trance that have been enlisted since the days of Frazer and Eliade. There are no definitive descriptions or interpretations of spirit possession and trance phenomena, which is one reason why attempts to understand them through rigid categorization are fraught with difficulty. Arguably, it is in the dialogue between multidisciplinary interpretations of spirit possession and trance – when the tension between competing perspectives is harnessed – that the most fascinating insights into such phenomena are revealed.

Notes

[1] To paraphrase Lisa Appignanesi's book title *Mad, Bad and Sad: A History of Women and the Mind Doctors from 1800* (2008).

[2] Interestingly, Crapanzano continues to define the possessed person in terms that correspond to Oesterreich's three-fold interpretation of the manifestation of the possessed spirit, as he describes the 'dramatic changes' within the 'physiognomy, voice and manner' of the one who is possessed (2005, p. 8687).

[3] To claim, as many scholars of spirit possession and trance do, that such 'experiences' entail the loss of control of body and/or mind, is to presume a distinction between body and mind. In interpreting spirit possession and trance we would do well to enquire into the role of the body – and physiology in general – and the extent to which it informs and shapes our conceptions. From Marcel Mauss (1935) we were taught that we should not view the human body as the 'passive recipient of cultural imprints' but as the '*self-developable* means for achieving a range of human objects – from styles of physical movement (for example, walking), through modes of emotional being (for example, composure), to kinds of spiritual experience (for example, mystical states)' (summarized by Asad 1997, pp. 47–8, emphasis Asad's). Similarly, Sarah Coakley criticizes ethnographic studies for its naïve approach to the value of the body. She argues that modern-day ethnographers continue to maintain that our 'bodies provide us with an Archimedean point, a "natural" datum of uncontentious physicality upon which religious traditions have then spun their various interpretations' (Coakley 1997, p. 3). Arguably, in order to understand religious experience more effectively we need to adopt an approach that does not get waylaid by the primary value we give to the body and its dichotomy with mind. Such an approach may be found in Geoffrey Samuel's understanding of the shaman, who, he claims, overcomes those states of being – such as mind and body – as we understand them. The shaman, in his mediatory role between our human realm of existence and being and that which is other (or what we may call 'non-being'), travels beyond our familiar constructs of meaning (Samuel 1990; and his chapter in this book).

Bibliography

Appignanesi, L. (2008), *Mad, Bad and Sad: A History of Women and the Mind Doctors from 1800 to the Present.* London: Virago.

Asad, T. (1993), *Genealogies of Religion: Discipline and Reasons of Power in Christianity and Islam*. Baltimore: Johns Hopkins University Press.

Asad, T. (1997), 'Remarks on the anthropology of the body', in S. Coakley (ed.), *Religion and the Body*. Cambridge: Cambridge University Press, pp. 42–52.

Bourguignon, E. (1973), *Religion, Altered States of Consciousness, and Social Change*. Columbus: Ohio State University Press.

Bourguignon, E. (1976), *Possession*. San Francisco: Chandler & Sharp.

Brown, K. M. (2001), *Mama Lola: A Vodou Priestess in Brooklyn* (updated and expanded edn). Berkeley: University of California Press.

Coakley, S. (1997), 'Introduction: religion and the body', in S. Coakley (ed.), *Religion and the Body*. Cambridge: Cambridge University Press, pp. 1–12.

Cohen, E. (2007), *The Mind Possessed: The Cognition of Spirit Possession in an Afro-Brazilian Religious Tradition*. Oxford: Oxford University Press.

Crapanzano, V. (2005), 'Spirit possession: an overview', in L. Jones (ed.), *Encyclopedia of Religion* (2nd edn). Detroit: Macmillan Reference USA, pp. 8687–94.

Eliade, M. (1989 [1964]), *Shamanism: Archaic Techniques of Ecstasy*. London: Penguin Books.

Frazer, J. G. (1911 [1890]), *The Golden Bough*. London: Macmillan.

Herskovits, M. J. (1948), *Man and His Works: The Science of Cultural Anthropology*. New York: A. A. Knopf Doubleday.

Johnson, P. C. (2007), *Diaspora Conversions: Black Carib Religion and the Recovery of Africa*. Berkeley: University of California Press.

King, R. (1999), *Orientalism and Religion: Postcolonial Theory, India and the Mystic East*. New Delhi: Oxford University Press.

Lambek, M. (1980), 'Spirits and spouses: Possession as a system of communication among the Malagasy speakers of Mayotte', *American Ethnologists*, 7 (2), 318–31.

Lambek, M. (1989) 'From disease to discourse: remarks on the conceptualization of trance and spirit possession', in C. A. Ward (ed.), *Altered States of Consciousness and Mental Health*. Newbury Park: Sage, pp. 36–61.

Lewis, I. M. (2003 [1971]), *Ecstatic Religion: A Study of Shamanism and Spirit Possession*. London: Routledge.

Lienhardt, G. (1963 [1954]), 'Modes of thought', in E. E. Evans-Pritchard et al. (eds), *The Institutions of Primitive Society*. Oxford: Blackwell, pp. 95–107.

Mauss, M. (1973 [1935]), 'The techniques of the body', *Economy and Society*, 2 (1), 70–88.

Métraux, A. (1972 [1958]), *Voodoo in Haiti*, trans. H. Charteris (original edn). New Schocken Books; New York: Oxford University Press.

Oesterreich, T. K. (1930 [1921]), *Possession: Demoniacal and Other Among Primitive Races in Antiquity, the Middle Ages, and Modern Times*. London: Kegan Paul.

Otto, R. (1936 [1917]), *The Idea of the Holy*, trans. J. W. Harvey. Oxford: Oxford University Press.

Parkin, D. (ed.) (1985), *The Anthropology of Evil*. Oxford: Blackwell.

Samuel, G. (1990), *Mind, Body and Culture: Anthropology and the Biological Interface*. Cambridge: Cambridge University Press.

Viveiros de Castro, E. B. (1992), *From the Enemy's Point of View: Humanity and Divinity in an Amazonian Society*. Chicago: University of Chicago Press.

Chapter 2

Animism rather than Shamanism: New Approaches to what Shamans do (for other animists)

Graham Harvey

What shamans do is sometimes said to involve possession by spirits. However, shamanism has also been defined in opposition to spirit possession. This chapter proposes that approaching shamans and their activities, ideas and communities via the perspective provided by recent re-examination and re-definition of 'animism' may improve and enrich scholarly understanding and analysis of the activities and involvements of shamans. 'Possession', like 'shamanism', deserves considerable debate, contest and care because it can be applied to diverse and contradictory phenomena and does not have one simple, self-evident or uncontested referent. The profligate variety of scholarly application of both terms is hardly disconnected from their invocation in a wide range of religious, social and therapeutic discourses. Judgements of the value of acts, ideas and experiences that can be so labelled vary wildly, and academics have not stood aside from these tangled polemics. At least part of the problem of understanding and researching putative shamanic and possession phenomena is that many of the terms in use are forcefully propelled by a heavy historical legacy that makes alternatives difficult to speak or think. If our observational lenses can easily turn into distorting mirrors so too can our analytic tools become burdensome hindrances. This is especially so when we fail to reflect radically on inherited 'Western' notions and approaches and thereby reduce the effectiveness of our scholarly work.

What is proposed here is that a significant alteration of the language used in relation to shamans will improve academic debate and knowledge about a range of phenomena. Current themes in academic debate may be seen in a new light if we attend to the possibilities and perspectives of alternative and, in this case, indigenous perspectives. In brief, this chapter's argument is that the activities of shamans, including their performance of what might or might not appropriately be called 'possession', deserve to be revisited in the wake of the recent rethinking about 'animism' (see especially Bird-David 1999; Harvey 2005a). Older notions of animism are implicated in still prevalent notions of shamanism and possession because these terms are frequently defined in relation to 'spirits'. A summary of this older approach to animism, associated with Edward Tylor, may aid understanding of what is distinctive in the new reconsideration, associated with Irving Hallowell. It will also anticipate some problematic themes in the study of shamans, spirits and possession. The new approach to animism aids a richer understanding of the relational activities of shamans, but it also requires more precision about the beings with whom shamans relate (co-operatively or aggressively) than the inherently vague term 'spirits' allows. Conversely, critical debate may be greatly enhanced if we attend to the complex resonances and associations of the term 'possession', especially by linking it to kinds of ownership and relationship rather than to putative inner states.

Tylor's Animism

In Edward Tylor's monumental proto-anthropology (1871), 'animism' is defined as 'a belief in souls or spirits' and is used as a synonym of 'religion'. Tylor had considered labelling his theory 'spiritualism', but that was already strongly associated with a particular religious movement. (It might be significant that spiritualism was gaining popularity in the late-nineteenth century, contrary to the decline of religion that Tylor anticipated.) The term animism, however, carried associations with the 'souls' and 'spirits' that Tylor saw as central, definitive matters of religious belief in *all* religions. It had been previously used by Georg Stahl (1708) in a failed attempt to define the difference between living bodies and dead matter as the presence of a physical, chemical element, *anima*. All that is left of this theory in Tylor's work is the implicit question: 'how are living beings distinguished from dead matter?', or, more simply, 'is it alive?' Religious people continue the 'primitive' error of interpreting dreams and hallucinations as evidence that souls and spirits animate living beings and sometimes possess others. Metaphysics (an error by definition in this rationalist discourse) posits the existence and effects of these constituent parts of beings to distinguish them from inert matter. In accepting such beliefs, religious people make a category error of projecting life where it does not exist (e.g. in rocks) or human attributes, such as intentionality, on to non-human creatures (e.g. eagles). From the belief in souls and spirits they also extrapolate a further false belief that these make their possessors at least potentially immortal. From there, vast edifices of different religious cultures evolved a panoply of supernatural notions. Of particular interest here is the ability of some spirits to possess other beings' bodies, perhaps even displacing the host spirit.

Tylor's evidence for this grand theory of the nature of religion was drawn from data gathered from colonial sources globally, as well as at home in Victorian Britain. Among many other kinds of religious practices, it includes both indigenous possession cults and British Spiritualist séances. It has an explicit polemical purpose: the furtherance of rationalism against the mistakes of religious belief. Tylor's animism should not be mistaken either for a categorization of a type of religion distinct from 'monotheism' or for the name of a particular religion distinct from 'Christianity'. Tylor's animism *is* religion. He claims to be defining religion as distinct from science, politics, entertainment or any other human endeavour. Nonetheless, because Tylor's animism is reputed to have arisen from the first thought mistake of a religious kind, its foundational nature contributed to a debate about what kind of religion was the earliest. The Victorian contest between prevalent styles of Christianity and nascent forms of evolutionary theory are visible in the replacement of the theory that religion derives from (monotheistic) divine revelation but has degenerated into diversity, sometimes and in some places at least, by the theory that 'primitive' spirit-belief religion slowly progressed towards its own replacement by rationalism.

It can seem possible to encounter Tylor's animists because many people in many places do talk about 'spirits' or 'souls', or use words that can be translated in this way. Some do talk as if the death of trees was as personally meaningful as the death of humans, or as if deceased relatives continued to communicate with their descendents. Alan Campbell illustrates this with reference to the Amazonian Wayapí, noting that their 'conversation shifts between' suggesting 'that all sorts of things round them are simply alive' and 'that all these things have a soul or spirit in them that makes them alive' (Campbell 1995, pp. 136–7). Nonetheless, Campbell objects to the use of 'animism' as a 'religious tag' of the sort used by people who produce 'colour-coded maps of the world' indicating where particular religions predominate. In these, much of West Africa and Amazonia can be labelled 'animist' where people are neither 'Christian' nor 'Muslim' (although this can depend on who is defining any of these religious complexes). Campbell does not, as he suggests, contribute to the sharpening of Tylor's blunt signpost (mixing his metaphors), but to the understanding of a different approach to animism that he discusses with reference to various kinds of shamanic actions and discourses.

Hallowell's Animism

The new approach to animism is appropriately associated with the increasingly influential research and writings of Irving Hallowell among the
Ojibwa of Beren's River in south-central Canada between the two world
wars (Hallowell 1960). The key question here is not 'is it alive?' but 'how
should we relate?'. The problem is not beliefs about something that might
distinguish life and death, but learning appropriate ways of behaving.
Among the Ojibwa, Hallowell learnt, animism is implicit in grammar and
becomes explicit in casual and deliberate discourse and performance.

In the Ojibwa language a grammatical distinction is made between animate and inanimate genders. A suffix, –g, is added to nouns that refer
to animate persons rather than inanimate objects. Verbs indicating the
actions of animate persons differ from those referring to acts done to
inanimate objects. For example, the plural form of the word *asin* (stone) is
asiniig, identifying stones as grammatically animate (Nichols and Nyholm
1995, p. 14). Ojibwa speakers use the same personal pronoun (*wiin*) for
masculine and feminine persons, grammatically making nothing of the
difference between masculine and feminine. But they use animate gender
terms for a wider range of beings than the English language officially rec-
ognizes. In practice some English speakers do talk about their ships, cars or
computers as if they were animate beings rather than inanimate objects,
giving them names, blessing or cursing them, and applying the personal
pronouns 'he' or 'she' rather than the impersonal 'it'. How far can this 'as
if' discourse be taken? In the French language, tables are marked as grammatically feminine, *la table* rather than *le table*. Do French speakers treat
grammatically female tables as female persons? Perhaps they do so in
poetry and children's stories, but what about in everyday reality? So the
question arises, do the Ojibwa treat grammatically animate stones as animate persons? Do they speak with stones or act in other ways that reveal
intentions to build or maintain relationships?

Irving Hallowell asked an unnamed old Ojibwa man, 'Are *all* the stones
we see about us here alive?' (1960, p. 24; original emphasis). Grammatically
all stones everywhere are animate, but did this man actually think that
particular rocks around him were alive? Did he treat them in some way that
showed them to be alive? The man answered, 'No! but *some* are'. He had
witnessed a particular stone following the leader of a shamanic ceremony
around a tent as he sang. Another powerful leader is said to have had a
large stone that would open when he tapped it three times, allowing him to
remove a small bag of herbs when he needed it in ceremonies. Hallowell

was told that when a white trader was digging his potato patch he found a stone that looked like it may be important. He called for the leader of another ceremony who knelt down to talk to the stone, asking if it had come from someone's ceremonial tent. The stone is said to have denied this. Movement, gift-giving and conversation are three indicators of the animate nature of relational beings, or persons.

Hallowell makes it clear that the key point in each account is not that stones do things of their own volition (however remarkable this claim might seem) but that they engage in relationships. For the Ojibwa the interesting question is not 'how do we know stones are alive?' but 'what is the appropriate way for people, of any kind, to relate?'. This is as true for humans as it is for stones, trees, animals, birds, fish and all other beings that might be recognized as persons. Persons are known to be persons when they relate to other persons in particular ways. They might act more or less intimately, willingly, reciprocally or respectfully. Since enmity is also a relationship, they might act aggressively – which is important when we seek to understand the need for shamans and the dangerous ambiguity of possession. The category of 'person' is only applicable *when* beings are relating with others. Perhaps 'person' is not a nominal category but a performance, and one that is both corporeal and corporate. This is quite different to the understanding of most European-derived cultures in which personhood is an interior quality, a fact about an individual (human) who is self-conscious. Hallowell recognized this by insisting that we are not talking here about different 'belief systems', epistemologies, but about different ontologies, different ways of being in the world. Indeed, we could say that the old Ojibwa man lived in a different world from Hallowell's until the latter learnt to see the world as his teacher showed it to be. Once he saw it, Hallowell had to find new ways to use the English language to write about what he had learnt. To talk of animism may have suggested a discussion of life (animation) versus death. To talk of persons may have implied notions about human interiority (belief, rationality or subjectivity). He has, in fact, been misread in both these ways. However, the 'animate persons' Hallowell introduced were relational beings, actors in a participatory world. His question is phrased in a way that indicates he had already appreciated some, at least, of what it meant to live in the unnamed old man's world: he did not ask 'are all rocks (universally) alive?' but inquired about nearby rocks. Hallowell was already recognizing the importance of relationship and participation.

Having learnt from his Ojibwa hosts, Hallowell coined the phrase 'other-than-human persons' to refer to the animate beings with whom humans share the world. He was not privileging humanity or saying that what makes something a person is its likeness to humans. He is clear that 'person' is not defined by human characteristics or behaviours. The term is a much larger umbrella than 'human'. All beings communicate intentionally and act towards others relationally: this makes them 'persons'. It is useful *for us* (humans) to speak about 'human-' and 'other-than-human' persons only because (a) we are humans talking to humans (if we were bears we might speak of 'other-than-bear persons') and (b) because English speakers are preconditioned to hear the word 'person' as a reference to other humans. The word 'persons' should be enough, and would be if English speakers had not learnt to privilege and separate humanity from other beings. This separation is also demarcated by the variously maintained boundaries between the 'natural' and 'social' sciences as much as by the peculiar way in which humans are separated from 'the environment' in contrast with the integrated placing of animals *in* their environment – and other constructions of culture–nature dualism.

Animists live in a different world: a community of persons all of whom are capable of relationship, communication, agency and desire. There is no mute or inert 'nature' but only the many competing conversations of a multi-species cultural community. Some of these conversations cross species boundaries. Another of Hallowell's informants told him that he had been visiting with an elderly couple during a thunderstorm. He said, 'There was one clap of thunder after another. Suddenly the old man turned to his wife and asked, "Did you hear what was said?" "No," she replied, "I didn't catch it"' (Hallowell 1960, p. 34). Hallowell comments that

> The casualness of the remark and even the trivial character of the anecdote demonstrate the psychological depth of the 'social relations' with other-than-human beings that becomes explicit in the behavior of the Ojibwa as a consequence of the cognitive 'set' induced by their culture. (p. 34)

After a lifetime living as animists this couple assumed that thunder is an act of communication. Acceptance of not having 'caught' what was said indicates another assumption: that not all communication is about us (humans in general or the hearers specifically). The elderly couple could carry on talking with their visitor while the thunder engaged in a separate conversation nearby.

By referring to relational beings, 'persons' invites us to consider what 'good persons' might be. In Ojibwa culture (and many other indigenous cultures) goodness too is relational: people are encouraged to be good towards one another, and they are recognized as being good when they reciprocate respect rather than enmity. Eating other 'persons' may place a strain on relationality but perhaps only if permission is not sought and placation offered (Tawhai 1988, p. 101). Predation may be conceived of as an ordinary act within the negotiated relational community of living beings, but it, too, may be pursued within the dynamic tension between respect and aggression. Totemism and shamanism may usefully point to ways of dealing with these negotiations and tensions. If the former entails cooperation, the latter is sometimes said to involve aggressive possession.

Totemism

In one of her excellent discussions of Aboriginal Australian relationships with their lands and other-than-human neighbours, Debbie Rose writes that not only humans, but also 'other animals like kangaroos have their own rituals and law, and ... they too take care of relationships of well-being' among all the inhabitants of an area or 'country' (1998, pp. 7, 11). All related beings share rights and responsibilities and are expected to be committed to and concerned for each other's 'flourishing in the world'. Rose uses the term 'totemism' to refer to these relationships and commitments that cross species boundaries, involving high degrees of mutual care. In her *Reports from a Wild Country* (2004) she further establishes the responsibility of local, multi-species communities for the well-being of all co-inhabitants, an obligation that is commonly identified as 'the Law' among Aboriginal people but also (re-)translated as 'Dreaming'. Tim Ingold's (2000) term 'dwelling' might be a more resonant equivalent. In this context 'wild' is not synonymous with 'nature' (either positively or negatively valued) but refers to places that have not been cared for appropriately: it is a result of the hyper-separation of humans from both place and the community of other-than-human persons. By drawing attention to the presence and absence of humans and ways of being in place this counter use of 'wild' contests the construction of 'wildernesses' and 'nature (p)reserves' which result from the removal of human dwellers. It reveals links between genocide and ecocide just as it invites the linkage of eco-responsibility and co-inhabitation.

  The word 'totem' originated among the Ojibwa and refers to clans that include humans and particular animals and plants. It has been used by academics to theorize about human–animal relations. Claude Lévi-Strauss established the notion that totem-animals are chosen not because they are 'good to eat' but because they are 'good to think' (1969, p. 89). Here, once again, a scholar has constructed an epistemology that marginalizes a term's originators. In Ojibwa and Aboriginal Australian totemism, animals are good to relate with. As Chris Knight says, 'Totemism is, therefore, embedded in animism as an aspect of sociality' (1996, p. 550). It is a more immediate and intimate mode of relating than the all-embracing relationality indicated by 'animism'. The title of another of Debbie Rose's books points to the central importance of totemic relationships in making people what they are: *Dingo Makes Us Human* (1992). The job that clans are supposed to do within the wider, inclusive, cross-species community posited by animism is to animate and locally enact the privileging of respect, co-operation and the bias towards resolving differences amicably rather than destructively. However, Rose is careful to point out that relationships and co-habitation are not always harmonious: they can lead to tension, conflict and competition. There is often a need for mediators or diplomats to intervene between groups and individuals to sort out problems – such people may be labelled 'shamans' for comparative and analytical purposes.

What 'Shaman' Means

It is too late to insist (although a few scholars still do) that nobody should be named a shaman beyond the territorial, cultural and linguistic boundaries of the Siberian Evenk people and related speakers of Tungus languages. A host of neighbouring and distant religious and/or social functionaries are regularly named 'shamans' alongside whatever local names might be deemed applicable. Without doubt, indigenous terms point to variations of some type or magnitude. In one place, the label 'shaman' might translate a local term pinned to a healer, in another to someone who gains knowledge about prey animals in unusual ways, and elsewhere to ritualists with expertise in communicating with the deceased or the divine. Campbell (1995) argues that among the Wayapí (and perhaps elsewhere) we have been misled into identifying 'shamans' where local people speak not in nouns but adjectives and even verbs that point to a range of acts and abilities widely available to everyone in the community – sometimes without any deliberate effort. Nonetheless, although 'shaman' does now label a wide range of phenomena, a quick skim through academic publications, let alone popular ones, will show that absolutely anything and everything can be (indeed probably has been) labelled 'shamanic' or 'shamanism'. This makes it hard to be clear on what any author means by 'shaman' and related terms. At least part of the confusion is caused by uncertainty about whether we are offered (or seeking) functional, lexical or real definitions (Baird 1971, pp. 1–16). As with 'religion', it is possible that 'shaman' no longer refers (if it ever did) to something 'real'. Its lexical history demonstrates a confusingly wide range of associations and putative referents. Now only a functional definition – selected precisely to draw attention to particular phenomena within the possible range – is helpful. In this regard, the intention of this chapter is to demonstrate the value of defining shamans as people who play specific but varying roles within (localized) animist communities. Contrasting definitions are not negated, merely deemed less interesting and less helpful in relation to much of what they purport to define.

Where should we begin to form a functional definition? What are the basic and central data to which it must refer? Many attempts to talk about shamans begin with the title's origins among the Evenk people and their neighbours. At first this seems obviously helpful: it was their word first, they ought to know what it means and what is expected of people to whom it applies. However, two portrayals (one visual, one verbal) of Evenk shamans immediately point to fundamental problems. The first is a wood-cut depiction of a shaman in Nicolas Witsen's 1692 book *Noord en Oost Tartarye* entitled 'Priest of the Devil'. The second is Piers Vitebsky's ethnography of the Evenk entitled *The Reindeer People: Living with Animals and Spirits in Siberia* (2005).

It is tempting to ignore Witsen's allegation that shamans have anything to do with the Christian devil but, if we do so, why should we trust anything about the portrayal at all? If Witsen is responsible for the devilish clawed feet portrayed here, how can we be sure he did not invent the drum or the posture? Ethnographic description from elsewhere might support these details, but our understanding is at least contaminated by Witsen's composite (if it is not a complete fabrication). But this is a small matter in comparison with the greater difficulty caused by Witsen's identification of this shaman as a 'priest'. Are shamans and priests really comparable? Do they serve the same, presumably religious, function? Many more recent scholars of shamanism categorically reject such assertions, even suggesting that no one could possibly confuse the two. Should we be swayed by such certainty? How helpful is it to define one term in relation (whether of comparison or opposition) to another that is, once we begin to think about it, similarly unclear and wide-ranging. What, after all, do Episcopalian priests have in common with Vodou leaders or officiates at ancient biblical or Roman ceremonies? Perhaps the answer here is 'sacrifice' (real or metaphorical) but, if so, does the categorical distinction between shaman and priest collapse among shamans who offer gifts, including blood sacrifice, to their ancestors? If, however, the term 'shaman' is indeed a local, indigenous term for 'priest', scholars already have a translation equivalent and need not mystify others by importing a foreign term. Similarly, if 'shaman' and 'priest' are equally translatable as 'religious leader' without further clarification or content-specific narrowness, they are equally vacuous.

Vitebsky (2005), meanwhile, nourishes the idea that reindeer herders who employ shamans live among animals and spirits. If we assume that 'animals' in the subtitle refers in particular to reindeer, an internet search for 'reindeer' returns many sites that present uncontroversial images, descriptions and even recipes. Certainly there are sites that offer stories of reindeer that might be alleged to commit the error of anthropomorphizing, projecting human-likeness of some kind. Others are plainly mythological or folkloric. Generally, however, 'reindeer' are recognizable denizens of a taxonomy of the deer family, the prey of humans and wolves. 'Animals' too, though a wider taxon, are readily understandable. 'Spirits', however, are far less easy to pin down. The few websites that offer any kind of illustration of spirits tend to use conventional symbols like candle flames rather than portrait photographs. Dictionaries evidence a widespread vagueness arising from the (reputed) intangibility of the word's supposed referents. But *if* spirits are, by definition, alien to the material world or embodied life, the means by which they cause effects that require shamanic intervention are hard to understand. Vitebsky's linking of animals (rather than reindeer specifically) and spirits might suggest that 'spirits' is a wider, more generic term. There might be as many kinds of spirits as there are kinds of animals. This is born out to some degree by illustrations in another of Vitebsky's books: *The Shaman* (1995) which will be commented on below. The question raised by Vitebsky's 'animals and spirits' subtitle is whether we really know what 'spirits' means in the same way that we know (or can easily find out) what 'reindeer' means. If the term is inherently vague, it is arguably more mystifying than conducive to understanding.

Whatever 'spirits' means, a common theme of discourse about shamans is that they are caught in a tension between opposing and co-operating with 'spirits'. Often these are played out in the domain of health or illness, healing and other therapeutic practices and discourses. Where shamans are healers they may be defined by the enabling relationship they have formed with 'spirits' and their opposition to the predatory acts of other 'spirits'. Where shamans are allies of hunters they may be defined by the mediation they conduct between potentially generous and potentially aggressive 'owners of (prey) animals or other food sources'. The precise form and content of shamanic acts and ideas is the subject of complex ethnographies and, if one is willing to embrace their inclusion, Western spiritual DIY manuals. (My *Shamanism: A Reader* [2003], and *Shamanism Dictionary* [2005], co-authored with Robert Wallis, are intended to promote debate about these and other definitional and boundary issues.) The point here is that if only some shamans are therapists and only some shamans inform hunters, these cannot inform a global, cross-cultural or critical definition of the term. If, as seems common opinion, some practice to do with something called 'spirits' is universal, then these practices and entities appear definitive.

Mircea Eliade's defining of the word 'shaman' – and his shaping of 'shamanism' in research and in practice – is (virtually) inescapable. Everything he wrote on the topic is an exposition of the words of his (1964) book title: *Shamanism: Archaic Techniques of Ecstasy*. His 'ecstasy' follows in the trajectory of earlier scholars in privileging states of consciousness. Marie Antoinette Czaplicka (1914), for example, summarized earlier and contemporary writing about the hysteria and mental illness of shamans, and Sergei Shirokogoroff (1935) wrote about the 'psychometrical complex of the Tungus'. Jeremy Narby and Francis Huxley say that 'Lévi-Strauss appeared to settle the issue by twisting it around and saying that shamans were more like psychologists than psychotics' (2001, p. 75; referring to Lévi-Strauss 1949). Others have agreed; for example, Morton Klass (1995, p. 72) asserts that shamans are neither frauds nor mentally ill, but intelligent and thoughtful individuals. Nonetheless, Eliade's insistence that shamans are essentially expert controllers of 'ecstatic' states has reinforced the psychological turn in shamanism studies and constructions. He has persuaded many that what shamans do is to perform 'techniques' that result in their own ecstasy. This allows them to benefit others – especially therapeutically – but it is the shaman's psychological state that is most important. Such techniques are 'archaic' when they derive from ancient, traditional or authorized origins. Eliade does not hide his claim to be able to authoritatively determine whether or not particular people practise 'archaic techniques'. For example, he condemns contemporary shamans for being 'degenerate' when they fail to adhere to his insistence on the centrality of an allegedly ancient tripartite cosmology. But even dabbling with the lower of the three proposed realms is deemed inadequate. Where 'possession' is not the condition shamans seek to cure in others, where it is something that overwhelms shamans themselves, it is a failing, and part of this degeneracy.

Eliade's position was greatly developed by Michael Harner (1990). Harner adapted shamanic initiation and Eliadean ecstasy into states achievable in a suburban living room or a New Age workshop. Consciousness could be altered by individual imagination aided by taped drum rhythms and other modernized and interiorized archaic techniques. 'Neo-shamans' cannot be criticized for converting frightening otherworlds into life-enhancing inner-worlds and conflating shamanism with quasi-Jungian therapy when Eliade, Harner and other academics required such a move (Jakobsen 1999). The task of distinguishing a 'shaman' from other therapists and seekers of personal growth is, however, made more difficult. The lack of fit between Eliade's model (or tight-jacket) and ethnographies of shamans and those they live among has only widened in parallel with the criticisms levelled at Eliade for purveying a single cosmology regardless of the data he claimed to be discussing. Nonetheless, the various Western forms of shamanism continue to constellate around 'spirits' if we allow that term to embrace 'inner', psychological or archetypal realities, and 'possession', whether this is something to be cured or, in metaphorical terms at least, a state of consciousness to be evoked. But since both terms mystify rather than aid understanding they cannot easily form helpful, scholarly definitions of what shamans are or what they do. We need to examine 'spirits' and 'possession' further.

Spirits

In Piers Vitebsky's *The Shaman* (1995) there are illustrations of what 'spirits' look like. Most impressively, spread across pages 20–21, there is 'A Shaman's-Eye Photograph of Non-ordinary Reality'. Or, rather, there might be – Vitebsky ends the caption with a question mark. The difficulty is compounded when Vitebsky discusses the photo. First he quotes the Tamu shaman's exclamation on being shown the photo that 'This is exactly what the god, the witches and the ancestors look like!' In the next paragraph he says that 'The shaman explained that the yellow line running right across the picture is what the ancestor spirits who come to protect the shamans look like as they arrive'. Another coloured line becomes 'the souls of witches' not just 'the witches' (1995, p. 20). The fact that these shifts in description are made by a careful presenter of rich ethnographic description and an enviable critical analyst indicates that even the best interpretations can lead to uncertainty. The term 'spirit' here and everywhere else is at best a religious term and at worst a word imported by observers who, whatever they intend, thereby make understanding less, rather than more, likely. If people are willing to claim that ancestors, stones or lightning communicate in various ways, or that witches and deities exist, or that trees can have good or bad intentions, the addition of the word 'spirit' is either empty of meaning or too full of meanings. If empty, the term can immediately be dropped and we can worry about what people mean when claiming that the dead or rocks participate in ceremonies. If full, the term is either part of a local taxonomy that requires translation (just as Evenk terms have been translated into 'animals' and 'reindeer' in Vitebsky's book title) or a remnant from the taxonomy of Western religious vocabulary. Since 'spirit' in Western discourses either refers to mysteries that transcend or romanticize ordinary reality or contributes to polemics about false (foolish or culpable) metaphysics, it is, again, not conducive to understanding or debate. The regular use of 'spirits' in association with the word 'possession' invites another approach to the range of questions we are asking about what shamans do and what shamanism is.

Possession

Just for now, let us assume that, on occasions at least, shamans see ancestors and witches (whatever these terms mean) and that animists communicate with animate stones. Let us try to cast out whatever associations the word 'spirit' might have if we were to add it to these or other terms. That done, we can ask what 'possession' might mean in the context of what shamans do and what happens to them and those among whom they live and serve. Some interpreters may conclude that 'possession' is best translated into other words that speak more plainly of psychological conditions or states of consciousness. They may be correct. People may mistake unusual or powerful 'inner states' for experiences of other beings. Experiences are always interpreted and never so immediate that we can know or speak about them unmediated by expectations, worldviews and contexts. Similarly, people absorb the expectations of their group or society and tend to perform in locally typical ways. Indeed, if they wish to be understood, it makes sense for them to share wider ideas, even about what is 'eccentric'. We do not need to agree with informants about their interpretations. However, if our first aim is to understand what shamans say they do and experience, it does make sense for us to begin with their discourse, their knowledge as expressed in locally relevant ways. It might also be true that the legacy of Martin Luther and René Descartes too easily persuades us to fit what people say and do into boxes that privilege individuality and interiority (belief, mind, consciousness) (see, e.g., Taylor 1998, p. 2; Koerner 2005, pp. 421, 433). Such boxes may be both inappropriate and uncritical. What is proposed here is that the wider associations of the term 'possession' with ownership and relationships (including complementary and conflicting ones) may enrich scholarly discussions of shamanic and other phenomena.

Descriptive data from many putatively shamanic contexts demonstrate the wide distribution of ideas of intimate relationships between shamans and otherworld beings. (The term 'otherworld' is admittedly another difficult or mystifying one. It is used here to suggest something like an aspect, perhaps plural aspects, of the world that is not encountered easily everyday by everybody. It may be conceived to be above or beneath the land or sea surface, or in a nearby but strange dimension, but is not as 'transcendent' as the heavens of monotheistic cosmologies. Its geography and inhabitants may be what the word 'spirit' claims to refer to, but these are not necessarily any less physical than this-worldly beings – just of a different order.) Sexual, seductive and marital language is used in many places to refer to the formation and maintenance of relationships between shamans and otherworld partners. These are sometimes paralleled or in conflict with similar relationships with human partners. Such discourses suggest, at least, a degree of complementarity but with an edge that at least hints at potentially ambiguous or fraught power imbalances. The seducer and seduced are not always either equals or entirely willing. More aggressive relational terms are also frequent and form the bulk of discourse about shamanic initiations. It is here that shamans are most likely to experience something closest to the phenomena elsewhere labelled 'possession': being overpowered and overwhelmed by an other. If the initiation is successful (i.e. if the initiate narrates this as an initiation), it is likely to lead to the formation of a working relationship in which the shaman is helped in future tasks. This typically involves claims that the shaman has gained control or mastery of the being who assaulted them, and is able to maintain control over them to the benefit of others. In particular, people in the shaman's human community who are assaulted by such beings might be aided by the shaman and the mastered being. This is the foundation of the claim that shamanism and possession are distinct phenomena. However, since members of 'possession cults' *voluntarily* undergo 'possession' by powerful others, and since their narration of such experiences so closely parallels that of shamanic relationships, it is hard to resist the notion that these are similar phenomena. It is sometimes claimed that people who are 'possessed' are controlled by others rather than gaining control over them – but descriptions of possession and of shamanic séances often include considerable ambiguity about who is in control. Performances contain phases and elements that illustrate a host of locally expected acts and motifs. Deities, ancestors, disease-beings, owners-of-animals could, in theory, act in a wide range of ways but tend to be recognizable within more-or-less stereotypical acts. This is, of course, to be expected in a context where something is being communicated.

Whatever we are to make of performative dramas among the possessed and among shamans, it is certainly helpful to note Caroline Humphrey's (1994) reminder that the important matter for shamans and their communities is rarely the individual's inner state of mind (which is considered inaccessible to others), but the fact that particular actions identifiable as 'possession' or 'trance' indicate that the shaman is communicating with helpers or journeying to gain knowledge and abilities beyond those of other people. Similarly, Ioan Lewis's demonstration of the close similarities between practices and discourses identified as shamanism in one place and possession elsewhere undermines any categorical differentiation. Lewis (2003) supports a definition of shamans as people who welcome 'possession' as an aspect of (sexual and/or marital) relationship with otherworld persons, and who are distinguished from the victims of unwanted possession – who may be the subject of exorcism by shamans (or other religious specialists where there is no acceptable form of possession).

Shamans, Spirits, Possession and Animism

If we refuse to psychologize shamans, and resist accepting that pre-existing Western (Protestant Christian and Enlightenment inflected) notions readily explain shamanic discourse and practice, we may need to drop the word 'spirit' even as we worry about what 'possession' entails. The (new) animism does not simplistically replace the word 'spirit' with the word 'person' but challenges a stress on interiority, spirituality or transcendence, and mystification. It points to relationality as a key to what happens in shamanic acts and communities. It makes it possible to understand shamans not as virtuosi dealing with their own psychoses and helping others with psychosomatic problems, but as necessary negotiators of communal well-being among people who understand themselves to be participatory members of wider-than-human communities. The radical personalist ontology of animism does not romanticize relationships but pays attention to ambiguities and even raises difficulties distinct from those known elsewhere. The problem of the need to eat those who are themselves 'persons' leads directly to conflicts about ownership of, and access to, what we might call 'resources'. Many animist communities require shamans because of issues of possession: who possesses the animals that hunters and cooks require? Who possesses the right to give and take life? Who possesses control over animals, health, wealth and well-being? If it is not individuals, are there powerful persons of some other-than-human but also other-than-animal kind whose aid and permission might be sought or whose anger might be placated? In communities with relatively diffuse authority patterns, who possesses the authority to define appropriate behaviour? When people are ill, who is in control and who can help? When people bring home food, who possesses it? Such questions about varied and mundane kinds of possession are raised to intimate that possession as a (putative) state of (awareness/ performance of) being controlled and/or in control of other beings is entangled with other senses of the word. Possession here becomes a way of talking about varied kinds of ownership implicated in particular kinds of relationship and particular kinds of performance.

In the version of shamanism popularized in a trajectory following Eliade and Harner the abbreviation 'ASC' has become popular, highlighting the centrality of 'Altered States of Consciousness'. This sums up a range of the problems of an interiorizing interpretation that devotes most attention to individuals and their consciousness. It is proposed here to re-use the abbreviation ASC to refer to 'Adjusted Styles of Communication'. Shamans are persons (human or otherwise perhaps) who learn to communicate across species boundaries within a richly animate world full of persons who deserve respect but who might be eaten and might aggress, and who might control and be controlled.

Conclusion

Earlier it was insisted that, despite the confusing cacophony of claimants to the title, it is too late to restrict the term 'shaman' within a Siberian religious or cultural box. Although there are local specificities that are identified by the Evenk as the activities of shamans rather than elders or hunters, there are commonalities as well as differences between Evenk shamans and other religious or cultural actors elsewhere. Engaging with similarities and differences in order to form working definitions rather than absolute ones is something scholars of religion are used to, precisely because 'religion' is amenable to so many definitions (Smith 1998, p. 281;

Chidester 2005, p. vii; Tweed 2006, p. 60). It has been suggested, in opposition to Nicolas Witsen's polemical image, that shamans are not priests, and, in concert with Vitebsky's suggestive subtitle, that they do have something to do with 'spirits' among people who live closely with animals (hunting and/or herding in particular). Now that the term 'shaman' is so widely used with reference not only to reindeer herders and those who deal with 'spirits', but also to agriculturalists and consumerists who utilize consciousness-altering techniques, the Evenk (and knowledge of the Evenk) cannot now say what 'shaman' means in all the books and websites where it now appears.

'Shaman', 'spirit' and 'possession' are Humpty Dumpty words: words that are made to work hard, sometimes in eccentric ways, and sometimes 'paid extra' for their work (as Humpty Dumpty claims to do in a bizarre conversation with Lewis Carroll's, 1872, *Alice 'Through the Looking Glass'*). It is argued here that the word 'spirit' is made to work too hard but is never paid extra: it is most often obscure or redundant. It should now be retired altogether. The word 'possession' works hard and is beginning to be paid its due, as evidenced in this book and in wider reconsideration and research. It promises to reward this careful attention with even greater insights into the richness of the human relationships, performances and experiences that it labels. 'Shaman' has certainly worked too hard and is only sometimes paid extra. This chapter has aimed to say something about animist shamans working among and for other animists because relationality needs mediations of various kinds. It has sought to introduce some of the benefits of speaking about shamanic relationships, including those that entail 'possession'. In this context, animist shamans might be defined as people who, for specific, locally meaningful purposes, welcome 'possession' by otherworld persons while also 'possessing' those persons as significant helpers and co-workers. 'Possession' here may be defined as a particular kind of relationship that arises from and affects the behaviour of both the shaman and the otherworld person. Whether these functional definitions describe reality (i.e. whether there really are otherworld persons) is not the point. The task is to see the world of those among whom we research and allow ourselves to be challenged to understand and communicate about them more richly than we would under the possessive constraints of our cultural context. To that end, the words 'person' and 'relationship' are offered as ways of understanding matters of importance in the scholarly debate about shamans and possession.

Bibliography

Baird, R. D. (1971), *Category Formation and the History of Religions*. The Hague: Mouton.

Bird-David, N. (1999), '"Animism" revisited: personhood, environment, and relational epistemology', *Current Anthropology*, 40, S67–S91. Reprinted in G. Harvey (ed.) (2002), *Readings in Indigenous Religions*. London: Continuum, pp. 73–105.

Black, M. B. (1977), 'Ojibwa power belief system', in R. D. Fogelson and Richard N. Adams, eds. *The Anthropology of Power*. New York: Academic, pp. 141–51.

Campbell, A. T. (1995), *Getting to Know Waiwai: An Amazonian Ethnography*. London: Routledge.

Carroll, L. (1872), *Through the Looking Glass*. Published in a combined volume in 1962 with *Alice's Adventures in Wonderland*. London: Puffin.

Chidester, D. (2005), *Authentic Fakes: Religion and American Popular Culture*. Berkeley: University of California Press.

Czaplicka, M. A. (1914), *Aboriginal Siberia: A Study in Social Anthropology*. Oxford: Oxford University Press.

Eliade, M. (1964), *Shamanism: Archaic Techniques of Ecstasy*. New York: Pantheon.

Hallowell, A. I. (1960), 'Ojibwa ontology, behavior, and world view', in S. Diamond (ed.), *Culture in History: Essays in Honor of Paul Radin*. New York: Columbia University Press, pp. 19–52. Reprinted in G. Harvey (ed.) (2002), *Readings in Indigenous Religions*. London: Continuum, pp. 18–49.

Harner, M. (1990), *The Way of the Shaman*. San Francisco: Harper and Row.

Harvey, G. (2003), *Shamanism: A Reader*. London: Routledge.

Harvey, G. (2005a), *Animism: Respecting the Living World*. London: C. Hurst/New York: Columbia University Press/Adelaide: Wakefield Press.

Harvey, G. (2005b), *Ritual and Religious Belief: A Reader*. London: Equinox/New York: Routledge.

Harvey, G. and Wallis, R. (2006), *Historical Dictionary of Shamanism*. Lanham, MD: Scarecrow Press.

Heusch, L. de (1982), 'Possession and shamanism', in L. de Heusch (ed.), *Why Marry Her? Society and Symbolic Structures*. Cambridge: Cambridge University Press, pp. 151–64.

Humphrey, C. (1994), 'Shamanic practices and the state in Northern Asia: views from the centre and periphery', in N. Thomas and C. Humphrey (eds), *Shamanism, History, and the State*. Ann Arbor: University of Michigan Press, pp. 191–228.

Ingold, T. (2000), *The Perception of the Environment: Essays in Livelihood, Dwelling and Skill*. London: Routledge.

Jakobsen, M. D. (1999), *Shamanism: Traditional and Contemporary Approaches to the Mastery of Spirits and Healing*. Oxford: Berghahn Books.

Klass, M. (1995), *Ordered Universes: Approaches to the Anthropology of Religion*. Boulder: Westview.

Knight, C. (1996), 'Totemism', in A. Barnard and J. Spencer (eds), *Encyclopedia of Social and Cultural Anthropology*. London: Routledge, pp. 550–1.

Koerner, J. L. (2005), 'Reforming the assembly', in B. Latour and P. Weibel (eds),

Making Things Public: Atmospheres of Democracy. Cambridge, MA: MIT Press, pp. 404–33.

Lévi-Strauss, C. (1949), 'L'efficacité symbolique', *Revue de l'histoire des religions*, 135 (1), 5–27.

Lévi-Strauss, C. (1969), *Totemism*. Harmondsworth: Penguin.

Lewis, I. M. (1998 [1971]), *Ecstatic Religion: A Study of Shamanism and Spirit Possession* (2nd edn). London: Routledge.

Lewis, I. M. (2003), 'Trance, possession, shamanism and sex', *Anthropology of Consciousness*, 14 (1), 20–39.

Narby, J. and Huxley, F. (2001), *Shamans Through Time: 500 Years on the Path to Knowledge*. London: Thames and Hudson.

Nichols, J. D. and Nyholm, E. (1995), *A Concise Dictionary of Minnesota Ojibwe*. Minneapolis: University of Minnesota Press.

Rose, D. B. (1992), *Dingo Makes Us Human: Life and Land in an Australian Aboriginal Culture*. Cambridge: Cambridge University Press.

Rose, D. B. (1998), 'Totemism, regions, and co-management in Aboriginal Australia', draft paper for the Conference of the International Association for the Study of Common Property. Available on-line at: http://www.indiana.edu/~iascp/ Drafts/rose.pdf.

Rose, D. B. (2004), *Reports from a Wild Country: Ethics for Decolonisation*. Sydney: University of New South Wales Press.

Shirokogoroff, S. M. (1935), *Psychometrical Complex of the Tungus*. London: Kegan Paul.

Smith, J. Z. (1998), 'Religion, religions, religious', in M. C. Taylor (ed.), *Critical Terms for Religious Studies*. Chicago: Chicago University Press, pp. 269–84.

Stahl, G. E. (1708), *Theoria medica vera*. Halle: Literis Orphanotrophei.

Tawhai, T. P. (1988), 'Maori religion', in S. Sutherland and P. Clarke (eds), *The Study of Religion, Traditional and New Religion*. London: Routledge, 96–105. Reprinted in G. Harvey (ed.) (2002), *Readings in Indigenous Religions*. London: Continuum, pp. 237–49.

Taylor, M. C. (1998), *Critical Terms for Religious Studies*. Chicago: Chicago University Press.

Tweed, T. (2006), *Crossing and Dwelling: A Theory of Religion*. Cambridge, MA: Harvard University Press.

Tylor, E. (1913 [1871]), *Primitive Culture*, 2 vols. London: John Murray.

Vitebsky, P. (1995), *The Shaman*. London: Macmillan.

Vitebsky, P. (2005), *The Reindeer People: Living with Animals and Spirits in Siberia*. London: Houghton Mifflin.

Witsen, N. (1692), *Noord en Oost Tartarye* (reprinted 1785; Amsterdam: Schalekamp).

Chapter 3

Possession and Self-Possession: Towards an Integrated Mind–Body Perspective

Geoffrey Samuel

We are often told that the Cartesian dualism between mind and body is at the root of many problems in the analysis of human society, and certainly spirit possession and trance seem to fit particularly badly into a conceptual framework built around a rigid mind–body distinction. It is less easy to find a convincing alternative. Much of the difficulty derives from the extent to which the categories of mind and body have been naturalized within most Western languages, and particularly within the English language, which has now achieved such dominant status within the academic world. It is possible to find ways of speaking that begin from an assumption of mind–body unity, but they tend to sound clumsy and artificial, at least to begin with, when phrased in a language such as English where the mind–body distinction is fully naturalized.

This is not sufficient reason to dismiss them. Many major advances in the history of science have involved rejecting what is obvious and commonsensical (the flatness of the earth, its central position within the universe, the solidity of matter) for alternatives which are at first sight far from intuitive; Copernicus, Galileo, Newton, Einstein, Schrödinger and Heisenberg all had to struggle to establish what gradually became a new orthodoxy. In the humanities and social sciences the task is in some ways harder, because we do not have the advantage of being able to express our hypotheses in mathematical language, and so to arrive at generally convincing demonstrations of the superiority of one approach over another. General relativity may be non-intuitive, but the mathematics based on general relativity describes the universe more accurately than that based on the Newtonian world view. The use of statistics in the social sciences is another matter, and certainly does not provide the level of conviction that is afforded by, for example, classic experiments in general relativity or quantum theory. In practice, theory change in the humanities and social sciences is often driven as much by the internal social processes of the university system (academic politics and generational change) and by wider intellectual and social fashions as by any genuine superiority of the new framework to the old.

It is this that led Thomas Kuhn to describe the social sciences as not yet having arrived at paradigms, in the sense that he used the term in the *Structure of Scientific Revolutions* (Kuhn 1970). The point would surely hold even more strongly for the humanities, and the successive waves of structuralist, Marxist, post-structuralist and other theoretical vogues in both social sciences and humanities since the time of Kuhn's classic work have not significantly changed the situation, simply further pluralized an already plural situation. Whether one accepts Kuhn's wording here is not really the point. Many social scientists have preferred to speak of a multiplicity of paradigms rather than of a pre-paradigmatic condition. It is nevertheless true that there is no consensus about what counts as proper evidence, or about what domains should be covered by our attempts at theoretical synthesis.

The recent growth of cognitive anthropology (also known as 'cognitive science of religion') is something of a case in point. Beginning with the works of Dan Sperber in the late 1970s onwards (Sperber 1975, 1985) and Pascal Boyer (Boyer 1996, 2000), this approach now has an international association and a book series.[1] It has already generated a substantial literature (e.g. Whitehouse 2000, 2004a, 2004b; Barrett 1998, 2004), including at least one substantial book on spirit possession, Emma Cohen's *The Mind Possessed* (Cohen 2007), which is discussed in Bettina Schmidt's chapter in this volume.

One can see the attraction of the approach. It is theoretically very simple and straightforward, focusing on a limited range of issues to do with the cognitive processing of religious categories, and offers the possibility of an effectively reductionist 'science of religion' at a time when the claims of religion to scientific status are becoming increasingly problematic for liberal democratic states.[2] In fact, it is striking how far the cognitive science approach reflects the existing biases and predilections of the Western European and North American mainstream, including the obsession with belief as the core of religion, and the preference for simplistic versions of evolutionary theory. This is an approach that feels natural and is easy to think with. It also looks scientific, and this counts for a lot in a world where knowledge remains dominated by the natural sciences.

At the same time, the cognitive science approach is only really convincing in so far as one accepts the fundamental assumption that cognitive categories – as distinct from, for example, emotional or motivational issues – are the main human variables that underlie religion. This radical assumption is a drastic break from previous schools of anthropology, such as the symbolic and interpretive anthropology of the 1960s and 1970s, though it echoes the nineteenth-century European tendency to see religion primarily as a (mistaken) explanation of the universe. It is intrinsically implausible and has never been effectively argued for.[3] Anthropologists and others are well aware that religion's role in most human societies has not been only, or even primarily, that of providing explanations.

Thus reducing everything to cognitive categories allows for a considerable elegance and simplicity, but at the expense of excluding much of what appears to be significant about the human condition. Bettina Schmidt demonstrates this quite effectively in her own chapter in this book, in which she discusses the cognitive science approach to spirit possession as exemplified by Emma Cohen's work. This approach answers certain questions quite well (e.g. why might brains with stereotypically female kinds of mental processing be more amenable to spirit possession than those which are stereotypically male?) but excludes other questions that one might find of more interest (e.g. what in fact is spirit possession and how does it operate, as a mode of human functioning, and why has it been significant within so many human societies?).

The integrated mind–body approaches are inevitably more complex, at least at first acquaintance, because their categories tend to work across our common-sense categories rather than to build upon them. Such writers as Gregory Bateson (*Steps to an Ecology of Mind*, 1973), Gilles Deleuze and Félix Guattari (*Anti-Oedipus*, 1984 and *A Thousand Plateaus*, 1987), or Francisco Varela (Maturana and Varela, *Autopoesis and Cognition*, 1980; Varela et al., *The Embodied Mind*, 1991), all of whom one might regard as situated within a generally neo-Bergsonian tradition (see Watson 1998), are undoubtedly harder to read than the cognitive science authors, because their assumptions conflict with our taken-for-granted categories.[4] None of these writers offers easy or straightforward accounts at first reading, yet all can become more convincing on further study, since they build plausible connections between aspects of human functioning that may otherwise be difficult to relate to each other. More explicitly, one might regard these aspects as including the mind and human consciousness, the body and its functioning at a physiological (including neural and hormonal) level, and the social or cultural aspects of human existence.

Much of this work is open and experimental in character, in part because of the difficulties, both scientific and particularly institutional or political, in building an effective research programme around it. However, these difficulties are not, as was perhaps the case with some of the theoretical excesses of postmodernism, a result of complexity for its own sake. They are, in part, intrinsic to the complexity of the models which attempt to mirror the complexity of the real world, and in part also a reflection of the political and institutional interests with which the scientific and academic field is invested. The possibilities that these approaches offer are nevertheless important because this general family of approaches remains the only serious contender for a genuine integration between the natural sciences, on the one hand, and the social sciences and humanities, on the other. Certainly, the over-simple reductionisms of evolutionary biologists such as E. G. Wilson (1975), Dawkins (1976, 1988), or Alexander (1982), or, in their way, of the cognitive science of religion group, will not lead to such an integration. At the end of the day, if we are going to move forward, we will have to find some way to bring together the insights from these different fields of human knowledge, rather than to look for the dominance of the field within which we are most at home ourselves.

I have provided at least one substantial contribution to this literature already (*Mind, Body and Culture,* Samuel 1990), but rather than repeat the approach taken in that book, I will work here from a different starting point. This is the concept of *āveśa* found in Sanskrit and related languages, which I discussed in a paper at the BASR conference in Edinburgh in 2007 (since published as Samuel 2008a).[5] The concept of *āveśa* has a long history within Indian thought, which may serve to give it a naturalness lacking with some of the more contemporary Western frameworks mentioned above. I tried to show in my 2007 paper, which took off in part from the work of André Padoux (1999) and Fred Smith (2006), that *āveśa* describes a subtly but significantly different approach to the question of human embodiment than that of typical Western modes of thought. I would suggest that this mode of approach to embodiment is worth taking seriously as a theoretical resource, specifically in relation to matters of shamanism and spirit possession, and that it can point the way to an account of such phenomena and practices that might integrate phenomenological, anthropological and natural scientific approaches.

First, however, I need to give some more content to what an *āveśa*-based model might be like. *Āveśa* is perhaps best translated in the present concept as 'pervasion', in the sense that the life-force (*jīva*) – a term to which we will have to return – pervades, controls and operates the mind–body totality of an individual human being (or, presumably, any other complex animal, to the extent that a similar process can be assumed).[6]

This is a model that assumes a dichotomy of a kind, but the dichotomy is between life-force and mind-body, not between mind (or soul) and body. We will return to what this might mean at a later point. If we are looking for a materialist reading of what is happening here, however, in the case of a specific human being, we can assume that it might be found in terms of factors such as the patterns of neuronal activity within the body, patterns of hormonal secretion and distribution within the body, and patterns of muscle relaxation and tension, of sensory awareness, and so on. How the *jīva* pervades the mind–body totality affects what the 'person' is consciously aware of, and also how sensory input is being processed unconsciously.

Such matters are in a sense 'habits' of the body. Here the echo of Pierre Bourdieu's *habitus* is intentional. Bourdieu respected the limits of Durkheimian social science and tended to treat the concept of *habitus* as something of a 'black box', a quantity or variable that was assumed within his theoretical approach but in whose inner workings he did not choose to enquire. He gave us little sense, however, of how the *habitus* might actually work in physiological or neurological terms, and it suited his approach better to leave it as a 'black box', as little more than a label for the ways in which an individual might internalize the habitual modes of functioning within a particular social and cultural milieu. If a truly scientific approach to human behaviour involves an integration of the social sciences and the biological sciences, this will require an investigation of what might be inside the 'black box' of the *habitus*.

Bourdieu's work nevertheless points us to the intimate relation between such habits and the social and cultural milieu. We might also note, following the suggestions of works such as Bateson's *Steps to an Ecology of Mind* (1973) and Maturana and Varela's *Autopoesis and Cognition* (1980), that these 'habits' pertain less to the individual human being than to the interaction between human being and social and natural environment. At one level, then, I suggest that the *habitus* consists of the kinds of matters I suggested above: the patterns of neuronal and hormonal activity within the body, which also have correlates at the level of consciousness in terms of patterns of sensory awareness (or the lack of it).

From the point of view of the individual, this is not a static matter but an ongoing flux in which the 'state' of the organism changes from moment to moment. Some of this change is at a gross level, between sleep and waking, for example, or rest and physical activity, but some takes place at much more subtle levels – as when one notices something moving out of the corner of one's eye, and a neuronal/hormonal shift in the body takes place in terms of readiness for what this movement might signify for the welfare of the organism. Modes of 'thinking' – what seems significant and how one might 'reason' about it – can be seen as derivative of the momentary state of this flux, rather than (as the cognitive anthropologists would have it) primarily explanatory variables.

From the point of view of the group or culture these matters are partly shared between individual members of the group or culture, though each individual is biologically unique, as well as differing in matters such as youth, age, physiology, gender, and social location. Thus one can speak of cultural patterns that are instantiated in specifically individual forms, depending, at least, on the specific mind–body formation of the individual.[7] It is also important to stress that these patterns are relational. They are about the way in which the 'individual' (a term which should not ultimately be given too much weight in any explanatory frame[8]) interacts with his or her environment.

With this general structure of ideas in mind, we can begin to examine some of the phenomena that have been classified under labels such as spirit possession, spirit mediumship and shamanic healing. Such phenomena are generally regarded as unusual and abnormal modes of human functioning ('altered states of consciousness' etc.), though the tendency to regard them as forms of psychopathology fortunately seems to be fading. The question of 'normality' nevertheless needs some discussion, and I shall begin with this. I then consider spirit possession as a response to organismic dysfunction, then turn to spirit mediumship, and finally to one of my current research topics: Tibetan longevity practice.

Normal Modes of Functioning

To speak of 'normality' is already problematic; Norman Zinberg quite rightly pointed many years ago to the implicit assumption behind terminologies such as 'altered states of consciousness': that there is a standard, normal state of consciousness. Zinberg preferred to speak of 'alternate states of consciousness' (Zinberg 1977), which at least conveys the message that human consciousness can alternate between a variety of states, none of them necessarily to be regarded as 'normal'.[9] Also, it is important to note that we are not just speaking of 'consciousness' here but of the body–mind complex as a whole, of which conscious awareness is only part. That complex is itself not ultimately separable from its cultural and physical environment.

However, it seems reasonable to suppose that there are, for most human beings, states of the body–mind complex that are part of the usual range of functioning and others that lie outside that range, such as those induced by severe illness, psychedelic substances or extreme ascetic practices. We thus speak of a range within which the various factors of the organism typically vary. Since they presumably do not vary independently of each other, we can also speak of a repertoire of usual states of the body–mind complex, each of which has its own associated consciousness and sense of self, its own ways of walking, holding the body, and so on.[10]

We can think of these states as part cultural and part individual.[11] They enable the individual to carry out his or her characteristic functions and roles in life. They change over time, as new behaviours are evolved or old ones are gradually dropped. While I speak here of separate states, what actually happens in life can be better considered as a flow made up of a shifting combination of these states, with the proportions of each varying from moment to moment.

One can see the advantage of speaking of *jīva*, a neutral term in relation to any particular state of consciousness or any specific sense of personal identity on the individual's part. Western vocabularies, because of their tendency to mind–body dichotomy, tend to treat the critical relationship as being that between the conscious self and the physical body (the 'ghost in the machine', in Gilbert Ryle's dismissive phrase; Ryle 1949). By introducing what is in effect a third term underlying both mind and body, this problematic relationship is decentred. Here, I am treating the specific assumptions of rebirth that are associated with the Indian model as secondary.[12]

Spirit Possession

In terms of consciousness of the self, these states of the body–mind complex correspond, in a normal mature human being, to a functioning and effective, if not necessarily entirely consistent, sense of self. What, though, of the situation where the individual is unable to find or access a state that provides an adequate response to what is happening (internally or externally) to him or her, where the *jīva* cannot find a way to inhabit satisfactorily the place its associated body–mind complex is occupying in social life, for example? In contemporary Western parlance, we are here in the area of psychological disorders, as mapped by typologies such as DSM-IV (American Psychiatric Association 2000). In many pre-modern and non-Western societies, such conditions are described in terms of soul loss or spirit possession.

I focus here on the latter. It is easier to argue in terms of specific examples, so I take as one 'typical' instance of spirit possession of a young woman in a South Asian society, such as India or Bangladesh, who is unable to handle the situation of being a newly married incoming bride, with the associated transfer from the relatively indulged status of a daughter in her parents' household to that of being a vulnerable and suspect outsider in her new husband's household. The woman's predicament might be intensified by a failure to bear male children, by her being made the scapegoat for conflicts within the husband's family, and so on. This is a classic context for spirit possession in South Asia, with a high proportion of cases of spirit possession being young women shortly before marriage or in the early years of marriage.

The situation described is characteristically South Asian, deriving from the specific patterns of kinship and family structures found in many South Asian societies, but could manifest in behaviour that might be diagnosed in Western terms as severe depression or other psychological disturbance, accompanied by an inability to carry out the work expected of her in her new household. We note that, in the frame of analysis adopted here, we do not need to make the (somewhat artificial) choice between the girl's condition being caused by endogenous factors or external factors. The two are interdependent. Not all women in similar situations will undergo severe psychological disturbance, in part presumably because not all have the same biochemical and neurological predispositions, in part because they have internalized different sets of personal and cultural resources as part of their 'normal' state repertoire. Equally, many of those who do experience severe problems might manage better if they were not placed in such a difficult situation, for example, if the husband's family was itself more supportive or less internally conflicted.

Gananath Obeyesekere and Bruce Kapferer's descriptions of Sinhalese spirit-exorcism rituals (Obeyesekere 1970; Kapferer 1979, 1983), or Graham Dwyer's accounts of healing at the Balaji shrine (1999, 2002), provide typical accounts, for Sri Lanka and India respectively, of the kind of treatment that might be provided. It might be noted that these modes of treatment, while quite various in detail, all (a) avoid labelling the individual,[13] (b) provide scope for negotiation within the social situation (here the actual or potential new marital family) and (c) provide a series of highly dramatic sequences during which there is scope for both the woman to develop a new 'self' (i.e. body of states) outside of the negatively labelled possession states, and for her family (marital and/or natal) to make appropriate adjustments in their own modes of interaction with her.

Of course, all this does not guarantee a successful outcome, either on an initial possession episode and treatment or as a result of a series of such episodes. In any case it depends on what one judges as success.[14] We are speaking here of a society with marked gender inequality, where young women are being required to adapt to a difficult and, in Western terms, perhaps even oppressive situation. The development of the strong autonomous sense of self that is favoured by Western psychiatry might not be either appropriate or possible. At the same time, whatever their social arrangements, people in all societies can be (and are) confronted by situations beyond their ability to cope adequately, and that are 'outside their repertoire'.

The key point here is that the 'sick' individual is caught in an unproductive pattern, or repertoire of patterns. The job of the ritual specialist (shaman or spirit-medium) who is attempting to deal with the situation is somehow to sense the way in which the patient is trapped in these patterns, and to bring into relief the 'dark' side – those areas of life-activity which are not adequately pervaded by conscious awareness. One might think here of Jung's concept of the shadow, although I am trying to sketch a vocabulary which is less metaphorical and more capable of reconciliation with the wider contexts of contemporary Western scientific knowledge.

Once the areas for which the patient's established patterns of response and behaviour are inadequate or self-defeating have been recognized, the possibility opens of allowing these areas to be expressed – in the form of the possessing spirit. Once they are brought to the surface in this way, it becomes possible to come to terms with them. The details here vary but the key issue would seem to be that the negative patterns are recognized as 'demonic', that is, as destructive to the interests of the individual and his or her wider social group, and also as capable of being driven out or, more typically, negotiated with. In South Asia, this typically takes place in the context of a healing temple, where the presiding deity, through his or her representatives, can force the possessing spirit to submit and to leave the individual. This does not necessarily provide a solution – cases of spirit possession may involve multiple visits to various healers and healing temples, and a positive resolution is by no means guaranteed. However, it does at least provide a space for negotiation between the stakeholders in the situation, both internal and external. The demon, after all, is there because certain patterns of behaviour and response have developed through the individual's lifetime; it represents certain real interests, even if at a considerable cost to the individual and the wider social group. Thus if the spirit is 'defending' the girl from an unwelcome marriage, or one which she is not prepared to embark on or not yet able to deal with, then possession offers both a breathing space and an opportunity for all involved to rethink where they are in relation to the situation.

Spirit Mediumship

Positively valued spirit mediumship is a different situation from spirit possession seen in negative terms, though in many societies it may arise as the resolution of a period of (in Western terms) psychiatric illness or breakdown. In such cases the resolution of a period of personal crisis is not the achievement of a 'normal' identity through the expulsion of the spirit, but the achievement of a new social role, that of medium for the spirit (here conceived of as at least potentially benign, and capable of being incorporated positively into the local social universe). In South Asia a woman might establish a positive identity as the medium for a local spirit or deity (e.g. Stanley 1988; Dietrich 1998). In the process, her relationship with her husband is also renegotiated. The positive establishment of a relationship with a spirit in the East African *zar* cult, or in Afro-American cults such as Candomblé, Santería or Vodou, involving controlled possession under ritually supervised circumstances, while not necessarily involving actual mediumistic activity, can be seen in similar terms.

From our present point of view the spirit-identity becomes, in effect, an additional and subsidiary repertoire within the individual's range of body–mind states, if substantially different in terms of subjective experience from the person's 'normal' range of states, and externally labelled as indicating a different identity (that of the spirit). This new subsidiary repertoire may provide a way for the social group as a whole to mediate its relationship with its wider social and natural environment (cf. Bateson 1970) or of assisting in the healing of others.

The role of spirit medium is, of course, by no means always preceded by a 'shamanic illness' of this kind. Selection of spirit mediums can take place on a variety of other bases, including a hereditary component; in some societies many people are thought of as capable of achieving it to at least some degree (see Samuel 1990). At any rate, a substantial proportion of the human population is clearly capable of developing body–mind states that can serve to actualize in some way the role of spirit medium. These may differ quite considerably from each other, and from those states that result from the resolution of a psychotic episode, but they have in common that they allow the person in question to carry out the role. Here one might think of some aspects of the Whitehouse-Cohen model, as described by Schmidt (this volume), where it is suggested that some patterns of brain functioning (the stereotypically female, empathetic and participatory) are more amenable to being able to take on such roles.

One of my favourite stories helps suggest the naturalness of such apparently exotic behaviour. Some years ago I interviewed a Tibetan lama in Orissa (Eastern India) who is well known for his activities as a visionary lama, having in effect built a central part of his career on his ability to convey messages, teachings and practices from the Tibetan deity and epic hero Ling Gesar. When Tashi Tsering, my co-worker on the project, and I asked him when he had first met with Gesar, he said that this was when he was a small child, and Gesar himself had appeared in the form of a young boy. I immediately thought of the frequency of imaginary playmates in early childhood within Western society. Such imagined friends are normally forgotten (at least to the conscious mind) as the child grows older, and is told by his or her parents that the playmate is not real. My interviewee, as the son of a distinguished hereditary lama family, was perhaps able to hold on to an imaginary playmate of much the same kind, since his status gave his childhood visions a legitimacy they would not have had in the UK or USA. In time, he was able to build his relationship with Gesar into a central component of his adult life and activity. Perhaps, given similar circumstances and encouragement, many people in the UK or USA could have done the same.[15]

Tibetan Longevity Practices

Finally, I discuss some material from a current research project, on Tibetan longevity practices (*ts'edrup* in Tibetan). I have described one particular set of practices of this kind in considerable detail elsewhere (Samuel 2008b). Here it is sufficient to say that *ts'edrup* practices involve creating a relationship with and imaginatively transforming oneself into a powerful, energized deity (often conceived of as in a state of sexual union with a consort). The deity, itself a manifestation of the enlightened nature of Buddhahood, is surrounded by an entourage of subsidiary beings seen as its subsidiary projections or emanations.

Thus the environment is imaginatively reconstituted in the shape of the tantric mandala, an idealized world of supportive and nourishing forces, taking the form of a highly ordered and symmetrical palace-structure centred on the principal deity, with assigned places for the various sub-sidiary figures. Lost life-energy (*la* in Tibetan) is recovered in a series of repetitive and functionally highly redundant ritual actions, in what can be seen as a transform of the idiom of soul-loss and soul-recovery common in many forms of Himalayan shamanic practice as elsewhere in the world. The identification with the deity is achieved through a series of structured steps, leading to the recitation of one or more mantras (ritual formulae) that represent the deity's innermost nature.

One can see how the repeated performance of such a scenario, alone in personal retreat or as part of a group of practitioners, might activate and strengthen the organism's immune response and self-healing abilities, by encouraging the building and strengthening of positive and healthy modes of interaction between the body–mind complex and the surrounding social and natural universe. From another point of view, one could see this whole process as a highly complex and sophisticated way of operating with what Western medicine knows as the 'placebo effect'.[16]

In terms of the current framework, one could see the process as learning more positive and constructive ways of operating with (or 'pervading') the mind–body complex. Since the Tibetans have their own version of the *āveśa* frame, the imagery is fairly closely related to that which we have discussed earlier, and is perceived of in terms of operations with the *tsa-lung-t'igle* (*nāḍī, prāṇa, bindu* in Sanskrit), an idealized model of the internal structure of the mind–body complex. I have suggested elsewhere that this might be seen as some kind of inner map of the central nervous system; in terms of our present vocabulary, it could be seen as a guide to how to achieve a positive structure for the mind–body complex in relationship to its external environment. This relationship is mediated in particular by the breath (*prāṇa*).

Tibetan Buddhist ritual aims at the transcendence of duality, and it tends to work towards this goal through successive stages in which dualistic structures are stated and then gone beyond. In the case of *ts'edrup*, this takes place both through the invocation of the tantric deities (who are imaginatively created 'within' and 'outside' the practitioner, with the two then being brought together), and through the duality between the visua-lization of deity and mandala on the one hand, and of the internal structure of *tsa-lung-t'igle* on the other. The aim always is to go beyond any particular dualistic structure to a condition of underlying non-duality. One might see these dualities as grounded in varying degrees in the neurophysiology of how human beings operate, with the holistic deity–mandala visualizations as linked with those functions generally specialized in the right hemisphere of the brain, and the more step-by-step, purposive manipulations of the internal 'energy' structure of *tsa-lung-t'igle* as related more to left hemisphere functions. This is a point I have developed at some length elsewhere and I shall not pursue it here (cf. Samuel 1990, pp. 153–5). The direction of the practices is nevertheless to move to a more unitive sense of oneself as in communion with rather than separate from the wider matrix of reality.

Conclusion

In conclusion, one might contrast two general approaches to dealing with the question of human embodiment, both of which form part of everyday human functioning. One operates in terms of step-by-step means–end sequences, and the other in terms of holistic imagery. These are not so much alternatives as different moments of experiencing and operating with the same process. One can see these moments, for example, in the process of learning to drive a car. One needs to learn what the controls do, but competent driving involves a move beyond this kind of stepwise operation to a more integrated mode of operation, in which most of the detailed functioning has been submerged below the level of conscious awareness. The process of learning a foreign language works similarly; one cannot speak fluently if one is translating word by word.

As Gregory Bateson pointed out in one of his best-known papers, 'Style, Grace and Information in Primitive Art', dating from 1967 (Bateson 1973, pp. 101–25), the ways in which human consciousness does this submerging, which tends to be driven by the logic of conscious reason, are inevitably incomplete and partial.[17] We are generally, and necessarily, aware of parts only of the wider networks of connectedness, between our various internal processes, between us and other human beings, and between us and the environment within which we live. The aim of techniques such as the Tibetan longevity practices is nevertheless to move to a more unitive sense of oneself as in positive communion with and not separate from the wider matrix of reality.

For Bateson, in his later years, there was a political point here as well as a spiritual one, or rather the two could not be disentangled from each other. Living with 'grace', to use the terminology he used in 'Style, Grace and Information', involved living in awareness of our connectedness with each other and our wider environment. In his last years, Bateson reiterated the message, but with a new sensitivity to the impact of human behaviour on the wider ecology, of which mind was an integral part. The conscious purposes of 'mind' (meaning, for Bateson, the emotional as well as the rational) needed some bringing into balance with the needs of the wider environment, or else pathologies of both the individual and the wider system would develop.

To return to spirit possession, I have suggested that this is a label for a certain kind of pathology of the self, where the self somehow fails to acquire the habits of operating with the mind–body complex that it needs to function as part of its social context.[18] Ideally, the spirit medium or shaman helps to rebalance the individual (and perhaps at the same time his or her family and friends) so as to repair the pathology. The question of the health of the wider system within those societies in which such 'shamanic mechanisms' (cf. Samuel 1990, pp. 106–20) are or were taken seriously is perhaps unanswerable, since our data on such societies inevitably refers to situations where the wider context has already been pathologized by the impact of imperialism and colonialism. That the wider global context of modernity has its pathological aspects is undeniable, driven as it is by processes of commercial exploitation and the creation of consumer needs on the one hand, and fear, poverty and disadvantage on the other. Ultimately, one would hope that an anthropology of mind–body processes might contribute to an awareness of this pathology and of its modes of operation, and to the creation of global mechanisms that might bring about a world which was both saner and, in the longer term, more viable.

Notes

[1] Details of the International Association of the Cognitive Science of Religion can be found at http://www.iacsr.com/Home.html (last accessed 25 March 2009). The book series, Cognitive Science of Religion, is produced by AltaMira Press and edited by Harvey Whitehouse and Luther H. Martin.

[2] Thus if the claims of cognitive science are taken at face value, the validity of religious claims can in effect be explained away by arguing that such claims take the form that they do because of cognitive constraints rather than because of anything they might have to say about reality.

[3] Sperber pointed, quite correctly, in his 1975 book and in later writings, to some of the problematic assumptions of the interpretive anthropologists. His work is regularly cited by the school to make this point (e.g. Cohen 2007, p. 71). However, to ditch interpretive anthropology because of the theoretical incoherence of some of its followers seems to me to be throwing the baby out with the bathwater. The interpretive contributions of the school are of major importance, and the theoretical incoherence is not intrinsic and can be remedied (cf. Samuel 1990). The central problem here is really the philosophical naivety of anthropologists as a whole. The strength of the discipline has always been in field research

rather than theory. It is doubtlessly clear enough that I see the cognitive science of religion group as sharing this theoretical naivety.

[4] There is a tendency to dismiss Bergson and others following in his tracks as idealist, 'vitalist', etc. The 'life-force' here (which can be seen, as below, as a kind of patterning of mind–body activity) is in fact no more 'theoretical' than anything else in science, and certainly no more than the variables of quantum mechanics or general relativity. It is not immediately accessible to observation or recording, but then neither are most scientific variables (what we measure and record is always a proxy of some kind, even with apparently straightforward variables such as temperature).

[5] This paper was written for a panel on spirit possession, again arising from an initiative of Bettina Schmidt's.

[6] The nearest English equivalent might be 'animation', but it is probably better avoided because of its close linkage with the specifically European and Christian body–mind (or body–soul) dichotomy; *anima* is the Latin for 'soul'.

[7] In my *Mind, Body and Culture* (Samuel 1990), I developed a sketch of how such patterns might be conceptualized. I suggested there that one might speak of a repertoire of such states at the individual level, and also a related repertoire of such states at the cultural level. I explicitly did not assume that cultures are sharply delimited and defined groups; the degree of closure might in fact vary very greatly between different situations.

[8] This is because the kind of 'individual' one is depends on the nature of the patterns through which one operates one's body–mind totality. One might think of the debate about the nature of 'individuals' in South Asian society (Dumont 1970; Marriott 1976, etc.). One does not have to accept Marriott's assertion that South Asians are 'dividuals' not 'individuals' to appreciate that modes of 'pervasion' may involve greater or lesser senses of separateness and distinction from one's fellow human beings.

[9] 'Normality' also has a political aspect, cf. the critiques of American psychoanalysis (especially the ego-psychology school) by Lacan and others as being essentially to do with 'adjustment' to the US social context, for example Lacan (1977) and Mills (2000).

[10] These states are the 'modal states' of the individual discussed in *Mind, Body and Culture* (Samuel 1990).

[11] In reality, this division is somewhat artificial, since culture does not exist separately from individuals, and vice versa, but culture is nevertheless instantiated in individual forms which depend on the specific aspects of that individual.

[12] It should also be noted that the *jīva* as used here is a theoretical term in a scientific theory, rather than something that is claimed as having ontological status. It is no more (but no less) real than, for example, gravity, a force that can in no way be observed directly, only postulated through its effects. Like gravity, it is also open to substitution by more 'fundamental' variables – for example, for the case of gravity, the 'curvature' of space-time in general relativity.

[13] Cf. here Obeyesekere (1985), who makes a similar point in relation to 'depression' in Sinhala culture.

[14] Note Kapferer's point that '[e]xorcism must be understood initially on its own terms and in its particular historical context. Only when this is done can one see

that Sinhalese exorcism is in many respects organized at complete variance from those principles on which Western psychiatry is informed-by Judeo–Christian principles of, inter alia, guilt and personal autonomy. Furthermore, Sinhalese exorcism addresses many other issues not reducible to or encompassed by Western medical concern' (Kapferer 1988, pp. 428–9). The approach in the present article may be seen as an attempt to work within a scheme general enough to include much of the specific contexts and purposes of a tradition such as that of Sinhalese exorcism.

[15] Mary Watkins has argued for seeing internal dialogue of this kind as potentially an effective and valued part of adult functioning, and in no way pathological or infantile (Watkins 1986).

[16] Cf. Moerman and Jonas (2002), who stress the role of 'meaning' in the placebo effect, and Samuel (in press), who develop the theme summarized here through an analysis of ritual healing.

[17] The use of the term 'primitive' in Bateson's title is perhaps unfortunate, since neither the Balinese art discussed by Bateson in the paper, nor the visualizations of Tibetan Buddhism and their artistic expressions, are in any way 'primitive' – but that was part of Bateson's point.

[18] 'Operating' here should be taken metaphorically, since we are not talking for the most part of a conscious process. The 'self' is itself constituted by these modes of operating with the mind–body complex.

Bibliography

Alexander, R. D. (1982), *Darwinism and Human Affairs*. Seattle: University of Washington Press.

American Psychiatric Association (2000), *Diagnostic and Statistical Manual of Mental Disorders: DSM-IV-TR Fourth Edition (Text Revision)*. Washington, DC: American Psychiatric Publishing.

Barrett, J. (1998), 'Cognitive constraints on Hindu concepts of the Divine', *Journal of the Scientific Study of Religion*, 37, 608–19.

Barrett, J. (2004), *Why Would Anyone Believe in God?* Cognitive Science of Religion Series. Walnut Creek, CA: AltaMira Press.

Bateson, G. (1970), 'An old temple and a new myth', in J. Belo (ed.), *Traditional Balinese Culture*. New York: Columbia University Press, pp. 111–36.

Bateson, G. (1973), *Steps to an Ecology of Mind*. Frogmore: Paladin.

Boyer, P. (1996), 'What makes anthropomorphism natural: intuitive ontology and cultural representations', *Journal of the Royal Anthropological Institute*, 2, 83–97.

Boyer, P. (2000), *Religion Explained: The Evolutionary Origins of Religious Thought*. London: Random House; New York: Basic Books.

Cohen, E. (2007), *The Mind Possessed: The Cognition of Spirit Possession in an Afro-Brazilian Religious Tradition*. Oxford and New York: Oxford University Press.

Dawkins, R. (1976), *The Selfish Gene*. Oxford: Oxford University Press.

Dawkins, R. (1988), *The Blind Watchmaker*. Harmondsworth: Penguin Books.

Deleuze, G. and Guattari, F. (1984). *Anti-Oedipus*. London: Athlone Press.

Deleuze, G. and Guattari, F. (1987). *A Thousand Plateaus.* Minneapolis: University of Minnesota Press.

Dietrich, A. (1998), *Tantric Healing in the Kathmandu Valley: A Comparative Study of Hindu and Buddhist Spiritual Healing Traditions in Urban Nepalese Society.* Delhi: Book Faith India.

Dumont, L. (1970). *Homo Hierarchicus. An Essay on the Caste System.* Chicago: University of Chicago Press.

Dwyer, G. (1999), 'Healing and the transformation of self in exorcism at a Hindu shrine in Rajasthan', *Social Analysis,* 43, 108–37.

Dwyer, G. (2002), *The Divine and the Demonic: Supernatural Affliction and Its Treatment in North India.* London: Routledge.

Kapferer, B. (1979), 'Mind, self and other in demonic illness: the negation and reconstruction of self', *American Ethnologist,* 6, 110–33.

Kapferer, B. (1983), *A Celebration of Demons.* Bloomington: Indiana University Press.

Kapferer, B. (1988), 'Gramsci's body and a critical medical anthropology', *Medical Anthropology Quarterly,* 2, 426–32.

Kuhn, T. (1970). *The Structure of Scientific Revolutions* (2nd edn). Chicago: University of Chicago Press.

Lacan, J. (1977), *Écrits: A Selection,* trans. Alan Sheridan. London: Tavistock.

Marriott, M. (1976), 'Hindu transactions: diversity without dualism', in B. Kapferer (ed.), *Transaction and Meaning: Directions in the Anthropology of Human Issues.* Philadelphia: Institute for the Study of Human Issues, pp. 109–14.

Maturana, H. R. and Varela, F. J. (1980), *Autopoesis and Cognition: The Realization of the Living.* Dordrecht: Reidel.

Mills, J. A. (2000), *Control: A History of Behavioral Psychology.* New York University Press.

Moerman, M. and Jonas, W. B. (2002), 'Deconstructing the placebo effect and finding the meaning response', *Annals of Internal Medicine,* 136, 471–6.

Obeyesekere, G. (1970), 'The idiom of demonic possession', *Social Science and Medicine,* 4, 97–111.

Obeyesekere, G. (1985), 'Depression, Buddhism and work of culture in Sri Lanka', in A. Kleinman and B. Good (eds), *Culture and Depression.* Dordrecht: Reidel, pp. 134–52.

Padoux, A. (1999), 'Transe, possession ou absorption mystique? L' āveśa selon quelques textes tantriques cachemiriens', *Puruṣārtha,* 21, 133–47.

Ryle, G. (1949), *The Concept of Mind.* London: Hutchinson.

Samuel, G. (1990), *Mind, Body and Culture: Anthropology and the Biological Interface.* Cambridge and New York: Cambridge University Press.

Samuel, G. (2008a). 'Possession and self-possession: spirit healing, tantric meditation and *Āveśa*', *DISKUS* (online journal of British Association for the Study of Religions), 9. Available at: http://www.basr.ac.uk/diskus/.

Samuel, G. (2008b), 'Tibetan longevity practices: the body in the 'Chi med srog thig tradition', paper for panel in 'Theory and practice of healing, medicine and longevity in Buddhism', *XVth Conference of the International Association of Buddhist Studies (IABS),* Atlanta, Georgia, pp. 23–8.

Samuel, G. (in press), 'Healing, Efficacy and the Spirits'. *Journal of Ritual Studies* Vol. 24 (to appear in 2010), ed. by W. S. Sax and J. Quack.

Smith, F. M. (2006), *The Self Possessed: Deity and Spirit Possession in South Asian Literature and Civilization*. New York: Columbia University Press.

Sperber, D. (1975), *Rethinking Symbolism*. Cambridge: Cambridge University Press.

Sperber, D. (1985), *On Anthropological Knowledge: Three Essays*. Cambridge: Cambridge University Press.

Stanley, J. M. (1988), 'Gods, ghosts, and possession', in E. Zelliot and M. Berntsen (eds), *The Experience of Hinduism: Essays on Religion in Maharashtra*. Albany: State University of New York Press, pp. 26–59.

Varela, F., Thompson, E. and Rosch, E. (1991), *The Embodied Mind: Cognitive Science and Human Experience*. Cambridge, MA: MIT Press.

Watkins, M. (1986), *Invisible Guests: The Development of Imaginal Dialogues*. New York: Analytic Press.

Watson, S. (1998), 'The new Bergsonism', *Radical Philosophy*, 92 (Nov–Dec), 6–16.

Whitehouse, H. (2000), *Arguments and Icons: Divergent Modes of Religiosity*. Oxford and New York: Oxford University Press.

Whitehouse, H. (2004a), *Modes of Religiosity: A Cognitive Theory of Religious Transmission*. Cognitive Science of Religion Series. Walnut Creek, CA: AltaMira Press.

Whitehouse, H. (2004b), 'Modes of religiosity in the cognitive science of religion', *Method and Theory in the Study of Religion*, 16, 321–35.

Wilson, E. O. (1975), *Sociobiology: The New Synthesis*. Cambridge, MA: Harvard University Press.

Zinberg, N. (ed.) (1977), *Alternate States of Consciousness*. New York: Free Press.

Chapter 4

Spirit Possession, Seduction and Collective Consciousness

Louise Child

Introduction

One of the questions arising from possession studies is concerned with the ways in which possession rituals may give rise to the expression of emotions and roles that are beyond the usual range for participants in everyday life. This is particularly problematic in the case of spirit mediums because there is a tension between assertions that the spirit (and not the possessed person) is the agent and the benefits that possession may provide both for the individual and her community. For example, it has been argued that possession ritual dramas may be one way in which people can express tensions related to gender identity and erotic fulfilment (Boddy 1994, pp. 415–22), raise issues rarely openly discussed (Lambek 1981, p. 78), or highlight and engage with issues and personalities related to colonialism (Henley 2006, p. 735; Stoller 1994, p. 636). While these notions do not necessarily entail the dismissal of the idea that spirits are also 'real', they do suggest that their characters and activities are shaped in part by the contemporary concerns of the medium and their surrounding community. In this sense, therefore, there is a 'social' aspect both to possession in general and the specific manifestations of spirits in any given time and place. I suggest that there are, however, inherent dangers with sociological analyses of possession that try to make direct links between structures of inequality and possession, not least because these inequalities often remain evident in societies with thriving possession cults, leading some sociologists to suggest that possession is a failed or extremely limited liberation strategy. My aim in this paper is to tackle the problem in three related ways. First, I suggest utilizing Émile Durkheim's theory of collective consciousness, as this theory explores links between ritual expression and its social context without restricting its understanding of social context to its most visible economic structures and forms (*Les formes élémentaire de la vie religieuse*, 1912;

Durkheim 1995). Secondly, I use the work of Jean Baudrillard (1990) to argue that possession, like seduction, may not be intended to operate as a system of redress within existing frameworks of inequality but, rather, may be a form of activity that subverts the foundation of social and psychological structures in important ways. Baudrillard's work on seduction can also help to re-conceive the erotic dimensions of the relationship between persons and possessing ancestors, deities and spirits because he critiques psychological models that rely on an 'economics of desire' and focuses instead on seduction as a radical and transformative relation between persons. Thirdly, I explore the relationship between possession, seduction and place.

Recent years have seen an increasing volume of scholarship that aims to examine spirits from a perspective close to that found in its indigenous contexts. Edith Turner (2006), for example, explores a growing trend in anthropological writings: namely, the inclusion of personal or eyewitness accounts of 'spirit experience' (often in the context of fieldwork), and the integration of this kind of experience into the theoretical foundations and findings of the works concerned. Turner rightly suggests that this material constitutes a series of important breakthroughs for the field and I would argue, following Bowie (2000), that its repercussions go beyond the implications for research and include suggestions for the ways in which we teach the anthropology of religion.

However, Turner's paper is not unproblematic for at least two reasons. First, she argues that 'a thing variously called spirit-energy is everywhere and is commonly accepted at the heart of the ritual of all the different societies' (2006, p. 33), and secondly she suggests that in order to explore it in more depth scholars have needed to reject the influence of Durkheim in favour of Victor Turner's own notion of liminality, which she argues was non-Durkheimian (E. Turner 2006, p. 38). Her first point, that spirits are everywhere, is an interesting notion. However, it does clash to some extent with anthropological trends that focus on local knowledge and spirits, which, far from being conceived universally, are often associated with particular places. For example, a local shrine for a goddess in Bengal may be activated by members of the community finding a stone that they believe is her manifestation (McDaniel 2004, pp. 32–3). In addition, the notion of place is complicated in particular ways in the religious expressions of African diaspora: first by physical dislocation from the soil on which rites were originally practised, and secondly by various political, economic and genealogical dislocations that are associated with diaspora itself and in particular its relationship with the slave trade.

Karen McCarthy Brown (2001, pp. 22–33) explores this to some extent in the story of Joseph Binbin Mauvant (great grandfather of Mama Lola, a Vodou priestess who conducts ceremonies that include spirit possession in Brooklyn). Joseph Binbin Mauvant had a special religious reputation in his community in Haiti because, although his father was a white Frenchman and his (black) mother was either a North American or Haitian, Joseph had been born in Africa. He was

> no ordinary man. He was . . . a true African. When he had healing work to do, he had no need to call the spirits as others did, using drums, candles, and other ritual paraphernalia . . . [he was] . . . completely African, and he had the spirits 'on him' all the time, all kinds of spirits. (Brown 2001, p. 29)

In this story, therefore, Africa is imagined as an important source of spiritual power, which Joseph tries to pass on to Mama Lola's mother, Philo, by vomiting up a stone which he offers to the child to eat (an offer which she refuses because she did not understand its significance at the time) (Brown 2001, p. 32). While the emphasis of this particular story is more on lineage than possession itself, it would argue that both questions are linked in important ways and suggests that spirit possession enables the evocation of a particular sense of place through the ancestor's ability to travel to the ceremony and participate through the bodies and voices of the participants. However, perhaps paradoxically, spirits are also susceptible to adaptation and change in response to changing social circumstances. For example, Brown suggests that spirit possession became much more central to Haitian religious expression than it was in the African context, partly because slaves had lost access to the musical instruments and altars that were present in Africa. Moreover, 'the possession performances of the spirits took on more of the specifics of time and place and more intimate detail of life. High liturgy became improvisational theater' (Brown 2001, p. 253).

Possession Amnesia and Collective Consciousness

Another important aspect of spirit possession is its sense of elusiveness and mystery, a quality which is not highlighted by Edith Turner's suggestion that spirit energy can be found everywhere. Nonetheless, this mystery contributes to the attraction of spirit possession for scholars because it raises profound questions about the nature of human identity. This idea has been explored by Mattijs van de Port, who suggests that it is the more disturbing and ineffable aspects of possession that make it powerful. In reflecting on his nervous reaction to a spirit possession ceremony in Bahia, van de Port notes his observations of behaviour that appeared to be

> a complete lack of control . . . no matter how possession trance is tackled theoretically, its most immediate experience escapes our understanding . . . the Otherness of the phenomenon (its uncanny inexplicability, its screaming incompatibility with Western notions of personhood, its seeming distain for self-control, its radical otherness) demands explanation, and this explanation highlights the inadequacy of our conceptual categories rather than the phenomenon itself . . . there is 'something' in possession trance that refuses to be signified. No matter how clever our attempts to break the mystery, something about possession trance remains enigmatic, unapproachable, resisting the word (van de Port 2005, pp. 150, 151; see also Boddy 1994, p. 407)

This resistance of the mystery to categorization is not confined to the academic outsider looking in. It is also noticeable within indigenous possession traditions, for although mythology

> may provide the phenomenon with an explanatory cosmological frame, the mystery as to exactly what happens is accepted for what it is: a mystery locked up in the here and now of bodily experience. The Candomblé priesthood is keen on repeating over and over again that there is 'something' in possession trance that is beyond human grasp. The mysteries, as they call it, cannot and should not be revealed. (van de Port 2005, p. 152)

An important aspect of these mysteries is the notion that the possessed person is not 'conscious' during the possession and therefore has no recollection of it. This blotting of consciousness or 'post-possession amnesia' is not uniform in character or extent across spirit possession traditions (Sered 1994, p. 189), but it is a feature at the heart of much academic debate about possession because it allows the possessed person to behave in ways that would normally be frowned upon. Sered, for example, cites Seth and Ruth Leacock's work on Afro-Brazilian traditions, noting that, 'Brazilian Batuque women mediums often engage in "male" behaviour such as smoking cigarettes or cigars, drinking alcoholic beverages and shouting vulgarities. (The entranced medium is unaware of all this and so cannot possibly be enjoying herself!)' (Sered 1994, p. 183). This idea, that mediums are given more room for certain kinds of expression in trance because they are not held responsible in the same way for their actions, underpins theories of possession that tend to see it in terms of unfulfilled social, psychological and sexual needs. For example, Walter Mischel and Frances Mischel, in their analysis of Shango worshippers in Trinidad, suggest that possession by spirits gives participants

> the sanctioned expression of behaviours which are otherwise socially unacceptable or unavailable. In a learning theory interpretation the sanctioned expression or release of otherwise unacceptable behaviour is not in itself reinforcing: rather, the consequences of the behaviour – for example, other people's reactions of praise or reproof – are the reinforcements and the determinants of whether or not the behaviour will be repeated. (Mischel and Mischel 1958, p. 254)

The behaviours they list include the power of the possessed person to issue commands to those around them, such as 'penance' acts, which may include rolling on the ground, tearing their clothing and beating themselves, expressing physical intimacy with persons with whom they have a 'much more restricted relationship in the normal state', a reversal of sex roles, and childish behaviour (1958, pp. 254–6). As Mary Keller argues, this kind of analysis is questionable, partly because it assumes on some level that forbidden desires of the possessed person's ego are given expression here, while participants insist that this ego has been temporarily subsumed by that of an ancestor, deity or spirit (2002, pp. 1–17). Moreover, sociological and psychological analyses of spirit possession tend to locate 'real' power in structures of inequality, suggesting that possession can, at best, merely relieve some of the resultant tensions of this inequality (2002, pp. 35–7). This focus on observable social structures can lead to circular lines of argument whereby, if possession trance does not radically alter social worlds or if its transcendence is only temporary, the practice can be regarded by scholars as failing to challenge the dominant culture (Smith 2006, p. 72). This kind of thinking, I believe, is mistaken because its definition of power is too narrow.

Rather, I aim to explore ways in which Durkheim's notion of the sacred can contribute to a conception of seduction that in turn can be used to explore indigenous accounts in more depth. In order to do so, I will try to counter Edith Turner's suspicion of what she regards as 'the Durkheimian view', by suggesting that her reading of Durkheim's work places too much emphasis on his interest in social structures and mistakenly assumes that he argues that these structures are fused directly with religion. This reading does not fully take account of the importance of social and emotional forces for Durkheim's conception of the relationship between religion and society. Rejecting the idea that his theory is a restatement of historical materialism, he argues that

> in pointing out an essentially social thing in religion, I in no way mean to say that religion simply translates the material forms and immediate vital necessities into another language . . . collective consciousness is something other than a mere epiphenomenon of its morphological base . . . if collective consciousness is to appear a sui generis synthesis of individual consciousnesses must occur. The product of this synthesis is a whole world of feelings, ideas, and images that follow their own laws once they are born. They mutually attract one another, repel one another, fuse together, subdivide, and proliferate; and none of these combinations is directly commanded and necessitated by the state of the underlying reality. Indeed, the life thus unleashed enjoys such great independence that it sometimes plays about in forms that have no aim or utility of any kind, but only for the pleasure of affirming itself. I have shown that precisely this is often true of ritual activity and mythological thought. (Durkheim 1995, p. 426)

These forces, by binding members of a social group together in a way that has at least some somatic aspects, are thought to generate the formation of social structures, but they are also in constant tension with them, a tension which Victor Turner arguably developed in his work on communitas so that, for example, Turner describes communitas as,

> existentially speaking, and in its origins, purely spontaneous and self generating . . . it is essentially opposed to structure, as anti matter is hypothetically opposed to matter. Thus even when communitas becomes normative its religious expressions become closely hedged about by rules and interdictions – which act like a lead container of a dangerous radioactive isotope. Yet exposure to or immersion in communitas seems to be an indispensible human social requirement. People have a real need . . . to doff the masks, cloaks, apparel, and insignia of status from time to time even if only to don the masks of liminal masquerade. But they do this freely. (V. Turner 1974, p. 243)

He is, however, also aware that

> Durkheim . . . is often difficult to understand precisely because, at differ-
> ent times, he uses the term 'society' to represent, on the one hand, a set
> of jural and religious maxims and norms, coercing and constraining
> the individual and, on the other, 'an actual living and animating force'
> closely approximate to what we are here calling 'communitas'. (V. Turner
> 1974, p. 251)

Debates about the medium's amnesia are not confined to academic
speculation. They also play an important role within spirit traditions, not
least because they are used by ritual practitioners competing with one
another for authenticity (van de Port 2005, pp. 153, 167–70). In the context
of possession trance, Durkheim's conception of the sacred may help one
explore the significance of possession amnesia because, for Durkheim, the
division between the sacred and the profane is profound and is transposed
within the individual into a tension between individual and collective forms
of consciousness (Durkheim 1995, pp. 36, 266–9). While collective consciousness remains an aspect of the individual's inner life during mundane
periods, Durkheim suggests that ritual activity is designed to generate an
excitation of social and emotional forces in the participants that enables
collective consciousness to predominate at these times.

> It is not difficult to imagine that a man in such a state of exaltation should
> no longer know himself. Feeling possessed and led on by some sort of
> external power that makes him think and act differently than he normally
> does, he naturally feels he is no longer himself. It seems to him that he
> has become a new being . . . and because his companions feel trans-
> formed in the same way at the same moment, and express this feeling by
> their shouts, movements, and bearing, it is as if he was in reality trans-
> ported into a special world entirely different from the one in which he
> ordinarily lives, a special world inhabited by exceptionally intense forces
> that invade and transform him (Durkheim 1995, p. 22)

This kind of immersion in collective consciousness can also be regarded
as a radically altered state of consciousness, because it is less amenable to
the expression of individuated thought through language. Therefore, if
possession states are related to experiences of collective consciousness, it
would follow that one cannot 'remember' being possessed in the same way
that one 'remembers' everyday experiences because there is a level of

incompatibility between everyday consciousness and possession. Another way of expressing this idea is to suggest that possession trance can be characterized as a kind of *seduction* of the individual by collective forces, which in turn express themselves through the social drama of the possession ceremony, an idea in harmony with Thomas Csordas's suggestion that spirit possession 'can be seen as a pure form of ritual drama, where the parts of deities are not played by humans, but where the deities in effect play themselves' (1987, p. 6; cited in Sered 1994, p. 191).

Possession, Eroticism and Seduction

The idea that there may be a link between possession trance and eroticism has been explored by a number of scholars. I. M. Lewis (2003) surveys a sample of this literature, including examples where there is marriage to a spirit (p. 30), but his observations appear at times to be too literal, emphasizing the physiological and psychological similarities between sexual orgasm (particularly the female orgasm) and trance (Lewis 2003, pp. 31, 32, 37). While actual sexual orgasm may be part of the trance experience in some cases, a purely physiological explanation begs the question – why bother with trance at all? What can it add to sexual experience? Moreover, this simple equation underplays the complexity and fluidity of relations with spirits that have an erotic dimension precisely because they are difficult to quantify, a quality attested to by the fact that no two possession rituals are exactly the same. It is partly for this reason that I would like to suggest that Baudrillard's work on seduction offers a more suitable framework for thinking about the erotic dimensions of possession, for he suggests that 'a direct sexual invitation is too direct to be true and immediately refers to something else' (Baudrillard 1990, p. 43). For Baudrillard, modernity's obsession with the female orgasm is directly connected with the contemporary West's exaltation of various quantifiable and productive structures and forms, including those of the economy and the libidinal theories of Freudian psychology, which together inform the logic of pornography (Baudrillard 1990, pp. 4, 29, 34, 53). Moreover, it is with 'the absence or denial of the orgasm [that] superior intensity is possible ... something arises that can be called seduction or delight ... sexual pleasure can be just a pretext for another, more exciting, more passionate game' (Baudrillard 1990, p. 18). Seduction, moreover, 'is stronger than power because it is reversible and mortal, while power, like value, seeks to be irreversible, cumulative and immortal' (Baudrillard 1990, p. 46).

One advantage of the more sophisticated implications of self surrender implied by seduction is that rather than trance being some kind of refined version of human sexuality it could be argued that in some cases sexual relationships may offer opportunities for self surrender similar to those experienced in trance states. What is crucial to this argument is the suggestion that on one level the engagement with spirits is expressed through individual mediums; it is, nonetheless, a collective engagement. Lewis's summary of Shirokogoroff's work illustrates this well for although he refers to a shaman 'mastering' the spirits there is also a sense in which

> His body is a 'placing' or receptacle, for the invading spirits during the séance . . . the rhythmic music and singing, and later the dancing of the shaman, gradually involves every participant more and more in a collective action. When the audience begins to repeat the refrains together with his assistants, only those who are defective fail to join the chorus. The tempo increases, the shaman with a spirit is no ordinary man or relative, but a 'placing' (i.e. incarnation) of the spirit; the spirit acts together with the audience and is felt by everyone. The state of many participants is now near to that of the shaman himself, and only a strong belief that where the shaman is there the spirit may only enter him, restrains the participants from being possessed en mass by the spirit. (Lewis 2003, p. 34)

Seduction, Narrative and Place

While seduction may play a particular role in possession trance, it has also been explored as an aspect of the anthropological project and its engagement with place more broadly, for example, by anthropologists asking questions about the dynamics of race, sex and power in the context of fieldwork experience (Kulick 1995, pp. 4–5). While some of these questioners may relate to the formation of sexual relationships with informants, others, such as Andrew Killick and Kate Altork, are concerned with the erotic dimensions of place itself. Killick draws from the work of J. M. Lotman to examine the suggestion that even if the anthropologist is literally female, the authorship of anthropological texts is a 'male' activity because they are narratives in which the heroic protagonist 'penetrates' a landscape (Killick 1995, pp. 83–5; Lotman 1979, pp. 167–8). Kate Altork, however, reflecting on her work with the temporary camps set up to facilitate the fighting of forest fires and the highly charged masculine atmosphere and camaraderie within these camps, suggests ways in which that atmosphere may penetrate the anthropologist with a suffusion of sensual information and she thereby characterizes these places as seductive (1995, pp. 109, 113, 114, 133).

Far from being unique to anthropology, however, narratives of place and their seductive powers have played a pivotal role in media as diverse as drama and tantric religious biography. Shakespeare's *Othello*, for example, appears to compare the power of these narratives with those of magic in its description of Othello's seduction of, and subsequent marriage to, Desdemona. When Brabantio, Desdemona's father, hears of their elopement he accuses Othello of bewitching her, suggesting that without spells or potions Desdemona would not have 'run from her guardage to the sooty bosom of such a thing as thou?' (Shakespeare 1958, p. 19). Othello, however, explains that Desdemona was captivated by tales about his life's battles, adventures, and experiences of places such as 'deserts, rough quarries, rocks and hills, whose heads touch heaven . . . and of the Cannibals, that each other eat; the Anthopophagi, and men whose heads do grow beneath their shoulders' and that 'she lov'd me for the dangers I had pass'd, and I lov'd her that she did pity them. This is the only witchcraft I have us'd' (Shakespeare 1958, pp. 29, 31).

Tales of foreign lands are also portrayed as seductive in tantric Buddhist biographies. The biography of Machig Labdron, for example, suggests that she initially rejected visionary indications that she should become Thopa Bhadra's consort. The terms consort is much debated, for while its essence contains an element of ritualized sexuality, scholars such as Ray have suggested that its implications, particularly in the context of tantric biographies, are much broader, with communication between the partners playing an important part (Ray 1989, p. 196). Machig had agreed to perform recitations of the *Prajnaparamita* (Perfection of Wisdom) texts for a wealthy benefactress, and the night before her journey she has a vision of two *dakinis* who advise her to unite with Thopa Bhadra, as means and wisdom (a phrase associated with the *Prajnaparamita* texts that suggests, among other things, a consort relationship). Just before she departs she sees seven white women who suggest that she has a former karmic connection with Thopa, and that she should therefore not be afraid to unite with him. However, Machig is unsure whether the apparitions are a demonic trick and remains ambivalent when she is greeted by the vision of a white girl riding a white mule who welcomes her on behalf of Thopa, who is waiting for her in Echung (Edou 1996, pp. 141–2). On reaching Echung, Machig's hostess introduces her to Thopa, a yogin with bloodshot eyes, who is performing the initiation rite of the tantric deity Cakrasamvara. When Thopa asks her if she is tired from her journey, she suggests that his coming to Tibet from India was a bit of a folly, and proceeds with her recitations of the *Prajnaparamita Sutra* in a private chapel.

> Only from time to time would she discuss some Dharma with the pandita or ask him for stories about India. But then on the evening of the seventeenth day there . . . Bhadra and Ladron entered the meditative absorption of skilful means and wisdom. Light pervaded the entire house and the benefactress Lhamo Dron, fearing that the butter lamps had set the house ablaze, ran up to have a look. All she saw was a five-coloured light, similar to a rainbow, which pervaded the entire house, and within this, all ablaze, were two moons in union, one white, one red. Apart from this she didn't see anyone, and frightened by it, she left the rooftop chapel and went back to sleep. (Edou 1996, pp. 143–4)

This episode is of interest, partly because it suggests that although a karmic connection determines the auspiciousness of a consort relationship between Machig and Thopa, there is a more human aspect to their courtship in which her disdain is overcome by his stories of India. A fascination with India as the country from which both the Buddha and teachers such as Padmasambhava originate is an important aspect of Tibetan religiosity.

The passage points to a relationship between seduction and bodily transformations (in this case the dissolving of the physical body into light manifestations), material that challenges conceptions of seduction which by its very nature suggests that it must entail the 'ruin' and subsequent abandonment of the seduced object (Kierkegaard 2007 [1843], p. 135). Although Baudrillard (1990, p. 80) does provide a sympathetic reading of Kierkegaard, he also suggests that seduction may be a mutually transformative process related to tensions between the maintenance and relinquishing of certain kinds of control when he states that 'love has nothing to do with sex drives . . . love is a challenge and a prize: a challenge to the other to return the love. And to be seduced is to challenge the other to be seduced in turn' (Baudrillard 1990, p. 22). These tensions are complicated in the context of tantric Buddhist consort relationships because consorts in union are not thought of simply as human beings; they are also (through explorations of the 'subtle body') manifesting tantric deities (a phenomenon implied by the transformation into light forms in Machig's story), so a double seduction/possession may be implied. The consorts not only seduce each other, they are also seduced by the tantric deities. This conception of the transformation into a tantric deity in terms of possession or seduction can be challenged on the grounds that the visualization techniques employed to generate or 'realize' an enlightened being are complex and require conscious mastery and control. However, once the 'completion stage' is reached, the person as enlightened being is thought to be devoid of a grasping self or ego in a way which implies that aspects of their usual personality have been subsumed or overcome. Geoffrey Samuel (2008), for example, draws from Frederick M. Smith (2006) among others to explore ways in which transformation into an enlightened being in tantric Buddhism can be thought of as having a degree of continuity with 'possession' by a deity. Moreover, links are often draw in the context of South Asian religions between deities, bodies and conceptions of place. Smith, for example, drawing from vedic material and Tamil literature, suggests that 'the acceptance of the multilocality of divinity must surely have contributed to the notion that the divine, or any other less benign force, could penetrate and divinize any receptive individual. In this way, the individual – the person in the form of a body – became a sacred site' (Smith 2006, p. 73). This dynamic can be explored further through an examination of the mandala, a symbolic structure found within a number of South Asian religions but explored here in the context of tantric Buddhism.

The Mandala

At its most basic level, a mandala is a circle that is often represented two-dimensionally but which denotes a three-dimensional sacralization of space with a centre point governed by a tantric Buddhist deity or a consort deity couple (Brauen 1997, p. 12). Concentric circles surrounding them may contain various figures that act as a retinue (not unlike the court of a king), including guardian deities and yoginis. In addition, the human body can also be regarded as a mandala (Brauen 1997, p. 11). The union between consorts has also been described as a mandala, one which facilitates transformations in consciousness and physical being through the mutual intersection and interpenetration of the partners (Dowman 1996, p. 41).

One example of a myth that closely links the mandala with sacred geography and the body is that of the Cakrasamvara mandala and the myth of its origin (Davidson 2002, p. 40). In this myth the Buddha Vajradhara emanates a fierce form, Heruka, who together with his consort, Vajravahari, subdues Mahesvara (a form of Siva) and his consort, Uma. A form of the Hindu Bhairava appears under the feet of Heruka, who together with his consort is depicted as having taken control of the summit of Mount Sumeru, with a retinue of twenty-four fierce tantric Buddhist deities taking control of twenty-four pilgrimage sites that were previously ruled by emanations of Bhairava (Gray 2001, pp. 480–9). Gray points to tensions in the employment of this mythology. While, on the one hand, there is a downplay of pilgrimage in favour of the internalization of Cakrasamvara, on the other,

> the spaces depicted in this myth were contested spaces: the myth depicts the entire Cakrasamvara mandala as hard-wired into the Indian subcontinent, with its nerve center at Kailash in Tibet . . . the Buddhists in Tibet used the myth of Cakrasamvara as a sacred narrative through which the very landscape could be sacralised. Important features of the landscape were associated with elements of Heruka's mandala, which could be materialised through the construction of landmarks such as stupas and temples. (Gray 2001, pp. 491–2, 503–4)

One of these locations is Tsari mountain in south-east Tibet, which has been explored by Toni Huber. His examination of Tibetan pilgrimage mythology and practices that surround Tsari mountain suggests that the mountain itself can be regarded as a body, partly because deities such as Cakrasamvara and Vajravarahi are thought to have taken residence within it. Therefore, 'the vital bodily substance of the chosen meditational deities can be found and extracted from the landscape itself, as their bodies are the body of the summit' (Huber 1999, p. 94). This may also help to explain one of the several possible translations of the name Tsari itself, wherein rTsa means a vital energy channel (in Sanskrit *nadi*) and the full title therefore translates as 'Psychic Energy Channel Mountain'. Huber suggests that,

> when conceived of as vital points within the yogin's body, the twenty four Tantric action sites (pitha/ne) of the Khorlo Dompa meditation system are arranged at points around this subtle channel network. Together, the sites and channels constitute the body mandala, which is a microcosmic version of the larger Pure Crystal Mountain mandala and the cosmic world system mandala. It is not uncommon in the Tibetan Tantric geographical traditions that actual landscapes are represented in terms of the subtle body structure. (1999, p. 82)

He therefore points to a complex transactional logic between pilgrims and the mountain. Care is taken when extracting substance from the landscape because, in effect, one is engaging with the body of a deity (Huber

1999, p. 96). However, pilgrimage is also regarded as an initiatory process that purifies the body, speech and mind of the pilgrim, thus bringing them closer to the ideal of enlightenment represented by the inhabiting deity, an idea that can also be expressed by suggesting that the subtle body of the pilgrim is 'purified' by pilgrimage and its powers are thereby more accessible. This purification could also be thought of in terms of a seduction, in that the pilgrim's subtle body is thought, by this process of purification, to resemble more and more closely that of the mountain deity.

Conclusion

A number of the main questions that scholars examining spirit possession have been asking revolve around the issue of the degree to which possession may be empowering, both for the possessed person and her community, and in what way. Baudrillard's work on seduction challenges many forms of feminist analysis because 'the feminine seduces because it is never where it thinks it is . . . the feminine is not found in the history of suffering and oppression imputed to it' (1990, p. 6). He suggests that the sexual revolution, far from liberating women, is itself a repressive force because it subscribes to 'a narrative of women's sexual and political misery to the exclusion of every other type of strength and sovereignty' including the strength of seduction (1990, p. 7). Nonetheless, according to Baudrillard, the women's movement is ashamed of seduction, not understanding that 'seduction represents mastery over the symbolic universe, while power represents only mastery of the real universe. The sovereignty of seduction is incommensurable with the possession of political or sexual power' (1990, p. 8).

Further to this, Baudrillard explores the politics of space, suggesting that

The external space, that of the palace, and beyond it, the city, that is, the political space, the locus of power, is itself perhaps only an effect of perspective. Such a dangerous secret, such a radical hypothesis, the Prince must keep to himself in the strictest secrecy: for it is the very secret of his power . . . politicians have perhaps always known that the mastery of simulated space is at the source of their power, that politics is not a real activity, but a simulation model, whose manifest acts are but actualized impressions. (Baudrillard 1990, p. 65)

This argument is particularly useful when possession or other kinds of altered states of consciousness are considered together with understandings of space or place. It is interesting to note in this context that the first concrete example of possession that Keller gives in her analysis is framed as one in which there is a conflict over the utilization of particular places in Malaysia between industrialists and ancestors and spirits.

> In 1979 a woman at a Japanese-owned factory saw a weretiger, screamed, and was possessed. She flailed at the machine on which she worked and fought violently as the foreman and technician pulled her away. Her supervisor recounted that the workplace used to be a burial ground, implying that the shop floor was likely to be haunted by angry spirits and that women who had weak constitutions needed to be spiritually vigilant so they would not be possessed. The juxtaposition of technology and spirits suggests that a complex and profound interaction of worlds was occurring, centered in the volatile bodies of possessed women. (Keller 2002, p. 1; drawn from Ong 1987, pp. 238, 204, 207)

Moreover, Paula Ben-Amos, focusing on spirit possession in the urban environment of Benin City in Nigeria, challenges the idea that possession merely provides a temporary relief from the structural inequalities or psychological difficulties suffered by women or low status persons within a given society (1994, p. 119). Her challenge rests on conceptions of Edo cosmology, which contrasts the dry land (ruled by the Oba, ruler of the Benin nation) and the realm of the deep waters (ruled by the deity Olokun) (Ben-Amos 1994, p. 119). Although material rule of the land is largely in the hands of men, priestesses of the cult are considered to be powerful because of their access to the realm of the waters during possession, and this latter realm, although in many ways parallel to that of the land, is thought to be superior (Ben-Amos 1994, p. 120).

However, in addition to exploring seduction, I have linked this idea with an analysis of Durkheim's notion of collective consciousness, suggesting that, if the fluidity and dynamism of this concept is fully appreciated, it becomes possible to utilize it to enhance our understanding of deities and spirits. In the context of spirit possession, deities, ancestors and spirits are not regarded as simply the products of individual phantasies because they are forms which are culturally recognized and replicated. This process of recognition and replication is not static – deities are subject to adaptation and change in response to the needs of a given community. Durkheim's theory of collective consciousness is a valuable tool in the study of possession; it can be used to explore the collective roots of phenomena and the ways in which dynamics of social change may have an impact upon it.

Moreover, as I have suggested elsewhere (Child 2000a; 2007b), although the idea of collective consciousness is usually applied to 'society' in the broad sense, it can also be used to explore the dynamics of more personal relationships, including sexual ones. I have suggested that the notion of seduction may help to refine analyses of the erotic aspects of possession trance more generally. I have also explored ways in which it may illuminate the relationship between the individual and enlightened beings in tantric Buddhism – that in cases where those persons are engaged in consort relationships a notion of 'double seduction' may provide a key to forms of transformative identity, rather than the destruction or ruin of one of the partners. Baudrillard's work may therefore contribute to possession studies in that both his perspective on seduction and many instances of spirit possession continue to challenge notions of power that focus on structural inequality in a given society. Both seduction and possession can be said to subvert power itself by demonstrating the virtues and pleasures of self surrender.

Bibliography

Altork, K. (1995), 'Walking the fire line: the erotic dimension of the fieldwork experience', in D. Kulick and M, Wilson (eds), *Taboo: Sex, Identity and Erotic Subjectivity in Anthropological Fieldwork.* London and New York: Routledge, pp. 107–39.

Baudrillard, J. (1990 [1979]), *Seduction*, trans. B. Singer. Houndmills and London: Macmillan Education.

Ben-Amos, P. G. (1994), 'The promise of greatness: women and power in an Edo spirit possession cult', in T. D. Blakely, W. E. A. van Beek and D. L. Thomson (eds), *Religion in Africa.* London: James Currey, pp. 119–34.

Boddy, J. (1994), 'Spirit possession revisited: beyond instrumentality', *Annual Review of Anthropology*, 23, 407–34.

Bowie, F. (2000), *The Anthropology of Religion: An Introduction.* Oxford: Blackwell.

Brauen, M. (1997), *The Mandala: Sacred Circle in Tibetan Buddhism.* London: Serinda.

Brown, K. M. (2001), *Mama Lola: A Vodou Priestess in Brooklyn* (rev. and expanded edn). Berkeley: University of California Press.

Child, L. (2007a), 'Subtle bodies, wrathful deities and men in Buddhist tantric traditions', *Religions of South Asia*, 1 (1), 29–45.

Child, L. (2007b), *Tantric Buddhism and Altered States of Consciousness: Durkheim, Emotional Energy and Visions of the Consort.* Aldershot: Ashgate.

Child, L. (2008), 'Possession in contemporary cinema: religious and psychological themes', *Diskus* (The Journal of the British Association for the Study of Religion), 9. Available at: http://www.basr.ac.uk/diskus/diskus9/child.htm.

Csordas, T. (1987), 'Health and the holy in African and Afro-American spirit possession', *Social Science and Medicine*, 24 (1), 1–11.

Davidson, R. M. (2002), *Indian Esoteric Buddhism: A Social History of the Tantric Movement*. New York: Columbia University Press.

Dowman, K. (trans.) (1996), *Sky Dancer: The Secret Life and Songs of Lady Yeshe Tsogyel*. New York: Snow Lion.

Durkheim, E. (1995), *The Elementary Forms of Religious Life* (1912), trans. K. E. Fields. New York: Free Press.

Edou, J. (1996), *Machig Labdron and the Foundations of Chod*. Ithaca, NY: Snow Lion.

Goulet, J. (1994), 'Dreams and visions in other life worlds', in D. E. Young and J. Goulet (eds), *Being Changed by Cross-Cultural Encounters: The Anthropology of Extraordinary Experience*. Ontario: Broadview Press.

Gray, D. B. (2001), 'On Supreme Bliss: A Study of the History and Interpretation of the Cakrasamvara Tantra'. Ph.D. Dissertation, Columbia University.

Henley, P. (2006), 'Spirit possession, power, and the absent presence of Islam: reviewing Les Maîtres fous', *Journal of the Royal Anthropological Institute*, 12, 731–61.

Huber, T. (1999), *The Cult of Pure Crystal Mountain: Popular Pilgrimage and Visionary Landscape in Southeast Tibet*. New York and Oxford: Oxford University Press.

Kapferer, B. (2000), 'Sexuality and the art of seduction in Sinhalese exorcism', *Ethnos*, 65 (1), 5–32.

Keller, M. (2002), *The Hammer and the Flute: Women, Power, and Spirit Possession*. Baltimore and London: Johns Hopkins University Press.

Kierkegaard, S. (2007 [1843]), *The Seducer's Diary*. London and New York: Penguin.

Killick, A. (1995), 'The penetrating intellect: on being white, straight, and male in Korea', in D. Kulick and M. Willson (eds), *Taboo: Sex, Identity and Erotic Subjectivity in Anthropological Fieldwork*. New York and London: Routledge, pp. 76–106.

Kulick, D. (1995), 'Introduction – the sexual life of anthropologists: erotic subjectivity and ethnographic work', in D. Kulick and M. Willson (eds), *Taboo: Sex, Identity and Erotic Subjectivity in Anthropological Fieldwork*. New York and London: Routledge, pp. 1–28.

Lambek, M. (1981), *Human Spirits: A Cultural Account of Trance in Mayotte*. Cambridge: Cambridge University Press.

Leacock, S. and Leacock, R. (1972), *Spirits of the Deep: A Study of an Afro-Brazillian Cult*. New York: Doubleday Natural History Press.

Lewis, I. M. (2003), 'Trance, possession, shamanism and sex', *Anthropology of Consciousness*, 14 (1), 20–39.

Lotman, J. M. (1979), 'The origin of plot in the light of typology', *Poetics Today*, 1 (1–2), 161–84.

McDaniel, J. (2004), *Offering Flowers, Feeding Skulls: Popular Goddess Worship in West Bengal*. Oxford: Oxford University Press.

Mischel, W. and Mischel, F. (1958), 'Psychological aspects of spirit possession', *American Anthropologist*, 60 (2), 249–60.

Ong, A. (1987), *Spirits of Resistance and Capitalist Discipline*. Albany: State University of New York Press.

Ray, R. A. (1989), 'Accomplished women in the Tantric Buddhism of medieval India and Tibet', in N. A. Falk and R. Gross (eds), *Unspoken Worlds: Women's Religious Lives*. Belmont, CA: Wadsworth, pp. 191–200.

Samuel, G. (2008), 'Possession and self possession: spirit healing, tantric meditation and āveśa', *Diskus*, 9.

Sered, S. S. (1994), *Priestess, Mother, Sacred Sister: Religions Dominated by Women*. Oxford: Oxford University Press.

Shakespeare, W. (1958 [1604]), *Othello*. London and New York: Methuen.

Smith, F. M. (2006), *The Self Possessed: Deity and Spirit Possession in South Asian Literature and Civilization*. New York: Columbia University Press.

Stoller, P. (1994), 'Embodying colonial memories', *American Anthropologist*, 96 (3), 634–48.

Turner, E. (2006), 'Advances in the study of spirit experience: drawing together many threads', *Anthropology of Consciousness*, 17 (2), 33–61.

Turner, V. (1974), *Dramas, Fields and Metaphors: Symbolic Action in Human Society*. Ithaca and London: Cornhill University Press.

van de Port, M. (2005), 'Circling around the *really real* spirit possession ceremonies and the search for authenticity in Bahian Candomble', *Ethnos*, 33 (2), 149–79.

Chapter 5

Analytical Psychology and Spirit Possession: Towards a Non-Pathological Diagnosis of Spirit Possession

Lucy Huskinson

Undermining the Tendency to Pathologize Spirit Possession

Analytical psychology does not differentiate between the many cultural or anthropological variations of 'spiritual' experience. Instead it conflates all transcendent phenomena – such as spirit possession and mystical experience – into one general kind of psychological experience. It refers to this experience as 'dissociation', or being in a 'dissociated state'. To understand the nature and underlying dynamic of spirit possession in terms of dissociation is not a *new interpretation* of spirit possession, per se.[1] However, 'dissociation' as it is understood in analytical psychology remains relatively unfamiliar to scholars of spirit possession and transcendent experience in general. The unheard voice of analytical psychology within debates on the nature of such phenomena is unfortunate as its contribution is noteworthy.

Perhaps the most notable contribution it makes is its departure from those psychological interpretations of spirit possession that pathologize and objectify its phenomenal variations, and consider them to be symptomatic of undesirable and maladaptive behaviour. Generally speaking, anthropologists do not pathologize spirit possession, but on the contrary, interpret it as an appropriate – even desirable – phenomenon of particular cultures and communities (cf. Kirmayer 1994). Arguably it is a general tendency of the Western mindset to reduce non-Western cultural experiences to its own rational terms. That is to say, to translate human experience into human knowledge and, subsequently, to reduce human behaviour to categories of explanation. As a consequence, experiences of 'spirit possession' have been identified with an array of psychological disturbances (such as paranoia, auditory and visual hallucinations, thought insertion, delusions, obsessions, amnesia, convulsive seizures, paralysis, heightened affects, and so on), and have subsequently been diagnosed as a variety of psychological and neurological disorders (including hysteria, dissociative identity disorder, epilepsy and schizophrenia).[2]

The parameters of what constitutes mental illness and health are not categorical; they are relative to cultural conceptions, and gradually evolve in light of changing cultural concerns.[3] It would take a paradigmatic shift of grand proportion in the Zeitgeist of Western culture for it to become less rationally oriented (or ego-centred) and more accommodating of non-rational values of interpretation. In the meantime, the tendency of Western psychological interpretation is arguably one that discriminates against spirit possession by explaining its behavioural presentation in terms of 'abnormality' and 'pathology'.

Dissociation is itself both a necessary and inevitable feature of a healthy psychological disposition to life and to everyday experience generally. Simply put, dissociation is a mechanism of the mind that enables one to establish what we might call the foreground of experience by splitting off from consciousness those thoughts, feelings, sensations and intuitions that are irrelevant to one's immediate concerns. For instance, if you are carefully reading this chapter you have successfully dissociated from other experiences that might otherwise concern you, such as the various sights and sounds that continue around you. According to the anthropologist M. J. Field, dissociation is the 'splitting of the stream of consciousness into parallel streams', and this he says is 'familiar to anyone who can "do two things at once", such as playing the piano and simultaneously planning a summer holiday, or driving a car "automatically" while thinking about something quite different.' (1969, p. 3).

Dissociation is thus the mechanism by which streams of consciousness are suspended and unavailable to experience. The activation of dissociation requires energy, and, consequently, the prolonged splitting of streams of consciousness can be very draining and fatiguing to the personality as a whole.

Dissociation operates within the context of a consciousness that is multi-faceted and which comprises different streams – or what we might call 'ego-states' – that are in dynamic relationship. In this model, the personality is conceived as a divided self that experiences the world according to the interplay of its parts; that is, according to whichever ego-state or combination of ego-states occupies consciousness at any one moment. Dissociation becomes problematic to the functioning of the personality when one ego-state seeks to dominate or annihilate others. In such cases, we may talk about dissociative *disorders* of the personality, where the overall personality becomes fragmented in such a way that the usual processing of information is disrupted.[4]

The parallel between dissociative ego-states and spirit possession is relatively clear. Thus, in the words of M. J. Field (1969, p. 3), 'The possessed person is in a state of dissociated personality whereby a split-off part of the mind possesses the whole field of consciousness, the rest being in complete abeyance.' Spirit possession and dissociative ego-states similarly describe a situation where a person seems to lose identity and the cohesiveness of his or her personality to become another person altogether. The obvious and often asked question is whether such experiences of possession are pathological. The answer to this, however, is not so obvious. Indeed, in this chapter I shall argue that, from the perspective of analytical psychology, it is in fact an inappropriate question to ask. According to analytical psychology, spirit possession defies diagnostic criteria; it cannot be explained in terms of pathology, or indeed, of health. In the course of this chapter we shall arrive at a different question – and perhaps one that is more appropriate to the aims of anthropological study, and more comfortable with its conclusions. We shall not ask whether spirit possession is itself pathological, but whether the ego of the possessed person can tolerate and integrate the possession experience into his or her personality as a whole. For, as I shall argue, possession merely *facilitates* mental health or illness according to the disposition of the ego. It is thus the disposition of the ego and not the phenomena of possession that lends itself to possible diagnosis of pathology.

Facilitating constructive dialogue between psychology and anthropology

Despite its healthy nature and its inevitable and frequent occurrence, the term 'dissociation' has received some bad press in anthropological studies of spirit possession, which is in no small part due to its perceived association with psychopathology (that is to say, its particular manifestation as 'dissociative disorder'). Arguably, this association has created an obstacle in communication between anthropologists and psychologists to the extent that the former often assume that the latter will inevitably cast negative judgement upon their subject matter. The anthropologist Morton Klass summarizes the problem thus,

The use of terms like *dissociation* and *dissociative state* without further analysis ineluctably implies that altered states of consciousness reflect some degree of psychopathology: used this way, *dissociation* runs the

danger of becoming merely an anthropological euphemism for the older
and supposedly discarded answer ('They are crazy!') to the question of
'what is really happening [in spirit possession]?' (2003, p. 69)

Klass implies that the terms 'dissociation' and 'dissociative state' in anthropological study have become so heavily entrenched in negative connotation
that they discourage anthropologists from investigating their potential
usefulness. This, I contend, is a great shame, for a deeper understanding
of the dynamics of dissociation is not only conducive to the aims of
anthropological study, but can lend insight to it.

This chapter goes some way to providing the 'further analysis' that
Klass implicitly calls for. That is to say, it offers an interpretation of the
non-pathological nature of dissociation, which is required if we are to
dispel the fictional notion that those people who are possessed by spirits
are, from a psychological perspective, inevitably *crazy*. The argument in
this chapter also proffers an hypothesis (not a definitive explanation) of
what is really happening in spirit possession, an hypothesis that – through
its interpretation of spirit possession as a non-pathological dissociative
state – can only facilitate improved dialogue between the disciplines of
anthropology and psychology. By the same token, the argument that I
expound is an attempt to ascertain *what is really happening* in spirit possession and dissociative states as they are conceived within analytical psychology itself. Analytical psychology originates in the ideas of the Swiss
psychologist C. G. Jung (1875–1961), but his accounts of the dynamics of
possession experience or dissociation in general are sketchy and ambiguous. This chapter attempts to determine and consolidate Jung's thoughts
on possession within the general theoretical framework of his analytical psychology, and subsequently to postulate a Jungian *theory* of spirit
possession.[5]

Jung does not regard spirit possession and its 'dissociative' underpinnings
as pathological, but, rather, as I shall argue, as healthy or unhealthy according to their *effects* on the development of the individual's ego-personality or
the communal ego or attitude of a group of people. Furthermore, these
effects are themselves determined by the disposition of the consciousness
that is possessed. Although spirit possession is not conceived as a mental
illness in its own right, its dissociative effects are believed to incite mental
illness (or health). The effects of dissociation can be devastating to the
ego-personality, with the likelihood of psychological damage or illness
increasing if the ego is unable to contain or make sense of the possession
experience. By contrast, if the ego is able to do so, the effects of dissociation

can be positively enriching for it: they can restore health to a neurotic personality and re-energize an unproductive community.

In order to ascertain how Jungian analytical psychology arrives at its non-pathological interpretation of spirit possession, I shall contrast its conception with that proffered by its prominent theoretical antagonist: (Freudian) psychoanalysis. We shall see that their different understandings of the nature of the unconscious and its dissociative effects on ego-consciousness inform their contrasting diagnoses of spirit possession. That is to say, the particular value given to the unconscious and its corresponding affects (dissociation) determines whether spirit possession is likely to facilitate health or illness. As we shall see, while analytical psychology regards the unconscious as an autonomous resource of creativity (and thereby construes possession of the ego by the unconscious as a potentially enriching experience), psychoanalysis, by contrast, regards the unconscious as a dumping ground for the ego's unresolved experience (and subsequently conceives its possession of the ego as a delusional experience of the ego's own making). I shall now turn to these competing perspectives to explain their contrasting diagnoses of spirit possession.

Jung and Freud on the Psychology of Possession

The name 'analytical psychology' was adopted by Jung to differentiate his theory of psychological development from Freudian 'psychoanalysis'. Jung's model departs considerably from Freud's in several respects. Arguably the most notable disagreement between the two concerns the nature of the unconscious; and it is this disagreement that underlies their different interpretations of spirit possession.

The spirit of the unconscious: a derivative of personal conflict or an autonomous source of personal enrichment?

Freud and Jung generally agree that human experience comprises several different aspects of the mind in dynamic interplay, and that mental health depends on the degree to which these aspects communicate to each other. In addition to intrapersonal dialogue between ego-consciousness and the unconscious, a person will inevitably encounter interpersonal dialogue between himself or herself and the people, society and world around him or her. Simply put, for both Freud and Jung, a mentally healthy personality is one that develops through the cultivation of these dialogues. A healthy relationship at the intrapersonal level will lead a person to feel appropriately integrated within his or her environment and to experience positive interpersonal relations, and these in turn will reflect back to the person an affirming acknowledgement of self. By contrast, a mentally unstable personality is one that splits off aspects of the mind and isolates these parts from each other, thereby preventing their creative dialogue and disabling the development of personality as a whole.

The disagreement between Freud and Jung concerns the dynamic nature of intrapersonal dialogue, and their respective interpretations of this are themselves informed by their different conceptions of the unconscious. Thus, according to Jung, the unconscious has an *autonomous* nature. That is to say, for Jung, unconscious processes express self-awareness and a sense of identity that is experienced by the ego as separate to its own. In this respect the unconscious is said to have its own agenda, as it behaves as if it were a second consciousness within the personality (which is commonly referred to as an 'alter ego'). Freud, by contrast, denies the unconscious its autonomy, regarding it instead as material of the ego that has been forgotten or repressed (1915, p. 148).[6] Although the ego in Freud's model may experience communications of the unconscious as uncanny and unfamiliar – as 'a cauldron full of seething excitations' (Freud 1933, p. 73) – they are nevertheless aspects that were once known and owned by the ego, and can again be known and owned. In Jung's model, however, the communications of the autonomous unconscious have never been known by the ego and remain resolutely unknowable. In this respect, the ego is the recipient of *new* material from a source outside it.

Arguably, the ego assumes a more central role in Freud's model than it does in Jung's. For Freud the ego determines the extent of its own capacity (to contain and assimilate its emotional experiences) and that of the unconscious, which it cultivates as a store-room for its more troublesome and unwanted experiences. Unconscious material in this scenario is repressed by the ego as a *defensive* measure to protect itself from the traumatic feelings that would otherwise overwhelm it. By defending against its unwanted material, the ego facilitates a split in the overall personality and rejects those aspects that are incompatible with its conscious requirements. The unconscious will always seek to reintegrate the repressed material of the ego back into ego-consciousness in order to maintain a cohesive and un-fragmented personality. But because the ego often does not want to engage in dialogue with it, the unconscious is forced to express its material to the ego in coded, symbolic language; for instance through neurotic disorders and symptoms (such as those Freud found in cases of hysteria where repressed feelings are *displaced* on to the physical body). In Freud's model, intrapersonal dialogue is regressive in the sense that the unconscious contains and communicates to the ego those experiences the ego has failed to process. The expression of unconscious material is likewise symptomatic of a disturbed instinctual life and even of 'a diseased psyche' as a colleague of Jung maintains (Jacobi 1959, p. 21).

Unlike Freud, Jung does not regard the unconscious as the mere 'gathering place of forgotten and repressed contents' (Jung 1954a, par. 2[7]). For Jung the unconscious has two different aspects: it is both *personal* and *collective.* While the personal unconscious is similar to the unconscious postulated by Freud, Jung's concept of the collective unconscious places his understanding of intrapersonal dialogue at variance with that of Freud. Jung regarded Freud's understanding of the unconscious as 'unendurably narrow' in its 'reductive causalism' (Jung 1950, p. xxiii); and he subsequently conceives the collective unconscious as a vast repository of (*archetypal*) material that transcends the realm of the personal, and impresses upon the ego's universal patterns or constellations of human experience. This unconscious material communicates itself to ego-consciousness through symbolic images that are often personified and always numinous in affect (Jung 1954b, par. 405; cf. par. 383). The universal patterns themselves remain unconscious, but their images are made particular according to the ego-consciousness that perceives them. For instance, the archetypal pattern or constellation of 'spirit' is universally applicable to every human being, but the ways in which 'spirit' is experienced and conceptualized are as different and as various as there are different intuitions, feelings, thoughts or sensations of 'spiritedness'. Thus, by entering into dialogue with the collective unconscious, the ego encounters a realm of experience infinitely larger and more archaic than the totality of its own limited perspective.

For Jung, intrapersonal dialogue is not a matter of *recovering* memories of unprocessed personal experience as it was for Freud, but, rather, of *discovering* the possibilities and potential of human experience. Such discovery is achieved, Jung claims, through unrestricted dialogue between the ego and the autonomous unconscious. Their healthy relationship or dialogue is characterized by Jung as *compensatory.* Thus, the more ego-consciousness is promoted as the primary function within the personality, the more the unconscious material strives for its realization, and vice versa (Jung 1954b, par. 425; 1914, par. 465). In this respect, the unconscious can be a helpful guide for the ego, as it redresses the ego's one-sided prejudices, and reorientates the ego within the wider concerns of the personality as a whole.

Broadly speaking, Jung's conception of the unconscious and its intra-personal dialogue with ego-consciousness is more optimistic than Freud's. While the Freudian model focuses on the ego's failure to assimilate its experiences of past events, and construes the unconscious as an expression of this failure, the Jungian model focuses on the ego's potential growth and its assimilation of new experiences acquired from an unconscious that is, in part, autonomous and collective. In contrast to the Freudian model, Jung's model allows for an unconscious realm free from the conflict and pathology of personal experience (see Jacobi 1959, pp. 25–6).

Spirit possession: delusional or life-enhancing?

To be possessed by a spirit means that the ego has identified with the unconscious and has thereby dissociated itself from its normal conscious state. The different conceptions of the unconscious formulated by Freud and Jung inevitably lead to different interpretations of spirit possession. Thus, for Freud – who regards unconscious expression as symptomatic of a disturbed and traumatized ego – spirit possession is nothing more than a neurotic delusion. Freud writes, 'demons are bad and reprehensible wishes, derivates of instinctual impulses that have been repudiated and repressed', and 'possession is the suffering and phantasy of a sick man' (1922, pp. 72, 100). Just as Jung criticized Freud's model of the unconscious for being too reductive with its focus on personal traumatic experience, Jung criticizes Freud's diagnosis of spirit possession for reducing the otherness of the experience to a pathological experience of the ego's making. Jung protests against Freud's attempt to reduce spiritual experience to the rational terms of the ego; or, in his words, to

> unmask as illusion what the 'absurd superstition' of the past took to be a devilish incubus, to whip away the disguises worn by the evil spirit and turn him back into a harmless poodle[8] – in a word, reduce him to a 'psychological formula'. (1939, par. 71)

Jung's diagnosis of spirit possession is more ambiguous than that of Freud. As we shall see, spirit possession for Jung facilitates the transformation of the ego-personality, and it is the condition of this new ego-personality – rather than the process that enabled it – that is considered healthy or unhealthy (Jung 1921, par. 383). Furthermore, the condition of the new ego-personality will depend greatly on the condition of its previous incarnation. In this respect, possession is a state of potential, rather like pregnancy, which can give birth to a new form 'or future personality' that may be healthy or unhealthy (Jung 1902, par. 136). Such a state

[D]oes not necessarily indicate inferiority. It only means that something incompatible, unassimilated, and conflicting exists – perhaps as an obstacle, but also as a stimulus to greater effort, and so, perhaps, as an opening to new possibilities of achievement. (Jung 1921, par. 925)

Spirit Possession by a *Complex*

It could be argued that Jung's conception of the dynamics of spirit possession shares greater affinity with the model of dissociation described by Freud's early antagonist, Pierre Janet, than it does with that of Freud himself. Indeed, Jung himself expresses his debt to 'the French psychopathologists, Pierre Janet in particular, for our knowledge today of the extreme *dissociability of consciousness*' (1948a, par. 202). Importantly, as we shall see, Jung's labelling of Janet as a psychopathologist does not mean that he thought dissociation – the process Janet is thought, by some, to have discovered – is in itself pathological.

For Jung and Janet before him, the conscious personality is essentially multi-faceted, and it is able to splinter off into separate, autonomous parts. Earlier in this chapter these parts were described as 'streams of consciousness' (by M. J. Field). Jung refers to them as *complexes*. These fragments of personality have their own peculiar character, including their own memories, and likes and dislikes; with some even developing their own sense of identity or self-awareness. These complexes are equivalent to the possessing spirit that invades the familiar personality. Indeed, when Janet began to develop his theory of dissociation he made a connection between dissociated states and spirit possession. Thus, he observed that his traumatized and hysterical patients, when under hypnosis, would often exhibit multiple personalities that were apparently aware of each other; and in some instances they would refer to themselves as '*daimons*' (Janet 1889; 1894).[9]

According to Jung, complexes manifest themselves as autonomous personifications of the split-off unconscious (1948a, par. 203). He writes,

The more the unconscious is split off, the more formidable the shape in which it appears to the conscious mind – if not in divine form, then in the more unfavourable form of obsessions and outbursts of affect. Gods are personifications of unconscious contents. (Jung 1948b, par. 242; cf. 1921, par. 204)

Thus, for Jung, the unconscious is unconscious by degree, so that its corresponding material can be construed as either having or not having the potential for conscious integration. The greater the autonomy of the unconscious complex, the more imposing and unfamiliar is the personified form of the 'possessing spirit'.

Two possessing spirits: personal and collective

As we have already noted, Jung propounds two types of unconsciousness – the *personal* and the *collective*. These two types comprise the different degrees of unconsciousness alluded to above. The personal unconscious is closest to ego-consciousness and comprises material that has been repressed by the ego; and the collective unconscious comprises material that can never be known by the ego. By referring to these two degrees of unconscious, we can postulate two different types of complex, and, subsequently, two different types of spirit possession. Thus, Jung writes,

> Certain complexes arise on account of painful or distressing experiences in a person's life . . . These produce unconscious complexes of a personal nature . . . But there are others [autonomous complexes] that come from quite a different source . . . At bottom they have to do with irrational contents of which the individual has never been conscious before. (1948c, par. 594; see also Jung 1938/1940, par. 22)

In other words, if a spirit possesses me I am either possessed by aspects of myself that have been split off from my ego-consciousness, and which subsequently appear outside of me and as having a disagreeable nature to me; or I am possessed by aspects that have never been part of my personality. The latter type of possession is possession by an *archetypal* personification of experience that pertains to the human race as a whole.

We might presume that those complexes or spirit possessions that originate in the personal unconscious – that *arise on account of painful or distressing experience* – are pathological (in the manner that Freud regarded them). While those complexes or spirit possessions that originate outside personal struggle – in the collective unconscious – evade pathological diagnosis on the basis that they are impervious to our rational scrutiny and to our diagnostic determinations generally. These presumptions are supported by Jung's colleague, Jolande Jacobi, who claims,

> Material deriving from the collective unconscious is never 'pathological'; it can be pathological only if it comes from the personal unconscious, where it undergoes a specific transformation and coloration by being drawn into an area of individual conflict. (1959, pp. 25–6)

Jacobi consequently postulates *morbid* and *healthy* complexes, with the former referring to material of the personal unconscious that has been repressed by the ego, and the latter referring to material that has 'grown out of' the collective unconscious; material that 'could never have been arbitrarily repressed' (Jung 1938/1940, par. 22; cited in Jacobi 1959, p. 22). In this instance, a spirit possession that originates in the personal unconscious (which entails an encounter with those unwanted and previously repressed experiences that demand conscious expression) is considered unhealthy, while a spirit possession that originates in the collective unconscious (which is an encounter with universal, previously undiscovered material) is deemed healthy.

However, Jung himself provides ambiguous support for Jacobi's hypothesis. In support of Jacobi's claims, Jung maintains that personal complexes are caused by traumatic experiences in a person's life (under such unfavourable conditions as 'distress', 'emotional shocks' and 'moral conflict' (1948a, par. 204), 'which leave lasting psychic wounds' (1948c, par. 595). Furthermore, with regard to complexes of a collective origin, he says that they can alter the ego-orientation of a person and the communal attitude of whole groups of people 'to *redeeming* effect' (1948c, par. 594; my emphasis). Yet, in contradistinction to Jacobi's assertions, Jung asserts that those complexes that originate in the personal unconscious are not in themselves unhealthy because the traumatic feelings associated with them are not indicative of illness.

> [T]he possession of complexes does not in itself signify neurosis . . . and the fact that they are painful is no proof of pathological disturbance. Suffering is not an illness; it is the normal counterpole to happiness. (Jung 1946a, par. 179)

Likewise, he concedes that those complexes that originate in the collective unconscious can lead to mental illness, and can be construed as 'pathological fantasies' when they are found to replace an ego-attitude of a person or group with one that is 'unrealistic'. That is to say, Jung maintains that complexes of a collective nature are detrimental to the overall personality when they overwhelm the ego completely, subsequently flooding it with archetypal material which dislocates the conscious personality from its grounding in reality (Jung 1948c, par. 595).

It is, therefore, inaccurate to presume both that the personal unconscious yields only complexes of a morbid or pathological nature, and that the collective unconscious proffers only non-pathological ones. Moreover, it is surely erroneous to regard a complex as having originated in *either* the personal domain *or* that of the collective, for the personal and collective unconscious cannot in themselves be so readily distinguished. The fact that the individual partakes in the collective unconscious (so that the personal unconscious – or the *shadow*, as Jung referred to it – is itself an archetypal constellation of the collective unconscious) muddies the waters. Indeed, Jacobi herself is unable to provide convincing clarification for their difference. In distinguishing between a complex that originates in the collective unconscious and one that originates in the personal unconscious, Jacobi describes the latter simply as the former with personal material '*superimposed* on it' (1959, p. 25).

We cannot diagnose the complex according to its origin. Instead, the complex is more appropriately evaluated according to its effects on ego-consciousness. Furthermore, as I shall argue, the disposition of the ego is crucial for such determination. In other words, spirit possession is not inherently 'morbid' or 'healthy', but it can facilitate illness or health in the possessed person depending on his or her capacity to endure and make sense of the experience (Jung 1948a, par. 209–10, 218).

Non-pathological complexes

Earlier we alluded to the capacity of the complex to possess ego-consciousness in a variety of forms and degrees of intensity. On this point Jung notes, 'They may take the form of fluctuations in the general feeling of well-being, irrational changes of mood, unpredictable affects, a sudden distaste for everything' (1934, par. 287). Jung elsewhere notes,

> They slip just the wrong word into one's mouth, they make one forget the name of the person one is about to introduce . . . they make the tiptoeing latecomer trip over a chair with a resounding crash. They bid us congratulate the mourners at a burial instead of condoling with them . . . [they have us say] 'Our Father, who are not in heaven'. (1948a, par. 202)

Likewise, on their intensity Jacobi writes, 'Some complexes rest peacefully, embedded in the general fabric of the unconscious, and scarcely make themselves noticed; others behave as real disturbers of the psychic "economy"' (1959, p. 9). Despite their noted variety, complexes describe the same dissociated ego-state. Thus Jung claims, 'there is in fact no difference in principle between a slip of the tongue caused by a complex and the wildest blasphemies' (1948a, par. 204).

Through Jung's notion of the complex we find that spirit possession is phenomenologically equivalent to the trivial parapraxes of everyday life. Thus,

> Even the schizoid phenomena that correspond to primitive[10] possession can be observed in normal people. They, too, are not immune to the demon of passion; they, too, are liable to possession by infatuation, a vice, or a one-sided conviction. (Jung 1934, par. 287)

Spirit possessions as complexes affect us all, irrespective of our particular mental disposition or cultural bias (they are 'the normal phenomena of life', Jung 1948a, pars. 218, 210; 1921, par. 925). Whatever *form* the possession or complex takes depends on the conscious disposition of the recipient. That is to say, the manner in which the complex becomes manifest is determined by the strength of its affect on the ego, and by the recipient's particular epistemological framework (his or her cultural, social or religious disposition). The strength of the affect of the complex is itself determined by the degree to which it is split off from consciousness. This refers both to the origins of the complex (in either the personal or collective unconscious), and to the propensity of the ego to allow the complex its expression.[11] We have already spoken at length about the implications of the unconscious origin of the complex, and we have touched upon the compensatory relationship of ego-consciousness and the unconscious. This latter dynamic is key to understanding how the complex can grow in stature and acquire its formidable form on the basis of the ego's resistance to it. Jung writes,

> All unconscious contents, once they . . . have made themselves felt possess as it were a specific energy which enables them to manifest themselves . . . But this energy is normally not sufficient to thrust the content into consciousness. For that there must be a certain predisposition on the part of the conscious mind, namely a deficit in the form of a loss of energy. The energy so lost raises the psychic potency of certain compensating contents in the unconscious. (1946b, par. 372)

The ego inadvertently increases the momentum of the complex through the depletion of its own energy reserves when it attempts to exert itself in its resistance to the complex. For the more the ego tries to assert itself the more the unconscious will compensate the ego's attempt to do so. The intensity of the swing of psychic energy, as it is redirected away from the ego and invests itself in the complex, is correlative to the intensity of the perceived form of the spirit possession. That is to say, the form of the possessing spirit will appear most formidable when both the complex originates in the collective unconscious and the ego musters all of its energy to resist the affect of the complex. In this respect Jung writes, 'any autonomous complex not subject to the conscious will exert a *possessive* effect on consciousness proportional to its strength and limits the latter's freedom' (1948b, par. 242 n.15; emphasis mine; see also Jung 1917/1926/1943, par. 111). Interestingly, the anthropologist Erika Bourguignon alludes to a similar compensatory relationship in her study of Haitian Vodou:

> The idea that human beings may resist possession by spirits . . . is considered to be a dangerous thing to try, and when possession trance occurs in spite of such efforts, it appears to be more violent and exhausting than under other circumstances. This makes good psychological sense: going into possession trance means that one 'lets go' and submits to the cues of the drums. . . . Resisting means that an opposite pull exists so that there is conflict and ambivalence in the individual; if this conflict is resolved by overcoming the resistance, the result may well be stressful. (1976, p. 23)

According to this compensatory relationship between the ego and the unconscious complex, the ego can reduce the powerful form of the complex if it is able to submit itself to the complex and not resist it. In light of this seeming paradox, Jung says, 'Everyone knows nowadays that people "have complexes"; what is not so well known . . . is that complexes can "*have us*"' (1948a, par. 200).

The myriad of ways in which a complex *can have us* – and indeed, whether we wish to call it a complex at all – are culturally determined. The cultural bias of those who experience the possession will determine the name of the experience and its subsequent value. Thus Jung notes,

> Where the primitive speaks of ghosts, the European speaks of dreams and fantasies and neurotic symptoms, and attributes less importance to them than the primitive does. (1948c, par. 573)

Also,

> Possession, though old-fashioned, has by no means become obsolete;
> only the name has changed. Formerly they spoke of 'evil spirits', now we
> call them 'neuroses' or 'unconscious complexes'. Here as everywhere the
> name makes no difference. (1945a, par. 1374)

And, perhaps the most cited passage in which Jung makes the point,

> We are still as much possessed by autonomous contests as if they were
> Olympians. Today they are called phobias, obsessions, and so forth;
> in a word, neurotic symptoms. The gods have become diseases. (1929,
> par. 54)

It is my contention – and also, I claim, one of Jung's – that spirit possession should not be diagnosed as either healthy or unhealthy according to
its presenting *form*, but rather according to the disposition of the person or
community that *experiences* it. In other words, spirit possession should not be
evaluated according to the intensity of its presentation, but according to
one's capacity to endure it. In this respect I do not diagnose supposedly
'trivial' manifestations of complexes – such as slips of tongue, falling over a
chair, and other 'accidents' – as inherently healthy experiences; and neither do I diagnose supposed demonic possession as inherently unhealthy.
Rather, I contend that all spirit possessions or dissociative ego-states – across
the spectrum of mild to intense presentation – lead to healthy or unhealthy
conditions *depending on* the disposition of the person or people who
encounter them.

Conclusion

The ego's disposition to the possessing spirit

Thus far I have argued that the form and intensity of the complex or
spirit possession is determined by the nature of its unconscious origin (as
personal or collective) and by the disposition of the consciousness that
encounters it. I have concluded that while the complex itself and its
unconscious origins are not accountable for the consequent mental health
or illness of the possessed personality, the disposition of the conscious ego
is. In this final part of the chapter I shall address the relationship between
the disposition of ego-consciousness and the affect of the complex in order

to outline its various permutations, and to postulate those circumstances in which the ego's response to its possession is likely to incite mental health or illness. In the course of our discussion we shall see that even in those dissociative states that seem most perilous and intense – where the ego-personality seems to have lost all sense of reality – the end result can be a more enriched and enlivened state of ego-consciousness.

I shall take as my starting point two well-documented ways in which the ego can respond to its possession: where the ego is present during its possession and is conscious of the experience; and where the ego appears to be absent – subsumed within the invading unconscious, and subsequently unable to experience the possession. These different scenarios represent two extreme dispositions of the ego – and their dichotomy is often adopted within anthropological and religious studies in order to classify spirit possession and varieties of 'spiritual experience' in general. For instance, Bourguignon distinguishes between 'possession belief' and 'possession trance', where the former refers to a form of spirit possession that *does not* affect the cohesion of the ego-identity of the possessed person, and the latter to a form that *does*, in such a way that the person feels himself or herself to be – or socially defined to be – a completely different person (1976, pp. 7–8).

We could go as far as to argue that these two scenarios of ego-disposition provide a universal standard or classification that enables us to examine as one the different cultural or anthropological variations of spiritual experience on the basis of their phenomenological equivalence. Thus, Bourguignon's notion of 'possession belief' is phenomenologically equivalent to T. K. Oesterreich's concept of 'lucid possession' (1930), W. T. Stace's extroverted form of mystical experience (1960), and to 'spirit possession' in spiritualist discourse (Peebles 1904). Likewise, Bourguignon's notion of 'possession trance' is phenomenologically equivalent to Oesterreich's concept of 'somnambulist possession' (1930), W. T. Stace's introverted form of mystical experience (1960), and to the spiritualist's notion of 'spirit obsession' (Peebles 1904). And I would stress here that psychological diagnoses of different degrees of dissociated ego-states are, similarly – and perhaps 'merely' – of equivalent phenomenological presentation. Jung alludes to the two extreme ego-dispositions in the context of the dissociated state of what he calls, 'demonism':

Demonism (synonymous with daemonomania = possession) denotes a peculiar state of mind characterized by the fact that certain psychic contents, the so-called complexes, take over the control of the total personality in place of the ego, at least temporarily, to such a degree that the free will of the ego is suspended ... in certain of these states ego-consciousness is present, in others it is eclipsed. (1945b, par. 1473–4)

So, how do each of these typical or representative ego-dispositions relate to mental health and illness? The answer is not so straightforward. It is certainly not the case that one represents a healthy response and the other an unhealthy one. After all, those egos that are present during their respective possession experiences are not necessarily going to behave or respond to their experience in exactly the same way as each other (for instance, an ego may be conscious and unaware of its possession; see Ellenberger's differentiation between overt and latent possession [1970, p. 14; cf. Jung 1954, par. 385]; and the same can be said for the ego that is presumed to be absent during its possession). Rather, I think it the case that the two different categories of ego-disposition represent for Jung different degrees of potential health and illness for the possessed personality. Thus, in the first scenario, where the ego is present and conscious of its possession, the ego's potential transformation is relatively minor. The ego can become ill, but, generally, not critically ill (such as we find in Jung's understanding of neurosis), or it can undergo a mild enrichment of personality (such as a temporary state of, what we might call, 'inspiration'). In the second scenario, where the ego is absent and has lost all sense of reality in its identification with the autonomous unconscious, the potential transformation of the ego is considerable. Here the ego can become severely ill and may never again find its grounding in reality (such as we find in Jung's understanding of psychosis); or it may return renewed with a more affluent orientation to life (such as we find in descriptions of conversion experiences).

Earlier I described spirit possession as a state of potential similar to pregnancy, and it is in the second scenario – with the full eclipse of the ego – that the greatest potential for the rebirth of personality occurs. In such a scenario Jung describes the personality as entering an 'incubation period', which occurs shortly after the complex's ' "spontaneous" activation' within ego-consciousness and before the occurrence of a 'sudden change of personality' (1946b, par. 373). 'During the incubation period of such a change', he says, 'we can observe a loss of conscious energy'. The change in personality finally occurs when it has 'drawn' from the ego enough energy to substantiate its manifestation. An absent ego is one that has been drained of most, if not all, of its energy. If the ego is absent during its possession, it may well be the case that the ego has become implicated within a change of personality of substantial proportion – a change that is either of significant benefit or detriment to the overall personality. Thus, Jung maintains that the 'lowering of energy [of ego-consciousness during the incubation period] can be seen most clearly before the onset of certain psychoses, and also in the empty stillness which precedes creative work' (1946b, par. 373).

I shall conclude this chapter by placing these two different scenarios of ego-disposition within the context of Jung's model of intrapersonal dialogue in order to clarify the extent to which spirit possession facilitates mental health or illness.

The resistant ego, refusing the unconscious its expression

If the ego is receptive to the vital communications of the unconscious, the subsequent maturation and development of the whole personality is relatively unproblematic and barely perceptible to the ego. If, on the other hand, the ego refuses to engage in dialogue with the unconscious and assimilate its material, the personality becomes 'stuck' in its development. The dynamic psyche postulated by Jung (and Freud) cannot function in this inert condition, and it therefore has in place mechanisms of self-care that ensure that, when such inactivity is threatened, the personality is 'kick-started' back into life. The uncompromising mechanism that it employs is *possession* of the conscious ego by the unconscious, which enforces an appropriate change in the ego-personality that encourages dialogue between the ego and the unconscious. I have claimed throughout this chapter that spirit possession is not in itself pathological, but is both an expression of the dissociation of the ego from its vital dialogue with the unconscious needs of the personality, and also the mechanism that enables the restoration of this dialogue. Possession of the ego by the autonomous complex is therefore crucial to the maintenance of mental health (Jung 1921, par. 925).

It is helpful to think of possession as a battle of wills, of ego and unconsciousness, each trying to dominate the personality with its own monologue. Ideally, the battle ends with a reconciliation of the two, and the reinstallation of their creative dialogue. If, however, the unconscious is temporarily in control of the personality – having drawn its energy from the now depleted ego – the ego is forced to relinquish its authority as the orientating perspective of the personality and allow the unconscious its expression. Possession can therefore be regarded as a test of ego, in its capacity to tolerate the new, broader perspectives of the personality that it has yet to assimilate. The sudden loss of control for the ego can be devastating. The ego may experience the sudden invasion of the autonomous unconscious as an annihilation of self – a tremendous experience from which it might not recover. Such an experience, Jung says, is often described as a loss of self or soul (1948c, par. 586; 1946b, par. 372). In extreme instances ego-consciousness is completely eclipsed by the unconscious, which means, phenomenologically speaking, there is no ego there to experience the possession. In this situation the ego is totally subsumed within the autonomous unconscious and identifies with the unconscious complex. If the complex is one that originates in the collective unconscious the possessed person is inflated to grandiose proportion, for his ego-personality is no longer grounded within personal reality, but in infinite possibilities of human experience. In this circumstance, the chance of psychosis or of a sustained loss of reality and ego-functioning is much greater than if the ego were present. The key issue for a possessed person in this scenario is whether his or her ego can return to take charge of consciousness, or whether it remains eclipsed and unaware of itself and the world around it.

If the ego is present during its possession and is aware of itself and is able to experience its possession, then we may assume the ego has not identified with the unconscious, and has not been destroyed by it. That is not to say, however, that the ego does not find its experience traumatic. It may well do; in which case it may dissociate from its difficult feelings, and thereby provide the possessing complex with more emotional affect, which will increase its charge and the likelihood of further possessions occurring in the future. However, the possession experience in this scenario is unlikely to lead to psychosis because the ego remains grounded in reality.

The presence of the ego throughout its possession may also indicate that it has not yet been able to surrender itself to the unconscious demands of the personality, and has therefore forfeited the opportunity to acquire valuable new insights into the wider personality (and to the human race as a whole). In this case, a neurotic disorder may result, which effectively means the ego is harassed by the demands of the personal unconscious, which wants the ego to reclaim the material it has repressed. If the ego is unable to do so, the unconscious will continually find ways to encourage it to do so by enticing further dissociated-states (or through the manifestation of other symptoms).

During a possession the ego must find within itself the resources to endure the emotional affects of the complex. The ego must tolerate the shattering of its prejudices if it is to accept the new insights revealed by the unconscious, and find itself again as an orientating force of the personality. The ego, Jacobi notes, 'requires courage, strength' (1959, p. 18) if it is to affirm the content of the complex as part of the wider personality of which it is also part. And yet, Jacobi also notes that the ego must find within itself the 'capacity to suffer'. That is to say, the ego must humbly accept its limitations and receive the communications of the unconscious without resistance. If it cannot do so, the energy employed by the ego in its resistance will compensate the invading complex, giving it a greater impetus and momentum in its possession of ego-consciousness.

The unconscious releases its grip on the conscious mind and 'de-possesses' the ego (Jung 1948c, par. 591) if the ego is able to harness its resources and subsequently begin both to detach itself from its identification with the unconscious complex and to assimilate some of the emotional content of the complex. When this happens the ego experiences a corresponding increase in power and finds itself again at the foreground of the personality, which has been – if all goes well – enriched and enlarged by the assimilation of hitherto unconscious material. The process of possession and then 'de-possession' of the ego by the complex

Always results in a new distribution of psychic energy. For the psychic energy that has been held fast in the complex can then flow off into new contents, and so bring about a new situation more propitious to psychic balance. (Jacobi 1959, p. 12)

Because the unconscious communicates a deeper and fuller knowledge of the individual's personality and – in terms of the collective unconscious – knowledge of the human race in general, to be possessed by the unconscious is to have immediate access to this wealth of information. A vulnerable ego that is weakened by its experience of possession is not able to digest this information; instead it becomes subsumed within it and identifies with it. By contrast, a strong ego (one that is able to reflect upon – and thus assimilate – its experience of possession) is enlightened and transformed as a result (Jung 1948c, par. 596). The strong ego experiences a sudden growth and acquisition of wisdom and 'new' insights when it is reoriented away from its previous one-sided, prejudiced concerns, and towards the more objective concerns of the personality as a whole. It is this reorientation or re-centring of the ego within the personality that may explain why spirit possessions are often regarded as profound, transformative and spiritually enlightening, and why the possessing spirit is thought to act with intelligence and purpose.

The process of possession and dispossession of the ego is not peculiar to the individual ego, but is, as we have noted, apparent in the collective ego or communal attitude of groups of people. Thus, prejudiced or stagnant attitudes and belief-systems of communities are, Jung claims, vulnerable to possession by the collective unconscious. Likewise, it is the response of the group that determines whether the possession leads either to the destruction or revitalization of their social cohesion and communal attitudes. Jung writes,

> [E]xperiences [of possession] occur either when something so devastating happens to the individual that his whole previous attitude to life breaks down, or when for some reason the contents of the collective unconscious accumulate so much energy that they start influencing the conscious mind. In my view this happens when the life of a large social group or of a nation undergoes a profound change of a political, social, or religious nature. Such a change always involves an alteration of the psychological attitude ... all those factors which are suppressed by the prevailing views or attitudes in the life of a society gradually accumulate in the collective unconscious and activate its contents. Certain individuals gifted with particularly strong intuition then become aware of the changes going on in it and translate these changes into communicable ideas. The new ideas spread rapidly because parallel changes have been taking place in the unconscious of other people. (1948c, par. 595)

The intuitive individuals alluded to by Jung represent the capacity of the ego of the group to assimilate the communications of the unconscious. We might refer to these intuitive individuals, who become aware of the seismic shifts in the attitude of the communal ego, as seers, shaman, prophets and so on. These people come before their time and are outside the social consensus. To others they may be perceived as mad or deluded; that is, to those others who are resistant to the change in attitude (and who thus represent the ego in retaliation to the unconscious). The madness or delusion that is projected on to those who are receptive to the unconscious by those who resist it represents the intrapersonal conflict (or 'battle of wills') of the possession experience. In continuation of the above passage, Jung notes that the intuitive individuals

> may feel threatened or at any rate disoriented, but the resultant state is not pathological, at least so far as the individual is concerned.

Nevertheless, the mental state of the people as a whole might well be compared to a psychosis. (1948c, par. 595)

The internal conflict between the group ego and the collective unconscious causes the personality or communal attitude to fragment. It is only when material from the unconscious is translated into communicable language and canalized into conscious ideas that the possession of the group ego can begin to have a 'redeeming' effect upon the communal attitude. Jung cites the miracle of the Pentecost as 'a well-known example' of the redeeming change in attitude caused by collective spirit possession.

From the point of view of the onlookers, the apostles were in a state of ecstatic intoxication . . . But it was just when they were in this state that they communicated the new teaching which gave expression to the unconscious expectations of the people and spread with astonishing rapidity through the whole Roman Empire. (1948c, par. 596)

In analytical psychology spirit possession, along with other presentations of dissociative ego-states, is not a pathological phenomenon. On the contrary, it is indicative of the self-care system of the personality. It is not so much a *defence* mechanism used by the ego to repress unwanted aspects of the personality, as it is a catalyst for growth and a mechanism of the psyche as a whole – which both restores mental stability and introduces new and vital insights to an otherwise unstable and stagnant conscious attitude (Jung 1921, par. 383; p. 112). In this respect the dissociated ego-state of possession may well be healthier than the familiar conscious ego.

Notes

1 Dissociation as an interpretation and explanation for the phenomenon of spirit possession can be traced back to the psychiatrist Pierre Janet. Janet is thought to have derived it from his clinical observations of hypnotized patients, who demonstrated the co-existence of multiple consciousnesses that were apparently unaware of each other. The term dissociation has since been widely adopted within anthropological research to explain trance and possession phenomena in pathological terms. For instance, Blacker (1986), Bourguignon (1968), Crapanzano (1977), Kleinman (1988), Lewis (1989 [1971]), Métraux (1972 [1959]).

2 However, it has been noted that trance and spirit possession phenomena – also understood and explained in terms of dissociation – may involve features specific to certain cultures that make these phenomena better categorized in cultural terms rather than psychological ones. Furthermore, it has been demonstrated

that undesirable spirit possessions may respond better to indigenous treatments than they do to Western psychiatric treatment (see, for instance, Loewenthal 2007).

3   Indeed, it is only relatively recently that spirit possession has received a diagnostic category of its own in the DSM-IV (the fourth edition of the *Diagnostic and Statistical Manual of Mental Disorders*, 1994), as 'Dissociative Trance Disorder' (Appendix B: Criteria Sets and Axes for Further Study'). This corresponds to a similar diagnostic category in ICD-10 (the tenth edition of the *International Classification of Diseases*, published by the World Health Organization 1992). The essential feature of this trance disorder is its involuntariness. It is described as an 'involuntary state' that is 'not accepted by the person's culture as a normal part of a collective cultural or religious practice that causes clinically significant distress of functional impairment' (American Psychiatric Association 1994, p. 727).

4   The diagnostic criteria of DSM-IV describes the essential feature of dissociative disorder as a 'Disruption in the usually integrated functions of consciousness, memory, identity, or perception of the environment. The disturbance may be gradual, transient, or chronic' (American Psychiatric Association 1994, p. 477).

5   There have been very few attempts to do this. Most notable is Jolande Jacobi's work *Complex/Archetype/Symbol in the Psychology of C.G. Jung* (1959) (originally published in 1957 in German as *Komplex/Archetypus/Symbol in der Psychologie C.G. Jungs*). In the foreword to this work, Jung himself acknowledges Jacobi's book as one that can be referred to alongside his own writings. I shall therefore consider Jacobi's work as a key source in the development of my argument.

6   After 1923, Freud discontinued equating the repressed with the unconscious, and in place of the unconscious he referred to the more encompassing notion of 'id', which also contains drives that do not need to be repressed (Freud 1923).

7   All such references to Jung's works are to paragraph number and not to page number, unless otherwise specified.

8   In referring to poodle, Jung is most likely alluding to the 'black poodle', that was one of Mephistopheles' manifestations or disguises in the legend of Faust. Interestingly, Freud acknowledges the resemblance between his case study of 'a seventeenth-century demonological neurosis' (1922), and Faustian legend. According to Jung, Freud seeks (and, indeed, demonstrates through his paper of 1922) to strip the spirit of its affective power as a supra-rational (other than ego) agent and reduce it to the level of a knowable, and unaffective object.

9   Janet regarded the *daimon* as an unconscious creation of the patient: a substitute personality that contains feelings too traumatic for the conscious ego-personality to endure. For Janet, the possessing demon is a natural survival mechanism that is generated in order to protect the patient from a traumatic experience that would otherwise overwhelm him or her. By communicating directly with the *daimon* (when the patient was under hypnosis), Janet could learn of the patient's deeply repressed traumatic feelings. By gradually reintroducing the content of the trauma to the patient at a conscious level, Janet could heal the patient and enable him or her to dispel the delusion of possession by an external agent. The possessing *daimon* could be construed as a personification of the personal unconscious postulated by Freud. In other words, spirit possession for Janet is the embodiment of repressed material that needs to be integrated and

thereby a problem that needs to be resolved. Although Jung is influenced by Janet's theory of dissociation and its subsequent relevance to spirit possession, he would not reduce the *daimon* or spirit to the mere delusion or embodiment of repressed traumatic material.

[10] Jung applies the term 'primitive' here to twentieth-century Western European culture in order to contradict its rational basis. He does not imply a value-judgement (see Jung 1948a, par. 218).

[11] However, Jung suggests that irrespective of the complex's strength of affect, its capacity to function at an intense level may be limited to a relatively short period of time: 'Certain experimental investigators seem to indicate that its intensity or activity curve has a wavelike character, with a "wave-length" of hours, days, or weeks.' (1948a, par. 201). Interestingly, anthropological studies report similar time frames for spirit possessions (see for instance, Bourguignon 1976, p. 46; and Field 1969, p. 3). That is not to say, however, that the complex does not manifest itself regularly and in multiple waves (or that its effects are not long-lasting). Indeed, the presentation of the ego during its possession experience may merely indicate that the ego has succeeded in its temporary suppression of the complex, and that the complex will reappear at the next suitable opportunity 'in its original strength' (Jung 1948a, par. 201).

Bibliography

American Psychiatric Association (1994), *Diagnostic and Statistical Manual of Mental Disorders, Fourth Edition (DSM-IV)*. Washington, DC: American Psychiatric Association.

Blacker, C. (1986), *The Catalpa Bow: A Study of Shamanistic Practices in Japan*. London: George Allen & Unwin.

Bourguignon, E. (1968), *Cross-cultural Study of Dissociational States*. Columbus: Ohio State University Press.

Bourguignon, E. (1976), *Possession*. San Francisco: Chandler and Sharp.

Crapanzano, V. (1977), 'Introduction', in V. Crapanzano and V. Garrison (eds), *Case Studies in Spirit Possession*. New York: John Wiley.

Ellenberger, H. F. (1970), *The Discovery of the Unconscious: The History and Evolution of Dynamic Psychiatry*. New York: Basic Books.

Field, M. J. (1969), 'Spirit Possession in Ghana', in J. Beattie and J. Middleton (eds), *Spirit Mediumship and Society in Africa*. London: Routledge and Kegan Paul.

Freud, S. (1915), 'Repression', in J. Strachey (ed.), *The Standard Edition of Complete Psychological Works of Sigmund Freud*, 24 vols. London: Vintage, 1953–73 (*SE*), vol. 14, pp. 141–58, 2001.

Freud, S. (1922), 'A seventeenth-century demonological neurosis', *SE*, vol. 19, pp. 67–105, 2001.

Freud, S. (1923 [2001]), 'The ego and the id', *SE*, 19, pp. 1–66.

Freud, S. (1933 [2001]), 'New introductory lecturers on psychoanalysis', *SE*, 22, pp. 1–186.

Jacobi, J. (1959), *Complex/Archetype/Symbol in the Psychology of C.G. Jung*, trans. R. Manheim, London: Routledge & Kegan Paul.

Janet, P. (1889), *L'automatisme psychologique: Essai d'psychologie experiementals sur les formes inferieures de l'activité humaine.* Paris: Felix Mean.

Janet, P. (1894), 'Un cas de possession et l'exorcisme moderne', *Bulletin de l'université de Lyon,* 8, pp. 41–57.

Janet, P. (1907), 'A symposium on the subconscious', *Journal of Subconscious Phenomena,* 2, pp. 58–67.

Jung, C. G. (1902), 'On the psychology and pathology of so-called occult phenomena', in H. Read, M. Fordham, G. Adler and W. McGuire (eds), *Collected Works,* trans R. F. C. Hull, 20 vols. London: Routledge & Kegan Paul, 1953–83 (*CW*), vol. 1, pars. 3–88.

Jung, C. G. (1914), 'On the importance of the unconscious in psychopathology', *CW,* 3, pars. 438–65.

Jung, C. G. (1917/1926/1943), 'On the psychology of the unconscious', *CW,* 7, pars. 1–201.

Jung, C. G. (1921), 'Psychological types', *CW,* 6.

Jung, C. G. (1929), 'Commentary on 'The Secret of the Golden Flower', *CW,* 13, pars. 1–84.

Jung, C. G. (1931), 'Analytical psychology and "Weltanschauung"', *CW,* 8., pars. 689–741.

Jung, C. G. (1934), 'The meaning of psychology for modern man', *CW,* 10., pars. 276–332.

Jung, C. G. (1938/1940), 'Psychology and religion (The Terry Lectures)', *CW,* 11, pars. 1–168.

Jung, C. G. (1939), 'In memory of Sigmund Freud', *CW,* 15, pars. 60–73.

Jung, C. G. (1945a), 'Marginalia on contemporary events', *CW,* 18, pars. 1360–83.

Jung, C. G. (1945b), 'The definition of demonism', *CW,* 18, pars. 1473–74.

Jung, C. G. (1946a), 'Psychotherapy and a philosophy of life', *CW,* 16, pars. 175–91.

Jung, C. G. (1946b), 'The psychology of the transference', *CW,* 16, pars. 353–539.

Jung, C. G. (1948a), 'A review of the complex theory', *CW,* 8, pars. 194–219.

Jung, C. G. (1948b), 'A Psychological approach to the dogma of the trinity', *CW,* 11, pars. 169–295.

Jung, C. G. (1948c), 'The psychological foundations of belief in spirits', *CW,* 8, pars. 570–600.

Jung, C. G. (1948d), 'General aspects of dream psychology', *CW,* 8, pars. 443–529.

Jung, C. G. (1950), 'Foreword to the fourth (Swiss) edition', *CW,* 5, pp. xxiii–xxvi.

Jung, C. G. (1954a), 'The archetypes of the collective unconscious', *CW,* 9i.

Jung, C. G. (1954b), 'On the nature of the psyche', *CW,* 8, pars. 343–442.

Kirmayer, L. (1994), 'Facing the void: social and cultural dimensions of dissociation', in D. Spiegel (ed.), *Dissociation: Culture, Mind and Body.* Washington DC: American Psychiatric Press, pp. 91–122.

Klass, M. (2003), *Mind Over Mind. The Anthropology and Psychology of Spirit Possession.* Oxford: Rowman & Littlefield.

Kleinman, A. (1988), *Rethinking Psychiatry: From Cultural Category to Personal Experience.* New York: Free Press.

Lewis, I. M. (1989 [1971]), *Ecstatic Religion: A Study of Shamanism and Possession* (2nd edn). London and New York: Routledge.

Loewenthal, K. (2007), *Religion, Culture and Mental Health*. Cambridge: Cambridge University Press.

Métraux, A. (1972 [1959]), *Voodoo in Haiti*, trans. H. Charteris (2nd English edn). New York: Schocken Books.

Oesterreich, T. K. (1930), *Possession and Exorcism Among Primitive Races, in Antiquity, the Middle Ages, and Modern Times*. London: Kegan Paul, Trench, Trubner.

Peebles, M. (1904), *The Demonism of the Ages, Spirit Obsessions so Common in Spiritism, Oriental, and Occidental Occultism*. Battle Creek: Peebles Medical Institute.

Stace, W. T. (1960), *Mysticism and Philosophy*. London: Macmillan.

World Health Organization (1992), *The ICD-10 Classification of Mental and Behavioural Disorders: Clinical Descriptions and Diagnostic Guidelines*. Geneva: World Health Organization.

Chapter 6

Possessed Women in the African Diaspora: Gender Difference in Spirit Possession Rituals

Bettina E. Schmidt

'Women are More Religious than Men' – but Why?

Spirit possession is one of the traits that can be found (in different forms and shapes) in all human societies. This has aroused the interest of cognitive scientists because they are trying to understand which factors occur under which conditions. Cognitive science of religion argues that 'significant features of the content, organization and spread of religious phenomena can be explained in terms of the ways in which panhuman, evolved psychological mechanism are activated' (Whitehouse 2005, p. 207). They challenge, therefore, the perception of religious phenomena as culturally and historically distinct. Harvey Whitehouse argues, for instance, that the collected data points 'to a massive amount of cross-cultural recurrence not only in the forms that religious systems take but even in relation to some aspects of doctrinal content' (2005, p. 207). Hence, cognitive scientists argue that 'human minds develop in fundamentally similar ways the world over, even though cultural settings differ widely' (Whitehouse 2008, p. 19).

This chapter is an attempt to include cognitive science into a wider debate about gender difference in spirit possession. The ethnographic focus is on one specific cultural setting, Yoruba-derived religions in Brazil and Cuba. The Afro-Brazilian religion Candomblé was traditionally described as dominated by priestesses (e.g. Landes 1947) while scholars tended to present the Cuban Orisha religion (formerly called Santería) as led by male *Ifá* priests (e.g. Cabrera (1992) [1954]; Sánchez Cárdenas 1978). Recent publications challenge these perceptions and, at the same time, present a contradictory development for Brazil and Cuba as will be explained below. Nonetheless, Landes's original observation about the predominance of women in Candomblé was supported by findings worldwide, in different cultural, religious and even historical contexts.

Throughout history it was reported that religious institutions and move-ments have recruited women 'far more successfully than men' (Stark 2002, p. 495), at least, whenever they were not excluded categorically from membership. And even when men dominate leadership positions, women predominate in the numbers of its members. Consequently, women are, in general, portrayed as 'more religious than men' (Miller and Hoffmann 1995). Ignoring for a moment the problem with cross-cultural generaliza-tions, one notices from the literature that there is still no agreement about the reason for it. Even the question of whether it is a gender or a sex difference is still open (see Thompson 1991, p. 382). Early explanations refer to 'feminine susceptibility' (Cross 1950, p. 178) and described women in general as more superstitious and less educated than men. Newer studies argue that it is the result of differential sex-role socialization, that women are trained to be more religious during childhood (see the overview in Kay and Francis 1996, pp. 10–13). Others, such as the anthropologist Melville Herskovits (1948), argued that women were less occupied and hence had more free time than men, but later studies did not substantiate the correlation between job occupation and religious commitment (Miller and Hoffmann 1995, p. 64). More recently, scholars have returned to physiological differences between the sexes (such as the level of testoster-one in a male body) as a means to explain the difference in risk behaviour and religious participation (e.g. Stark 2002).

While it may not be possible to come to a general conclusion about women and religion due to its many variables, perhaps 'spirit possession' presents a better-defined category, despite all problems with defining 'pos-session' (see also the introduction to this volume). A dominant explanation for the spread of spirit possession in general, and the predominance of women in particular, is societal variability, in particular socio-economical inequality such as class stratification and the level of jurisdictional hier-archy above the local level (Cohen 2007, p. 186). For instance, I. M. Lewis (2003 [1971]) points to the impact of structural factors, such as gender discrimination and oppression, on gender difference in possession practice. Other scholars refer to the female body (e.g. Sered 1994) and, as mentioned above, some turn to cognitive science and argument based on brain activity types and mind activities (e.g. Cohen 2007). Despite the rich debate on the predominance of women in possession rituals, there is still no common explanation. In recent decades, scholars collected a vast amount of rich ethnographic descriptions that illuminate the various cultural settings of spirit possession but do not offer a universally applicable explanation. As an anthropologist I am in favour of case studies and respond reluctantly to universal explanations that ignore cultural diversity. Categorization in ready-made boxes might help to structure new observations and experiences, but it also conceals mixture, change, diversity and polyphonic readings within one context, let alone between different cultures (e.g. Schmidt 2008a). Durre Ahmed (1997, p. 27) even goes a step further and challenges all Western theories of religion because of the influence of Western education on scholars. In particular, religious traditions that are not considered to be part of the mainstream religious tradition are connected in the collective imagination with women because of their 'inferior' social status, according to Ahmed (2002, p. 9). Despite some persuasive points, I disagree with Ahmed's very polemical argumentation. In order to understand why women dominate in religious activities such as spirit possession, we need to go beyond a simplistic challenge of the Western way of thinking. This chapter demonstrates, therefore, that cognitive science can offer an interesting new approach – despite my preference for the ethnographic one.

The Research Field: Orisha-Religions in America

J. Lorand Matory, a US–American anthropologist who worked extensively in West Africa before switching his research area to Brazil, challenges the presentation of Candomblé as a matriarchal religion (2005, p. 189). He states that the number and authority of male priests equal or even exceed those of priestesses in the Òyó religion (Nigeria), Pernambucan Xangô (Brazil), Cuban Ocha, and Haitian Vodou, and therefore asks the question why Candomblé is portrayed differently. He argues that the portrayal of Candomblé as a matriarchal cult and as the legitimate standard practice is based on misinterpretation by early anthropologists, in particular US–American scholars such as Margaret Mead and Ruth Landes, whose influence on Brazilian academia he regarded as so immense that the latter 'helped to make real in Brazil her own subaltern North American vision of a primitive matriarchy' (Matory 2005, p. 190). Instead, Matory stresses the importance of male priests in Candomblé, even within the possession practice. He even presents material that contradicts Landes's observations during her research period in the 1930s. His argumentation is very plausible and his book increased my suspicion that Candomblé is not a world exclusively staffed by priestesses, in particular after visiting three Candomblé *terreiros* led by *pãe de santos* (male priests).

Mary Ann Clark, also a US–American anthropologist who works on the Cuban religion but who generalizes her observation as representative of Orisha-religions all over the world (hence, from Nigeria and Niger to Cuba and Brazil and the United States), states the opposite. She interprets possession in Orisha-religions as a gendered female practice that turns devotees into women, 'and sometimes, when the possessing Orisha is gendered male, women into men' (Clark 2005, p. 83). Clark regards all mediums as gendered female and concludes that the Orisha-religion valorizes feminine virtue and action. The Orisha-religion is, according to Clark, the only religion where female is normative (2005, p. 143). In the Orisha-religion the anatomical sex of women is 'no longer seen as a limitation on the participation'; quite the opposite, the gender role provides women 'the most important focal point of the entire ritual process' (Clark 2005, p. 120). Consequently, as she argues, it attracts more women than men.[1] Her observation is very different from my own. I studied the Cuban religion in Puerto Rico, originally with the aim of writing about female religious healers, but had to adjust my topic and ended up writing my thesis about religion and ethnicity. The reason for the change was that leaders and members of several religious communities insisted that there is no difference between the sexes. I was told that every person can enter spiritual communion with an Orisha or a spirit; it depends only on the spiritual ability of a person but not on physiology or sex. And the *Ifá*-cult is, as already mentioned, dominated by male *babalawos*. Clark (2005) argues that the representation of the *babalawos* as the high priests of the Orisha-religion is a misinterpretation of early male scholars. She insists that not *Ifá* but shell divination (called *diloggun*) is the most important form of divination – at least in the Americas (2005, p. 55). Both rituals aim to get answers from the deities but with a difference: *Ifá* is directed only to Orula (Orunmila, the Orisha of wisdom, sometimes also called the Orisha of divination) while *diloggun* is open to any Orisha (except Orula). And while it is possible to practise the Orisha-religion without access to *Ifá* (as it is done in Brazil[2]), it is not possible to conduct the major rituals without *diloggun*. The different divination ritual defines the gender of the priest who may perform the ritual: *Ifá* is open only to men (the *babalawos*) while *diloggun* is open to anyone, including women (Clark 2005, p. 69). My observations in Puerto Rico and later in New York led me to the conclusion that the Orisha-religion is divided into two branches: the *regla de ifá* (dominated by male priests) and the *regla de ocha* (open to both priest and priestesses), both used by devotees according to their needs (see Schmidt 2008b). Nonetheless, Clark's observation of an increase in female participants contradicts

Matory's interpretation. He has also stated elsewhere that in the traditional Oyo-Yoruba religion in Nigeria, femininity has been made 'a privileged status in the delegation of politico-religious authority' and its authority derived from references to the imperial past (Matory 1993, p. 58). But this status has changed throughout time. In modern Oyo-Yoruba, women's sexuality is used only as a metaphor for ritual and historical narration; they are antithetical to the dominant forms of contemporary Nigeria. Matory's argument is that we have to take into account the changes due to colonialism, missionary influences, and globalization (see also Lambek 1989, pp. 50–1; Stoller 1994).

We have here (in short) two very different interpretations of the gender distinction in Yoruba-derived religions in America. Matory points to male priests and their ritual importance, though he also acknowledges femininity in the Oyo-Yoruba tradition. Clark presents a religion that is dominated by female ritual activities and participants and concludes that female is the norm in the Orisha-religion worldwide. The critical point in both interpretations is the way the incorporation of the Orisha is seen: gender-value-free or gendered. I will come back to this question later, after a short overview of anthropological explanations of the predominance of possessed women.

The Predominance of Possessed Women in Anthropology

The most important study about possession and gender is still the one published by I. M. Lewis in 1971. He divides the ecstatic phenomena such as trance and spirit possession in central and peripheral cults according to the position they occupy in society. In a second step he then describes the two categories according to the dominant gender of the main figures: 'Where central and marginal possession religions exist side by side in the same society, the first is primarily reserved for men, while the second is restricted essentially to women, or men of lower status' (Lewis 2003 [1971], p. 121). Male-dominated cults are important for sustaining the moral standard in society; the priests are leaders of the community and in control. Women, on the other side, are regarded as weak and vulnerable, hence easily to be overcome by spirits which, 'flatteringly, are believed to be attracted by their beauty' (Lewis 2003 [1971], p. 75). These categories are only prototypes, as Lewis elaborates in a later work; one always has to include the possibility of exceptions, hence it is not always a man who is in control and it is not always a woman who is possessed by peripheral spirits.[3] However, Lewis sees spirit possession as a widespread strategy 'that gives women the opportunity to gain ends (material and non-material) which they cannot readily secure more directly' (2003 [1971], p. 77). When men enter into trance, they represent authority and morality. Consequently, he interprets women's possession cults as part of the sex-war in traditional societies 'where women lack more obvious and direct means for forwarding their aims' (Lewis 2003 [1971], p. 26).

Lewis's distinction between male-dominated central cults and the women-dominated peripheral ones has been influential – but not unchallenged – in studies about spirit possession and gender. The starting point of Janice Boddy, for instance, who challenges Lewis's interpretation in many aspects, is the suppression of Sudanese women by their husbands or fathers. She interprets the female predominance in *zar* as a kind of counter-hegemonic process, 'a feminine response to hegemonic praxis and the privileging of men that this ideologically entails' (Boddy 1989, p. 5). While Lewis interprets *zar* as female subculture, Boddy insists that it is not peripheral. The dominance over men is not just a fantasy for the women possessed by a *zar* spirit; it is a holistic social reality (Boddy 1989, p. 136) that allows women to become an exercising agency. Susan Sered criticizes both interpretations for the underlying hypothesis that possession is something 'abnormal'. She argues that spirit possession should be regarded as a normal human experience; women's involvement in possession should be seen as a normal human ability and not as a reaction towards oppression (Sered 1994, pp. 190–1). She explains the predominance of women by reference to the female body and women's experiences during childbirth and heterosexual intercourse. The boundary between a woman's self and the other is thinner than for men, and hence women are more receptive to others. But she also challenges the scholarly interpretation of women's religious practices, in particular the tendency to categorize female experiences as spirit possession and male experiences as trance (Sered 1994, p. 182, with reference to Bourguignon 1976). Hence, she disagrees with the gender difference between trance and possession because of its underlying biased assumption towards women made by scholars.[4] Ahmed also points to the cultural attitude towards the female body and the reproductive system as an explanation for the biased interpretation of women's participation in religions. She argues that certain female body functions such as menstruation and birth make male scholars uncomfortable. Consequently, they overlook the fact that rituals for women are special because of the female body and that they even lead to a different consciousness (Ahmed 2001, p. 34 fn 8). But instead of celebrating the Divine as feminine (Ahmed 1997, p. 41), women's religious practices and experiences became the legitimization of the subordination of women in society (Turner 1997, p. 25).

Mary Keller follows a different path in her critique of the theories about possessed women by stressing the importance of the possessing agencies, the spirits who choose 'who will act as their instruments' (2002, p. 52). Keller states that scholars 'attribute it [the predominance of women in possession cults] to women's inferior gendered status in patriarchal culture. These analyses suggest that possessions are symptoms of the women's social and psychological deprivation that happen to find expression in culturally specific religious traditions' (2002, pp. 2–3). But these scholars pay no, or little, attention to the possessing agency, the spirit, despite its importance. I agree with Keller and will refer in my chapter to all three components of spirit possession: the spirit host (the medium), the possessing agency and the other human participants (the observers or clients), though in an unstructured way.

The Perception of Possessed People as 'Wives'

In the Orisha-religions, the relationship between Orisha and human beings is in general described in terms of 'wife' and 'husband'. However, the descriptor 'wife' for a possessed human does not indicate that the person is always female or becomes female. It is still possible for a man to remain in a heterosexual relationship with a (human) woman despite being the 'wife' of an Orisha. In addition, even Oshún, a female Orisha, is the dominant 'husband' in this relationship with her 'children'.[5] The term 'wife' has to be seen as a metaphor describing the bond between human being and Orisha but without the limitation to one specific anatomical sex. It does not refer to the female body but to control and subordination. Oyèrónké Oyêwùmí (1997, p. 29) goes a step further. She states that the Yoruba language is gender-free and lacks many of the linguistic categories we are used to in the West. Consequently, the supernatural beings, the deities and spirits, too, have to be perceived without a fixed, static gender. Olodumare, the Supreme God, has no clear gender identification at all. The Orisha, who are regarded as manifestations of the attributes of the Supreme Being, are described with inconsequential sexual distinctions. And the ancestors, the third pillars of the traditional Yoruba religion, are female and male, both venerated equally by members of their lineages (Oyêwùmí 1997, p. 140). Oyêwùmí insists that sexual distinction was not important in the Yoruba tradition.

The main distinction between people, animals and so on was the role in reproduction, not sexuality.

Her explanation might explain why I was told to forget my research question about the role of women in popular religions in the Caribbean. It confirms the Orisha theology that the spirits do not distinguish between men and women, and only the individual ability of a person is important. However, it has its limitation when applied to current practices because it ignores the perception of devotees today who regard Orishas as gendered entities, not only in America but also in West Africa. Oyeronke Olajuba, for instance, refers to Oshún as the only female being among the seventeen primordial divinities sent by Olodumare to earth, and states that 'the conduct and interaction of goddesses in African religious narratives provide models for female roles at the religious and social levels' (2005, p. 3401, with reference to Olajuba 2003). Nonetheless, Olajuba, too, describes the gender construction in African indigenous religions as fluid and complex. They 'exhibit ritual features of transvestism and interchangeable gender characteristics' (2005, p. 3402). Within the ritual sphere (e.g. during possession) the cultural fluidity of gender relations reinforce complex gender constructions.

Clark disagrees with the presentation of fluid gender construction. She harshly criticizes Oyêwùmí for ignoring 'facts that suggest that among the Yoruba certain characteristics are attributed to women . . . and that these characteristics have an important place in their understanding of traditional religion in Africa and among Orisha worshippers in the Americas' (Clark 2005, p. 38). Clark overlooks not only that Oyêwùmí is writing only about Nigerian Yoruba and not about the African diaspora, but also that she explicitly describes Yoruba 'genderlessness' not as androgyny or ambiguity of gender: 'It [Yoruba] is not genderless in terms of a presence of both male and female attributes. Instead it is genderless because human attributes are not gender specific' (Oyêwùmí 1997, p. 174). However, we have to consider the political changes over the last centuries due to the influence of Islam (since the seventeenth century), Christianity (since the nineteenth century) and British colonialism (in the twentieth century). All carried a different gender perspective to Nigeria and affected Yoruba tradition. In particular, as Olajuba writes, Christian missionaries relegated women to the domestic domain (2005, p. 3402). This was a radical change because during the seventeenth century Oyo Empire women (the royal wives) had served as delegates of kings and played a crucial role in the protection of the Oyo royal power (Matory 1993, p. 60). Few of these 'wives' were wives in the conventional sense. The term was given to a corps of delegates that were considered loyal to the king and free from the influence of subordinate chiefs. Hence the term 'wife' was used as a metaphor to define absolute submission to royal power and was applied to male priests as well as to 'royal wives' (Matory 1993, p. 65). Male Shango[6] possession priests presented together with the royal wives the majority of the palace delegates and functionaries. But in the nineteenth century the role of women changed. Matory refers, as explanation, in particular to the collapse of the Oyo Empire in 1830 because the new political centre Ibadan became dominated by the cult of Ogun, a non-possessing, non-royal god of war. Women were increasingly marginalized or even excluded from rites because possession became less relevant (Matory 1993, p. 67). But Christianity started to affect gender, too. Nonetheless, women still occupied an important position in nineteenth-century society as traders and financiers. But even this role was taken away from women in the twentieth century. The only privileged role for women today seems to be in reproduction. Spirit possession is still practised and through it 'specific political orders of the past' are recalled (Matory 1993, p. 59). However, the political importance of possession has decreased (Matory 1993, p. 69). Possession religions 'have fallen increasingly under the control of women and untitled rural men' (Matory 1993, p. 70), socially marginalized groups. Possession offers an alternative historical vision and power base; hence rites of possession present a politico-religious order from which the modern and secular king and chiefs dissociate themselves. Going back to Lewis's distinction between marginalized female possession cults and central male possession cults, we can see here that Lewis's theory reflects the power relation between the genders of the postcolonial secular society, hence a society largely affected by powerful interferences such as colonialism and globalization. The traditional meaning was different.

The increasing marginalization of women in society is reflected in the religious sphere. As Oyêwùmí (1997, p. 141) argues, Christianity has introduced a male bias in the Yoruba religion and has led to the masculinization of religion: Olodumare, the Supreme Being formerly without gender identification, became Father in Heaven, female Orisha became less powerful than male ones, and ancestry became increasingly restricted to forefathers. As Oyêwùmí (1997, p. 174) writes, this development reflects that the Yoruba world today 'is not isolated from other worlds, particularly the Western world'. Consequently, possessing agencies are perceived in West Africa and America as gendered entities, and Yoruba mythology contains many stories about gendered Orisha with human characteristics. However, Marcio Goldman distinguishes between these Orishas whose stories are told in myths, and the Orisha who possess a human. He categorizes the first as 'generic' and declares that initiation never involves the consecration of the initiate to one of these generic Orishas; initiation means 'the ritual production of two individualized entities out of two generic substrates' (Goldman 2007, p. 112). The initial possession ritual is, therefore, the crucial moment in which the individuality of a person and of the Orisha is construed. Goldman bases his interpretation on the perception that a person 'is presumed to be multiple and layered, composed of agencies of natural and immaterial elements', including a main Orisha and a number of secondary Orishas, ancestral spirits and a soul (2007, p. 111). An uninitiated human being is regarded 'close to Non-Being', only the initiation finishes the creation process, hence a person is 'made' during the initiation. Similar to the human being, the Orisha has also no individuality prior to the initiation; hence the initial possession transforms a generic Orisha into an individual entity and an unfinished, undifferentiated human being into a structured person (Goldman 2007, p. 112). Let me explain his theory with an example: the myths tell stories about Shango, the Oyo king, for instance, about his marriages, his infidelity, his escape from Oyo in female clothes during the siege by his brother and much more. But this happened in mythical time, we can learn their meaning and their incorporated cultural and ethical values, but this Shango is – despite his human characteristics – distant and generic. This is not the Orisha who will possess a human body and become part of the person. The Shango whom I encountered in a Candomblé *terreiro* in Salvador da Bahia, Brazil, was a very special Orisha, with his own characteristics and individuality, different from the one I encountered in Santurce, Puerto Rico, some years earlier. Goldman provides us, therefore, with an explanation why there are different variations of one Orisha. Each initiation ritual creates one specific being within the human; possessed agency and possessing agency are inseparably connected by the initial possession ritual. It also affects the gender attributions of an Orisha because it is possible that one variation stresses female aspects while the other favours male aspects. It is therefore possible for devotees to consult a very specific and individual Orisha during a possession ritual. Similar to individual preferences for a doctor or a dentist, a devotee can also choose to consult a specific Orisha with the characteristics they prefer in a specific moment (depending, of course, that different variations are present during the ritual).

Goldman's argumentation echoes Klass's distinction between biological organism and personhood, but with a fundamental difference. While Klass (2003, with reference to Radcliffe-Brown 1940) regards personhood as a characteristic of every human being, Goldman argues that a human being is imperfect until the initiation, and hence he distinguishes between two different stages. Goldman writes that in Candomblé a person is regarded as not born ready-made but constructed during the long process of initiation (2007, pp. 111–12). Goldman distinguishes here between an unstructured human being and a structured person similar to the difference between a generic Orisha and an individual entity. Klass, on the other side, regards 'individual' and 'person' as different aspects of every human being. He refers to Radcliffe-Brown who has defined an 'individual' as a biological organism, 'a collection of a vast number of molecules organized in a complex structure, within which, as long as it persists, there occur physiological and psychological actions and reactions, processes and changes', while 'person' signifies 'a complex of social relationships' (Radcliffe-Brown 1952, pp. 193–4). Social personality (or 'personhood' as Klass writes) is dynamic, adaptable and even multi-dimensional, a cultural construct of human beings (Klass 2003, p. 113). It refers to the ability to position oneself in a social system, to be a member of a particular social structure; hence it includes a degree of identity that only human beings experience. Because spirit possession is connected to this ability, it is common only among human societies. During the possession an identity is present that is perceived as 'real' as any other identity because every identity is a cultural construct. Here, Klass comes back to Durkheim's argument that divinities are expressions of community unity, though expressed with a different set. Emma Cohen writes that 'our intuitive notions about agency are so bound up with our expectations about human psychological properties that we are predisposed automatically and easily to make gods in our own image' (2007, p. 122). Hence, our minds are used to represent divine beings such as the Orishas in specific forms, mostly as humans, and with specific, usually human, characteristics. Gender is one important characteristic of human beings, and it seems logical for us to regard Orishas as gendered beings. However, it is important that gender is seen not as a given category but as a social, cultural and historical construct. In the traditional Yoruba society seniority and not gender was the primary principle of social organization (Oyêwùmí 1997, pp. 31, 79). The perception of possessed agencies as 'wives' contains a fluid connotation; its meaning depends on the cultural context in which the possession is located. Possession reflects 'the constructive capacity of the person in the context of the culture' (Klass 2003, p. 125). Consequently, we need to take the emic assessment into consideration when we study spirit possession. We need to follow the expectation and assessment of the community to which the possessed belongs. Klass

(2003, p. 115) supports Sered's argumentation and insists on a bias-free interpretation of spirit possession. Possession is no mental disorder when the behaviour receives the support and approbation of the society (Klass 2003, p. 109). Possession, therefore, needs the community; it has to be situated in a ceremony that includes other human beings, observers or clients. These observers can identify the possessing agencies with their human resemblances; they can even comment on the ability of the host medium to express the spirit. The observers are vital for the success of a possession ritual because they are necessary to deliver the message (Crapanzano 2005, p. 8693). Some scholars even argue that 'possession is not possession unless it is recognized as such by both the individual and the community' (Smith 2001, p. 204, with reference to Rouget 1985). As various scholars have pointed out in recent decades, possession has a vital social function for the community, for instance, healing, oracle reading, counselling and communal activities. But, as Cohen summarizes the debate, it is also about 'resituating identity, [. . .] it is used as a medium of resistance, a social critique, a theatrical parody, a political act, moral statement, mimetic compulsion, embodied aesthetic' (2007, p. 132).

Cognitive Approach to Spirit Possession as a New Avenue to Understand Spirit Possession?

As mentioned at the beginning, cognitive science of religion follows a different path from that taken by most anthropologists of religion. Spirit possession is regarded as a universal cultural phenomenon whose spread can be explained by a universal mechanism. In order for a possession to occur, the belief in spirits needs to be present. 'Environments and socio-cultural systems do not affect people's thoughts and actions unless they are somehow registered by their perceptual systems, resulting in responses generated by intricate and flexible processes of mentation' (Whitehouse 2005, p. 221). Certain contexts may encourage or prevent the presence of spirit belief in one's mind or the inhibition of certain cognitive concepts (Cohen 2007, p. 220 fn 4, summarizing Whitehouse 1995, 2000, 2004). And even if the knowledge is successfully transmitted, not every member of the society will experience it in the same way, as the gender difference in spirit possession practice demonstrates. Emma Cohen, a student of Whitehouse, argues that, in uncontrollable situations (e.g. terminal illness, but also unpredictable environment), individuals use various strategies to maintain a sense of control, and one can be the involvement in religious practices such as spirit possession. Stress (caused by ill health, anxiety, crop failure or other factors) and uncontrollability increase the emergence of beliefs in spirits or other supernatural agents, hence Cohen argues that there is a correlation between stress/oppression/uncontrollability and the high incidence of spirit phenomena. One could argue that women experience more stress than men due to their role as main supporters of their children but this argumentation is stereotypical and does not offer a universal explanation for the predominance of possessed women. At this point, cognitive anthropologists such as Whitehouse and Cohen refer to the Theory of Mind (ToM). Simon Baron-Cohen, one of the key figures in this discussion, explains that 'by theory of mind we mean being able to infer the full range of mental states (beliefs, desires, intentions, imagination, emotion, etc.) that cause action. In brief, to be able to reflect on the content of one's own and other's mind' (2000, p. 3). The idea behind Theory of Mind is that human beings not only live socially but also think socially; as Wellman and Lagattuta explain, human beings 'develop numerous conceptions about people, about relationships, about groups, social institutions, conventions, manners and morals. . . . [and] certain core understandings organize and enable this array of developing social perceptions, conceptions and beliefs' (2000, p. 21). Based on the ToM, Whitehouse argues that any religious practices, but in particular spirit possession, require sophisticated ToM capacities because possession involves 'keeping track of at least two mental entities (the possessing spirit and the host) at the same time, and typically a number of such entities' (2008, p. 22). Not only the host but also the observers need to 'keep track' of many things at the same time in order to understand the social implications of the information given by possessing spirits. At this point gender becomes crucial because Baron-Cohen, who studies in particular Theory of Mind deficits, has discovered that women (at population level) have higher developed Theory of Mind capacities than men. He explains the gender difference with different brain types involving two opposed capacities: systematizing and empathizing. Women score higher on empathy measures and men score higher on systemizing measures. And because empathizing is crucial for any religious practice because it is necessary for analyzing the social world, for understanding the behaviour of other people (Cohen 2008, p. 200, with reference to Baron-Cohen), Whitehouse argues that spirit possession is a 'domain of religious activities that will tend to involve higher levels of participations from women than from men' (2008, p. 22, with reference to Baron-Cohen 2003). Although this theory does not indicate that there is an absolute difference between men and women (Cohen 2007, p. 201), it led scholars such as

Cohen to the understanding that the Theory of Mind differences between men and women are 'a causal factor in the high incidence of female sensitivity to the actions and intentions of supernatural agents' (2007, p. 202). Cohen argues that Type E individuals (and among them a majority are female) predominate religious activities 'in which spirits, gods, and other supernatural agents also participate' (2007, pp. 202–3) because they are more likely to be more sensitive 'to the perspectives, motivations, beliefs, and desires of the spirits that possess others as well as of the spirits that they themselves are host to' (2007, p. 203). Type E individuals are better at detecting and decoding social communication which is important for a spirit host as well as for the observers. Cohen concludes therefore that women predominate in possession activities, 'both as clients, or devotees, and as hosts of possessing spirits', due to the causal mechanism based on Type E brain activity.

Conclusion

Where do these new explanations of the gender difference lead us in search of an explanation for the developments of the Orisha religions in Cuba and Brazil? As in other cross-cultural theories mentioned above Whitehouse ignores social and cultural conditions that affect the gender division in religious practices. He presents a theory that may explain why spirit possession has spread globally and why in many cases we will find more women involved in possession rituals than men. But it does not explain the vast amount of variations and differences. However, Cohen's case study about possession in Afro-Brazilian religious traditions in the northern Brazilian city of Belém[7] tries to apply the cognitive approach to a specific case of possession practice in order to show the applicability of Whitehouse's theory to anthropological studies. Nonetheless, the danger remains that the correlation between brain type activities and a cultural phenomenon such as spirit possession is too simplistic. Whitehouse acknowledges the limitation and lists together with biological variables (such as ToM) also technological, socio-political and cultural variables that influence the activation of universal cognitive mechanism (2008, pp. 22–4). The neuroscientist and biologist Steven Rose goes even further. He questions the possibility 'to identify a biological – presumably genetic or neuro-developmental – cause to any difference in the way men and women think and act' and argues that the problem is that from the moment of birth, boys and girls are treated differently, which shapes both their growing bodies and brains and how they are expected to behave. It is not just that the biological is expressed through the social and cultural, but that the social and cultural in turn shape the biological. (Rose 2009, p. 787)

We need, therefore, a polyphonic, multi-layered approach to spirit possession. There is no one single answer but a combination of possibilities why more women than men are involved in spirit possession. There are no physiological reasons to exclude men from spirit possession but there may be physiological reasons (such as the specific role in reproduction and cognitive abilities) why one sex is more drawn to this practice than the other. But we have to be careful not to become blind towards the other sex as Matory's research in Brazil has shown. The new generation of scholars, who are no longer handicapped by the perception of the religious domain as feminine, influences the way we study religious practices such as spirit possession, even though the public viewpoint is still affected by the image of religion as a 'feminine' institution (Thompson 1991, p. 392). But in addition to the physiological dimension we need to include, in any plausible model, social and cultural conditions. Gender-orientation and sex-role socialization have an impact on the way women and men behave in certain situations, including the religious sphere. And this might affect long term the way women and men think, and hence it might have an impact on brain activity. Brain activity is regarded as something people are born with, but can it not also be changed or learnt? I argue that social and cultural conditions influence brain activities and vice versa; brain activity influences the way we express ourselves culturally and socially. It might be impossible for a person without any empathizing skills to develop them but it might be possible to increase low empathizing skills by learning. Otherwise the use of education would be limited. Why should we send, for instance, a child with brain type E to mathematics classes? And why should we try to teach someone with brain type S social skills? The current contradictory developments in Brazil and Cuba support my argumentation. The two religions are basically similar; both are derived from the West African Yoruba tradition but have developed a little differently due to social and political conditions. *Ifá*, as already indicated above, did not survive the oppression of slavery in Brazil, only in Cuba, but has recently experienced a revival. Nonetheless, possession is the core practice in both religions. During possession the worlds of gods and humans converse and, as Goldman writes, adept and Orisha *almost* overlap. Hence, being possessed does not mean that a person transforms into an Orisha but that he or she becomes an 'almost' divine entity (Goldman 2007, pp. 112–14). Goldman argues here that 'becoming' is not identical with transformation; it includes the view of an active and creative process that will not (necessarily) result in a transformed entity but includes a movement. This creativity of the liminal stage can have different outcomes as Victor Turner (1986) has pointed out. But it always involves the community, and hence is not limited to the possessed individual. Turner's observations can help us to understand the instrumental and expressive function of possession, for example, what possession does and what it means for the participants and observers (see also Cohen 2007, p. 132). The belief in Orisha is a culturally transmitted trait both in Brazil and in Cuba, part of the national repertoires of cognitive elements. It comes to the surface and increases its importance, as Cohen argues, during certain situations in which individuals suffer lack of control, whether it is caused by a personal problem such as terminal illness or a communal one such as natural disasters (see also Malinowski 1954 [1925] about religion's main function). Hence, we have here a combination of cognitive traits and social and cultural conditions that influence involvement in spirit possession.

The structural location in society has, as Lewis, Boddy and others have pointed out, an impact on the selection of mediums, but also the socialization of women, hence the way they are brought up. Religious activities are regarded in most societies as being part of the feminine section of society, as an extension of the household activities and concern for family well-being. Although it is a cultural construct, it has spread through the world due to colonization. However, the current increase in men participating in the upbringing of children will have an effect on religious participation, despite the current masculine role-model in industrialized societies (such as Brazil) that traditionally weakens religious activities. A changed socialization of children will also impact on the cognitive capacities of both girls and boys. My guess is that brain activity E (empathizing) will increase and will no longer be predominately connected to women.

In conclusion, I argue here that we should approach the question of gender distribution in possession rituals from a different angle. Instead of trying to understand why more women are drawn towards spirit possession, we should study why men avoid this ritual practice.[8] It is not women who decide to dominate the field of spirit possession but men who decide to withdraw from it because it is perceived as feminine. Spirit possession is not a feminine practice but open to everyone who chooses to become involved in it and who has the capability to surrender to an alien power. Currently women dominate due to various cultural and socio-political factors. When these conditions change, the gender distribution will change too, despite the fact that women seem to be more able than men in handling the presence of more than one mind.

Notes

[1] While Clark insists that sex and sexual orientation of a person is not important, she mentions a strong participation of gay men and lesbians (30–50 per cent) in the Orisha-religion (Clark 2005, p. 148).

[2] Stefania Capone reported at a conference in Paris in 2008 a revival of *Ifá* in Brazil due to Cuban influences (unpublished paper, 2008).

[3] In one of his early articles he states that he disagrees with the assumption that spirit possession in general is a product of the deprivation of women in male-dominated societies (Lewis 1967, p. 626; see also 1983, p. 413).

[4] Look also at Coakley's collection (Coakley 1997), in particular Asad's chapter about anthropological studies about the body (Asad 1997).

[5] A human being whose body can incorporate an Orisha is usually called a 'child' of this Orisha.

[6] Shango is considered an early king of Oyo though he is now seen as Orisha.

[7] The Afro-Brazilian tradition in Belém has many resemblances to Candomblé in Bahia but with some non-African-derived elements. Seth Leacock and Ruth Leacock labelled this mixture 'Batuque' (Leacock and Leacock 1972) but Cohen prefers the term 'culto afro' (Cohen 2007, p. 16).

[8] William Kay and Leslie Francis present a similar approach in their study about the attitude towards churches in the UK: 'The drift from the churches may not be a phenomenon so much characteristic of men as a phenomenon characteristic of individuals who emphasize the personality characteristics of masculinity at the expense of the personality characteristics of femininity' (1996, p. 21).

Bibliography

Ahmed, D. S. (1997), 'Women, psychology and religion', in R. Dhunjibhoy (ed.), *Women and Religion: Debates on a search*. Lahore: Heinrich Böll Foundation, pp. 23–45.

Ahmed, D. S. (2001 [1994]), *Masculinity, Rationality and Religion: A feminist perspective*. Lahore: ASR Publications.

Ahmed, D. S. (2002), 'Introduction: the last frontier', in D. S. Ahmed (ed.), *Gendering the Spirit*. London: Zed Books, pp. 3–34.

Asad, T. (1997), 'Remarks on the anthropology of the body', in S. Coakley (ed.), *Religion and the Body*. Cambridge: Cambridge University Press, pp. 42–52.

Baron-Cohen, S. (2000), 'Theory of mind and autism: a fifteen year review', in S. Baron-Cohen, H. Tager-Flusberg and D. J. Cohen (eds), *Understanding Other Minds: Perspectives from Developmental Cognitive Neuroscience*. Oxford: Oxford University Press, pp. 3–20.

Baron-Cohen, S. (2003), *The Essential Difference: The Truth about the Male and Female Brain*. New York: Basic Books.

Boddy, J. (1989), *Wombs and their Spirits: Women, Men and the Zar Cult in Northern Sudan*. Madison: University of Wisconsin Press.

Bourguignon, E. (1976), *Possession*. San Francisco: Chandler and Sharp.

Cabrera, L. (1992 [1954]), *El Monte* (7th edn). Miami: Ediciones Universal.

Capone, S. (2008), 'Le pai-de-santo et le babalawo: interaction religieuse et réarrangements rituels au sein de la religion des orisha', unpublished paper presented at the *Journée d'études ANR-SUD, Religions afro-américaines et dynamiques transnationales*. Paris: Université de Paris X-Nanterre.

Clark, M. A. (2005), *Where Men are Wives and Mothers Rules*. Gainesville: University Press of Florida.

Coakley, S. (ed.) (1997), *Religion and the Body*. Cambridge: Cambridge University Press.

Cohen, E. (2007), *The Mind Possessed. The Cognition of Spirit Possession in an Afro-Brazilian religious Tradition*. Oxford: Oxford University Press.

Crapanzano, V. (2005), 'Spirit possession: An overview', in L. Jones (ed.), *Encyclopedia of Religion* (2nd edn). Detroit: Macmillan Reference USA, pp. 8687–94.

Cross, W. R. (1950), *The Burned-Over District*. Ithaca: Cornell University Press.

Goldman, M. (2007), 'How to learn in an Afro-Brazilian spirit possession religion: ontology and multiplicity in Candomblé', in D. Berliner and R. Sarró (eds), *Learning Religion: Anthropological Approaches*. New York and Oxford: Berghahn Books, pp. 103–19.

Herskovits, M. (1948), 'Review of The City of Women', *American Anthropologist*, 50, 123–5.

Kay, W. K. and Francis, L. J. (1996), *Drift from the Churches: Attitude Toward Christianity During Childhood and Adolescence*. Cardiff: University of Wales Press.

Keller, M. (2002), *The Hammer and the Flute: Women, Power and Spirit Possession*. Baltimore: Johns Hopkins University Press.

Klass, M. (2003). *Mind over Mind: The Anthropology and Psychology of Spirit Possession*. Lanham: Rowman & Littlefield Publishers.

Lambek, M. (1989), 'From disease to discourse: remarks on the conceptualization of trance and spirit possession', in C. A. Ward (ed.), *Altered States of Consciousness and Mental Health*. Newbury Park: Sage, pp. 36–61.

Landes, R. (1947), *The City of Women*. New York: Macmillan.

Leacock, S. and Leacock, R. (1972), *The Spirits of the Deep: A Study of an Afro-Brazilian Cult*. Garden City: Doubleday Natural History Press.

Lewis, I. M. (1967), 'Spirits and the sex of women', *Man*, 2 (4), 626–8.

Lewis, I. M. (1983), 'Spirit possession and biological reductionism', *American Anthropologist*, 85, 412–13.

Lewis, I. M. (2003 [1971]), *Ecstatic Religion: A Study of Shamanism and Spirit Possession* (3rd edn). London: Routledge.

Malinowski, B. (1954), *Magic, Science and Religion and other Essays*. Garden City: Doubleday (the essay 'Magic, Science and Religion' was first printed in 1925).

Matory, J. L. (1993), 'Government by seduction: history and the tropes of "mounting" in Oyo-Yoruba religion', in J. Comaroff and J. Comaroff (eds), *Modernity and Its Malcontents*. Chicago: University of Chicago Press, pp. 58–85.

Matory, J. L. (2005), *Black Atlantic Religion: Tradition, Transnationalism, and Matriarchy in the Afro-Brazilian Candomblé*. Princeton: Princeton University Press.

Miller, A. S. and Hoffmann, J. P. (1995), 'Risk and religion: an explanation of gender differences in religiosity', *Journal for the Scientific Study of Religion*, 34 (1), 63–75.

Olajuba, O. (2003), *Women in the Yoruba Religious Sphere*. Albany: State University of New York Press.

Olajuba, O. (2005), 'Gender and religion: gender and African religious traditions', in L. Jones (ed.), *Encyclopedia of Religion* (2nd edn). Detroit: Macmillan Reference USA, pp. 3400–06.

Oyêwùmí, O. (1997), *The Invention of Women: Making an African Sense of Western Gender Discourses*. Minneapolis: University of Minnesota Press.

Radcliffe-Brown, A. R. (1940) [repr. 1952], 'On social structures', *Man*, 1, 1–12. Reprinted 1952 in *Structure and Function in Primitive Society: Essays and Addresses*. Glencoe: Free Press, 188–204.

Rose, S. (2009), 'NO: Science and society do not benefit. Commentary to: Should scientists study race and IQ?' *Nature*, 457, 786–8.

Rouget, G. (1985), *Music and Trance: A Theory of the Relations Between Music and Possession*. Chicago: Chicago University Press.

Sánchez Cárdenas, J. A. (1978), *La religión de los orichas. Creencias y ceremonias de un culto afro-caribeño*. Hato Rey: Ramallo BROS.

Schmidt, B. E. (2008a), *Caribbean Diaspora in USA: Diversity of Caribbean Religions in New York City*. Aldershot: Ashgate.

Schmidt, B. E. (2008b), 'Oshún visits the Bronx – possessed women in the Cuban Orisha Religion', *Diskus, The Journal of the British Association for the Study of Religions*, 9. Available at: http://www.basr.ac.uk/diskus/diskus9/schmidt.htm.

Sered, S. S. (1994), *Priestess, Mothers, Sacred Sisters. Religions Dominated by Women*. New York: Oxford University Press.

Smith, F. M. (2001), 'The current state of possession studies as a cross-disciplinary project', *Religious Studies Review*, 27 (3), 203–12.

Stark, R. (2002), 'Physiology and faith: addressing the "Universal" gender difference in religious commitment', *Journal for the Scientific Study of Religion*, 41 (3), 495–507.

Stoller, P. (1994), 'Embodying colonial memories', *American Anthropologist*, 96 (3), 634–48.

Thompson, E. H. (1991), 'Beneath the status characteristic: gender variations in religiousness', *Journal for the Scientific Study of Religion*, 30 (4), 381–94.

Turner, B. S. (1997), 'The body in Western society: social theory and its perspectives', in S. Coakley (ed.), *Religion and the Body*. Cambridge: Cambridge University Press, pp. 15–41.

Turner, V. (1986), *The Anthropology of Performance*. New York: PAJ Publications.

Wellman, H. M. and Lagattuta, K. H. (2000), *Understanding Other Minds: Perspectives from Developmental Cognitive Neuroscience*, ed. S. Baron-Cohen, H. Tager-Flusberg and D. J. Cohen. Oxford: Oxford University Press, pp. 21–49.

Whitehouse, H. (1995), *Inside the Cult: Religious Innovation and Transmission in Papua New Guinea*. Oxford: Oxford University Press.

Whitehouse, H. (2000), *Arguments and Icons: Divergent Modes of Religiosity*. Oxford: Oxford University Press.

Whitehouse, H. (2004), *Modes or Religiosity: A Cognitive Theory of Religious Transmission in Papua New Guinea*. Walnut Creek: Alta Mira Press.

Whitehouse, H. (2005), 'The cognitive foundations of religiosity', in H. Whitehouse and R. N. McCauley (eds), *Mind and Religion*. Walnut Creek: Alta Mira Press, pp. 207–32.

Whitehouse, H. (2008), 'Cognitive evolution and religion: cognition and religious evolution', in J. Bulbulia et al. (eds), *The Evolution of Religion*. Santa Margarita: Collins Foundation Press, pp. 19–29.

Chapter 7

Somali *Saar* in the Era of Social and Religious Change

Marja Tiilikainen

It is Saturday night. Around forty women have gathered in a private apartment. After dinner the dancing starts. Most of the women stand in the circle, clapping their hands and singing. Somebody bangs a drum with a wooden ladle from the kitchen. A woman is dancing in the middle, her head covered with a red scarf. Suddenly something happens: her eyes seem to turn around and her neck bends backwards. She goes around and I am afraid that she will fall on us. Every now and then the woman stops, she is not pleased but gives instructions to singers. In the end she falls down and other women help her to rest on a mattress. She does not seem to feel well, and holds her head. After a while she enters the floor again, and the drumming and singing continues. During the dance the woman talks and wants to have something from her handbag. She is given a silver bracelet. The woman continues dancing in a trance. After about five or ten minutes the trance seems to end and the woman goes to the kitchen. After a while I hear a strange male-like voice shouting. Others explain to me that *mingis*, the spirit inside the woman, is hungry and needs something to eat. Later I am told that the woman had *mingis* since she was a little girl. Now *mingis* was angry because the woman had not taken care of it, for example, by burning special incense, since she left Somalia . . .

The excerpt above is from my field notes from October 2000, when I was doing PhD research on Somali women in Finland (Tiilikainen 2003a). During that time Somali women explained that sometimes they experienced illnesses that could not be treated by Finnish medical doctors, and they needed either to rely on traditional and religious healers in Finland or, alternatively, consult healers in the Horn of Africa. Possession by *saar* spirits – *mingis* spirit mentioned in the quotation is one type of them – was among the given reasons why Somali women needed to rely on traditional healing practices.

The aim of this chapter is to provide new perspectives on Somali *saar*, which mainly has been described and understood through the analysis of I. M. Lewis, who conducted extensive fieldwork in northern Somalia in the 1950s and 1960s (e.g. Lewis 1956, 1966, 1991). The impact of changing social, religious and political conditions – in particular the civil war in Somalia and the flow of refugees – on the spirit possession cult *saar* has rarely been discussed (see, however, Pelizzari 1997).

In the quotation above, the explanation that the *mingis* had become angry because the woman had ignored it since her arrival in Finland is a key phrase that will be addressed in this chapter. Why had she not taken care of the spirit any more? One of the underlying reasons why Somalis, both in exile and in the Horn of Africa, discontinue the practice of *saar* seems to be Islamization of the Somalis at large. At the same time, however, I argue that Somali women do not necessarily stop practising *saar* altogether, but *saar* takes new forms and becomes visible through alternative ritual contexts such as women's *sitaat* rituals and wedding parties.

This chapter draws mainly from my on-going postdoctoral study.[1] I conducted ethnographic fieldwork in north-western Somalia, often referred to as Somaliland, in the summers of 2005 and 2006, and in the winter of 2007, for a total of four months. The population of the secessionist Republic of Somaliland (the former British Somaliland) is estimated to be around two to three million. Compared to the southern part of Somalia, the area has been relatively stable since the mid-1990s but has been struggling to create democratic governance. The fieldwork was concentrated mainly in the largest city, Hargeysa, and its surroundings. As part of the data collection, I interviewed local healers and patients from the diaspora, and also attended healing rituals. Healing rituals included a few *mingis* rituals organized by one healer in Hargeysa. Moreover, I participated in women's religious *sitaat* rituals that will be described and discussed later. My Somali language skills are rudimentary and hence, during the rituals as well as in many interviews, I was assisted by female or male assistants, depending on the situation. In addition to fieldwork in Somaliland, I use my recent discussions and interviews conducted with Somali migrants in Helsinki, London and Toronto as well as the data regarding *saar* collected during my PhD research. In the text, I use the Somali orthography. In order to pronounce Somali words properly, Somali 'x' can be thought to correspond to the English 'h', and 'c' to an apostrophe ['].

Saar and Religious Change in Somalia

In order to understand spirit possession and its changing role in Somalia, it is necessary to provide a brief background of the local political and religious context. Most Somalis are Sunni Muslims and they belong to the *Shafi'ite* school of Islamic jurisprudence. Traditionally, the practice of religion in Somalia has been Sufist. The most important Sufi orders in Somalia have been *Qadiriya, Ahmadiya* and *Salihiya* (e.g. Lewis 1998). Until recently, Sufi orders have had a great influence in Somalia and Somalis have been moderate in their religious views.

The rise of Islamic movements in Somalia began in the 1970s as part of the international Islamic revival, and as a reaction to Somalia's tangled national and international politics. Islamic political activity in Somalia has increased significantly during the past decade (Menkhaus 2002, p. 110). Islamist groups have gained wide support particularly in southern Somalia, where no government so far has managed to establish stability. Islamic groups have gained support among ordinary people by providing schools, orphanages, aid agencies and services to poor people who have suffered tremendously during the war (Menkhaus 2002, p. 114).

As a consequence of the increasing influence of new Islamic movements, political upheavals and civil war in Somalia, religious practices and interpretations in Somalia are changing. *Al-Waxda*, Unity, was the name of the first Islamic organization in Somalia, founded in Hargeysa in the 1960s (Hassan 2003). Nowadays, the term *waxda* is commonly used by Sufis in Somaliland to refer to supporters of new Islamic movements – two main groups being *Jama'at al-Islah* and *al-Ittihad al-Islami* – or, in general, Muslims who are seen to be different from traditional Sufis in the ways they practise religion. Sufis claim that they follow the right path, the original Islam, whereas *waxda* have distorted it, or not seen yet what Sufis have seen.

Islam is an integral part of everyday life in Somaliland and gives it a certain rhythm. Islam underpins the basic values as well as everyday chores and practices. However, as a result of Islamizing tendencies in the Horn, Sufi practices such as the annual commemorations of popular Sufi sheikhs seem to be in decline. Islamization is visible also in new ways of dressing, as an increasing number of women cover themselves with large veils, *jilbaab,* and also face veils, *niqab,* which is a new dressing code in Somalia. Moreover, Islamization influences the local healing traditions: a new phenomenon is the establishment of Islamic clinics, *cilaaj,* where sheikhs claim to heal by purely Islamic healing methods contrary to practices such as *saar,* which are condemned as forbidden.

Somali *saar* belongs to a wider spirit-possession phenomenon, which Lewis calls the *zar-bori* cult. According to Lewis, the complex of cults originates from Islamic West Africa and from Ethiopia, with both Islamic and Christian elements. The *zar-bori* cult has spread to Somalia, Sudan, North Africa and the Middle East. The *saar* spirit-healing cult is syncretistic. In addition to Islamic and Christian influences, it has preserved pre-Islamic and pre-Christian features. Moreover, it has influenced the development of local interpretations of these world religions (Lewis 1991, pp. 2, 10). As a phenomenon, spirit possession is widely known also on the East African coast and its hinterland. Despite different cultural and historical characteristics, the basic structures in the different areas are usually quite similar (e.g. Boddy 1989; Lewis et al. 1991; Lambek 1993; Nisula 1999).

Spirit possession in *saar* refers to diverse states, where a spirit, for one reason or another, has entered a person. A spirit can be inherited from a near relative, in particular the mother. Or it may enter a person through strong emotion like anger or love. Possessions of a person who has a spirit, such as clothes or shoes, may also transmit spirits. Spirits can cause various illnesses, symptoms and other problems. Common symptoms connected to spirits include, among others, fear, anxiety, general malaise, unhappiness, sleeplessness, tiredness, feebleness, lassitude, mental confusion, nausea, fainting, persistent headache, unwillingness to eat, loss of weight, unwillingness to talk, vomiting, sadness, 'madness', feeling of pressure in the chest, unspecified aches in muscles and bones, fertility problems, violent bodily agitation, blindness or paralysis without apparent organic cause and epilepsy (Boddy 1989, p. 145; Lewis 1998, p. 109).

In Somalia *saar*, which includes many different cults and spirits, for instance, *mingis, boorane, sharax, wadaaddo* and *numbi,* is common in all social classes. Different spirits, however, have their own specific ritual practices, which may also vary in different areas and groups. Healing rituals often include special incense types, different dance styles, music and animal sacrifices (Antoniotto 1984, p. 164; Ahmed 1988, pp. 241–2; Pelizzari 1997). According to Lewis's early study in Somaliland (1966, p. 314), Somali men alleged *saar* possession to be more common among the wives of the wealthy men, whereas women stated that there were spirits which attacked the wealthy, and others which possessed the poor.

Saar can be seen as a part of the religious, spiritual and moral order of the Horn of Africa, although, today, many Somali Muslims reject any connection between *saar* and Islam (Boddy 1989, p. 278; Lewis 1991, p. 3). Generally speaking, in many East African Muslim communities, where everyday life is divided according to gender, the existence of spirits is a cultural fact. Furthermore, many researches have shown that women in particular seem to be prone to spirit possession (e.g. Boddy 1989; Lewis et al. 1991; Nisula 1999). I. M. Lewis (1966, 1998) regards *saar* as a deprivation cult, through which marginalized Somali women try to enhance their position. But *saar* has also been approached as a complementary cultural practice in relation to Islam and men's public role in Islamic rituals (Nisula 1999, pp. 160–3), and as an inseparable part of women's cultural values and moral principles in their everyday life as Muslims (Boddy 1989, p. 276). As Islam spread to the Horn of Africa, *saar* spirits were often classified as a kind of *jinni* so that they could fit better into Islamic categories (Lewis 1998, p. 28; Boddy 1989, pp. 27, 278); in the Islamic world spirits are generally referred to as *jinn*.

At various times and places there have been attempts to interfere and outlaw spirit cults either by colonial and post-colonial governments or by increasing orthodox Islamic influences (on the Swahili coast of East Africa, see Giles 1995, pp. 92, 102; in colonial Aden, see Kapteijns and Spaulding 1996). In 1955, the British Somaliland Protectorate Advisory Council agreed that legislation was needed to make the practice of *saar* illegal (Lewis 1956, p. 147). Spirit possession rituals as well as other dances were also banned in Somalia during the rule of Maxamed Siyad Barre (Declich 1995, p. 208). More recently, the Union of Islamic Courts, which took power in Mogadishu in spring 2006, banned *mingis* rituals (Hiiraan 2006).

In Somaliland, it is still possible to find people who take part in *saar* or work as *calaqads*, leaders of the *saar* cult. However, according to my observations and interlocutors in the field, the general opinion about *saar* is increasingly negative because it is regarded as being against Islam. The opponents of *saar* say that: in the rituals spirits are called for even though they should be avoided; men and women may mix; and, moreover, substances considered forbidden in Islam such as blood and alcohol may be used. During the fieldwork in Somaliland I encountered *saar* rituals very seldom but, at the same time, I participated in several *sitaat* rituals. Interestingly, even though the aims of the two rituals are different, it is easy to observe many strikingly similar features between them.

Sitaat in Somaliland

Sitaat in practice

Sitaat,[2] also known as *Nebi-Ammaan, Hawa iyo Faadumo* and *Abbey Sittidey*, is a unique expression of Somali women's Sufi religiosity. *Sitaat* means Somali women's *dikri*, where women praise Allah, Prophet Muhammad, Sufi saints, and, in particular, the distinguished women of early Islam such as the Prophet's mother, wives and daughters. *Sitaat* is only sung by women and the events are organized and led by women. *Sitaat* is part of religious Somali poetry (Orwin 2001), but it is not well known. Important studies of *sitaat* include the works of Lidwien Kapteijns with Mariam Omar Ali (1996) and with Maryan Omar (2007), and Francesca Declich (2000).

I was introduced to three different *sitaat* groups by local friends. I visited mainly the groups of *Skeekhad*[3] Khadra and *Sheekhad* Nadiifa.[4] The third group, which I call the group of *Sheekhad* Zahra, had been initiated by a woman who had a personal interest in *sitaat* and who wanted to create an opportunity for herself and other women to practise it. The group seemed to lack clear leadership, but *Sheekhad* Zahra was one of the main characters in the group. The smallest gatherings consisted of about twenty women and the largest of about one hundred. *Sheekhad* Khadra and *Sheekhad* Nadiifa had practised *sitaat* for about thirty years. The first group gathers at the home of *Sheekhad* Khadra, where a room is dedicated for *xadra*.[5] The walls are covered with green and white silk textiles with Arabic writing and some pictures of tombs, in honour of Sufi sheikhs such as *Sheekh* Isaaq and *Sheekh* Madar. Along the wall there are long wooden rosaries, *tusbax*, which women use before the *sitaat* starts. The *Sheekhad* also has religious books with Arabic texts, some of which are recited during the *sitaat*. The same room serves both women and men. In the afternoons women have *sitaat*, and after they finish, men gather for their own *dikri*. The other two groups rent a room where they gather. Before each *sitaat*, carpets are spread to cover the floor.

All of the three groups have regular weekly meetings, ranging from one to four times a week. I was told that the usual days for *sitaat* are Fridays, Mondays, Wednesdays and Thursdays. Specific weekdays are dedicated to different persons – Friday to the Prophet, Monday to the Prophet's daughter Faadumo Rasuul, Wednesday to *awliyo* (saints, holy persons) such as *Sheekh* Jilani (the founder of the *Qadiriya* brotherhood), *Sheekh* Madar and *Sheekh* Isaaq, and Thursdays for *awliyo* in general. One informant mentioned that *sitaat* can also be arranged on Sundays, and then it is dedicated to Hawo (Eve) and Adam. The specific days, however, may differ according to the group. For instance, a woman explained that in the group that she knew best, Thursday was specifically dedicated to *Sheekh* Isaaq. Moreover, *sitaat* is arranged during specific periods such as the month of the death of Faadumo Rasuul.

A *sitaat* session usually starts after afternoon prayer, *casar* (around 3.30 p.m.), and ends with the prayer after sunset, *makhrib* (around 6.30 p.m.). In one of the *sitaat* groups women usually continued even after they had prayed the *makhrib* prayer together. Each participant contributes to *sitaat* by bringing a small amount of money, perfume, incense or food/drinks. They may also bring gifts to the leader of the group. Incense and perfume are an important part of the ceremony. As a woman explained, 'Whoever mentions the Prophet's name should smell nice'. Occasionally, a woman goes around with a bottle of perfume, *cadar*, and participants stretch out their hands in order to be perfumed. Moreover, an incense burner creates heavy smoke. Sweet black coffee, *bun*, in contrast to otherwise common tea, is served during a pause. Most of the women who arrive are married, divorced or widowed women. I have been informed that unmarried young women usually are too busy with other things and they start thinking more about religion only after they have had children.[6] The socio-economic background of the women who arrange and take part in *sitaat* seems to vary. I have seen *sitaat* arranged in affluent homes and some of the women come from the upper classes, whereas some of the women are seemingly poor.

Women sit in a circle on the floor and all of them wear a large, covering scarf. One or two women beat a drum/drums with wooden sticks, and women begin to chant. Different groups may sing different songs or use different words, and the order of the songs may differ according to participating women's desires. Moreover, women compose new verses and songs. First, however, women praise Allah and the Prophet. According to Kapteijns and Ali (1996), after the Prophet, 'Abd al-Qadir al-Jilani, who was the founder of the *Qadiriya* brotherhood, and other *awliyo* like local saints or *Sheekh* Isaaq, the ancestor of the Isaaq clan that is a dominant clan in northern Somalia, are praised. After these introductory songs, the main songs are sung to the distinguished women of early Islam: after greeting Aadan (Adam), Hawo (Eve), the first mother of humankind, is praised. Other women addressed and honoured in *sitaat* are, among others, the Prophet's mother Aamina (Amina), his foster-mother Xaliimo Sacdiyya (Halima Sa'diyya), Xaajra (Hagar), mother of Ismaaciil (Ishmael), Maryam (Mary), the mother of Jesus, the Prophet's wives and daughters, in particular Faadumo (Fatima) (Kapteijns and Ali 1996, pp. 126–8). One of my interviewees, however, stressed that in her group after the songs for the Prophet, they next praise the women, and only after that *awliyo* such as *Sheekh* Isaaq, because women existed before the *awliyo* and were their mothers.

Daughters of Faadumo Rasuul: religious and social experience

All the women participate in singing and clapping the hands. The language of the songs is mostly Somali, but also some Arabic songs and/or words are included. One or two women may stand up and dance. When the songs pass, the atmosphere in *sitaat* becomes more intense and women become emotional. They swing their bodies in the rhythm of the songs, they may draw the scarf over the face, and gradually reach a religious trance, *muraaqo* or *jilbo*. A woman explained: '*Muraaqo* means a religious condition, a strong emotion. A woman feels deep love towards the person that is being praised. Sometimes she also may see this person.' The breathing becomes heavier and she may stand up and bend the body back and forth at the waist. Sometimes a woman overreacts: she does not control herself any more, but movements get wider and wilder, and finally she may fall down unconscious.

'In *sitaat* we praise Hawa, the wife of Ibraahim, the daughters of the Prophet and the relatives of Ismaaciil. They are our ancestors, and in the hereafter we may become neighbours with them', *Sheekhad* Zahra reported. And not only in the hereafter, or afterlife, but Faadumo and other distinguished women and mothers are believed to be concretely present among women who are performing *sitaat*. For example, *Sheekhad* Nadiifa said in a *sitaat* to participating women that Faadumo Rasuul was among them, but they did not know who she was. However, she could sit beside anyone and therefore everyone should be treated in a friendly way. At some point in the evening, women shook hands with women sitting near them – this meant that at the same time they shook hands with Faadumo Rasuul. The *Sheekhad* identified her group as 'daughters of Faadumo Rasuul' and welcomed also the researcher to become part of it.

According to the women, after *sitaat* a person may get what she desired or hoped for. In addition to singing, participants also pray together. A leader of the group, or whoever feels like it, may read *duco* (prayer, blessing) and ask God, for example, for good health, a husband for unmarried and divorced women and good children for mothers. A *Sheekhad* also gives general religious advice and instructions. A participant may ask others to pray for her if she is ill or has other problems. Once I was present when a woman started crying and as a result other women gathered around her, prayed and patted her on the back. Women also discuss and interpret their dreams and visions together. Dreams may carry religiously important symbols and messages (in Egypt, see Hoffman 1997). For example, a lion that appears in a dream is a symbol of *awliyo*. A *sitaat* group may also collect money if one of the women needs economic support. Each participant contributes according to her economic resources. The main purpose of the *sitaat* group is, however, to practise religion:

> The only reason for the existence of a *sitaat* group is to praise God, to practise religion, to teach these ladies about religion and to warn about bad things. This is not for the tribe or personal interest; the main purpose is God. God said that if two persons gather because they love God, not because of personal interest, money or tribe, God will reward them. This is the only reason we come here. We do not care about colour or clan; we are equal. We like each other, because we all worship God. According to our religion, we have to respect all people, whatever religion they have . . . Unbeliever or believer, our religion does not allow us to harm another person. We have to live together in a peaceful way. We do not have to look at their origin or to abuse them because of it. It is not allowed that you eat yourself, if your neighbour is not eating. If someone is going to take your property or to harm you, regardless of the religion, you are allowed to defend yourself. Otherwise, give peace to existing people, of whatever religion or clan they are. (*Sheekhad* Khadra)

Unity between women and all humankind was often stressed as one of the basic values. In the case of a dispute between two women, the other members of the group may try to mediate. If that does not solve the problem, the *Sheekhad* has to interfere, and if needed, pronounce a punishment to the person who is creating problems: *Sheekhad* Khadra reported that in those cases they will arrange a celebration in *xadra* and read the Koran, and the person has to pay the costs.

In addition to regular *sitaat* groups, *sitaat* experts can be invited when a woman is pregnant in her ninth month: *sitaat* is arranged in order to ask for an easy delivery and a healthy child. *Sitaat* can also be specifically arranged when someone is ill. Moreover, it is nowadays common to arrange *sitaat* when a woman from the diaspora visits Somaliland and is about to return to a resettlement country: through *sitaat* a safe return and continuous blessing can be asked. The event is usually videotaped and, hence, can be remembered later back in the diaspora. I have also seen *sitaat* at a wedding, where it was more like a cultural performance, and played out together with traditional women's dances. And once I also attended *sitaat* that was organized by a women's association. I was informed that their association had been running only a few months, and they wanted to receive blessing for their new activities.

A new arena for the expression of *saar*?

I have been told that the performance of *sitaat* has changed after the war, and a new element, dancing, has been added. A participant in *sitaat* complained:

> Before the war we did not dance in *sitaat*, it was forbidden to stand up. Every person had her own place where she sat, we did not watch others, we concentrated on ourselves and praising. But now a new generation has come; it does not know the tradition, they do what they want, dance.

Another woman reported:

> *Sitaat* has changed, it has been renewed. When I left Somalia 20 years ago, there was no dancing in *sitaat*. People sat when they experienced *muraaqo*, they just swayed themselves sitting. At that time, women who came to *sitaat* were usually poor. But now everyone comes to *sitaat*, regardless of income or social class. Now there is also dance in *sitaat*, I was surprised when I came back 9 years ago. *Sitaat* has become a party. I do not believe that *sitaat* is going away. When I came here [*sitaat*] today, I was stressed, but now I feel refreshed.

The *sitaat* sessions that I have observed have had very different levels of emotional intensity. On some occasions, indeed, *sitaat* looks like a party: women have dressed up in beautiful, expensive clothes, they have on make-up, they seem to enjoy themselves and they smile, dance, and have fun together. But even in this 'light' *sitaat*, emotional feeling gradually grows. On other occasions, women seem to concentrate more on their inner experience; they sit down and sway their bodies. They do not dance, but stand up and bend the body rhythmically when they become very emotional. The leaders of the two regular *sitaat* groups that I followed most were quite strict regarding the way women should behave in *sitaat* and the leaders stressed the religious content and meaning as well as the seriousness of the ritual.

My views on whether the practice of *sitaat* is in decline or not are somewhat contradictory. On one hand, I have often been told that the number of women who take part in *sitaat* is decreasing. This has been explained by the influence of *waxda*, who do not accept praising the Prophet Muhammad and *awliyo*. 'Women and Somali people in general are forgetting their own culture and the historical way of doing things. *Xadra* was originally religious culture, not Somali culture. Nowadays most women are going to a mosque', *Sheekhad* Khadra explained. Another explanation given is that many women who used to practise *sitaat* before the war are now either dead or have moved abroad. Moreover, a woman explained that nowadays women do not have time to attend *sitaat* regularly, because they have to work and participate in earning the family income. Hence, according to her, *sitaat* is mainly arranged when someone asks for it. On the other hand, I have been told that the number of women in *sitaat* is increasing. And indeed, in many celebrations that I have attended, we have been sandwiched in overcrowded rooms. One of the *sitaat* groups regularly attracted seventy to one hundred women. The group had plans to raise funds and build their own house for *sitaat*. I suggest that among other factors (see Tiilikainen, 2010), reasons for the continued practice of *sitaat* even in the midst of negative views from the side of '*waxda*', are its ability to absorb new elements such as dancing and to give space for those women who previously used to take part in *saar*. Thus, modifications in *sitaat* and a party-like atmosphere may attract new women to participate. *Sitaat* is a rare place of relaxation and joy for women who otherwise struggle with everyday stresses and worries. Like a woman commented, *sitaat* is '*halal* dance'.[7]

The aims for doing *sitaat* and *saar* are basically different as *sitaat* praises the distinguished women of early Islam together with Allah, Prophet Muhammad and Sufi saints, whereas *saar* aims to pacify a spirit that causes suffering and illness. However, both rituals share similar features: slaughtering animals and eating together, drumming, clapping the hands, singing, dancing, the use of perfumes and incense, and the togetherness of women. Moreover, both rituals may lead to trance. Lewis pointed out that there are similarities between *dikri* and *saar* dance, and he suggested a syncretism between the two ceremonies (Lewis 1998, pp. 28–9). In addition, Janice Boddy has emphasized linkages between Sudanese *zar* and Islam; for example, founders of the Sufi brotherhoods have parallels in *zar* spirits, and in the beginning of the *zar* rituals, after greetings to Allah and the Prophet, they are called before other spirits (Boddy 1989, pp. 275, 278). Today, Somali *ulema*, religious scholars, as well as many ordinary people, regard *saar* as a non-Islamic ritual and hence, forbidden. In addition, *sitaat* is frequently seen as not a proper Islamic practice, and it is often confused with spirit possession *saar*, especially by Somali men who are not familiar with *sitaat*. Somali women who participate in *sitaat*, however, make a clear distinction between these two rituals, and stress that *sitaat* has nothing to do with *saar*. A *Sheekhad* explained:

A *jinni* cannot come here [to *sitaat*], he will be burned here, he escapes this area. *Saar* and *mingis* are forbidden. We have here *dikri*, we have *nasri* [religious things; also success, victory]. *Jinn, saar, mingis, rooxaan* [spirits] do not come; they are *xaraam* [forbidden]! (*Sheekhad* Nadiifa)

According to women in *sitaat, muraaqo*, religious trance, and a trance caused by *jinn*, are different states: a person who experiences *muraaqo* is not ill, but a person who enters a trance caused by *jinn* is. Most of the participating women seem to admit, however, that it is possible that sometimes a *jinni* inside a person becomes active during *sitaat* and causes a trance. This can be noticed when a woman reacts very strongly, is uncontrolled, screams, dances fiercely and finally falls down on the floor unconscious. A few times I witnessed this behaviour and other women around discussing whether the reason could be *jinn*. *Sheekhad* Khadra explained:

Sometimes when women come to *xadra*, some of them have *jinn*, something called *saar*, we do not know. When they are new to our group and the *saar* is with them, they may fall down with *saar* and become unconscious. But if they join us, *saar* leaves from these women. *Saar* cannot stay long with these women who stay with us. *Saar* is always looking for a group who likes it. Some *jinn* come with women and try to hide with them. Every group joins its own group. When *saar* does not find its own group here, it leaves. The person becomes normal. (*Sheekhad* Khadra)

Sheekhad Nadiifa also wondered if those women who were eager to dance in *sitaat* had previously participated in *saar*. This suggestion makes sense to me. As the participation in *saar* has become strongly labelled as non-Islamic and, hence, something to be abandoned, at least some of those women who used to attend *saar* rituals may find in *sitaat* an alternative ritual setting. The similarities in rituals lead to similar reactions in both rituals. Thus, according to Somali women, a spirit inside a possessed woman may remain peaceful and dormant or it may be suppressed for long periods of time, but at some point the spirit will manifest itself through illness symptoms or in trance. Trance, however, requires a specific ritual context: in addition to *saar* ritual itself, *sitaat* or even a wedding ritual may provide a sufficient ritual setting.

Saar in the Diaspora

Islamization of the Somali society is not restricted to the Somalis in the Horn of Africa, but reflects also on Somalis in the diaspora. Religious awakening, the increased importance of religious identity and an attempt to differentiate between religious and cultural traditions and practices as a consequence of politicization of Islam and life as refugees have been documented by several studies (e.g. Berns McGown 1999; McMichael 2002; Tiilikainen 2003a, 2003b). As a result, Sufi practices such as Somali women's *sitaat* have given way to more puritanical interpretations of Islam. According to my interlocutors in the Metropolitan Helsinki, London and Toronto, *sitaat* is sung only occasionally, for example, for a woman who is on the ninth month of pregnancy or at a woman's funeral. Hence, compared to Somaliland, *sitaat* in the diaspora seems to be rare. In addition to new religious interpretations, a reason not to arrange regular *sitaat* rituals in the diaspora probably also has to do with time constraints and difficulties in finding a location where drumming, singing and consuming incense and perfume could be done without disturbing neighbours.

For the same reasons, *saar* rituals are likewise unusual. Furthermore, in the diaspora it may be difficult to find a *saar* specialist to conduct a ritual locally (also Filippi-Franz 2009). An elderly lady who used to be a *calaqad*, a leader of *mingis* cult, related in February 2009 that she had stopped practising *saar* because a couple of sheikhs had come to her in Toronto and told her to stop doing *saar* as it was against Islam. This does not mean that *saar* would have totally ceased to exist, but it has gone 'underground'. During my PhD research, I participated in *saar* arranged in Finland twice. Both events were organized on small scale, and only some trusted relatives and friends were invited to take part. Possessed Somali women who came to Finland and other resettlement countries as refugees took their spirits along when they crossed national borders. In some cases, spirits might have been peaceful for long periods, or women have ignored their needs like in the example in the beginning of this chapter. If a woman falls ill, she may arrange a small *saar* ritual in the diaspora and/or travel back to the Horn of Africa, where a big celebration may be arranged (see also Tiilikainen 2007, pp. 218–25). Alternatively, she may turn to a mosque and try to get relief by using other healing methods such as religiously appreciated reciting of the Koran in order to exorcise spirits.

In addition, *saar* spirits may appear in another ritual setting – in a wedding party. Actually this is not unexpected; Boddy (1989) has shown that a *zar* ceremony is an allegory of a wedding. In a Somali wedding, it is customary to arrange a separate party for women where they may wear beautiful, transparent *dirca* dresses and make-up, undisturbed from the glances of men. The party customarily starts with traditional *buraanbur* songs, where women stand in a circle and one or two women at a time enter into the middle of the circle, the ritual space, to dance. Participating women clap hands to the rhythm of the music, accompanied with a drum or a plastic container drummed with a stick. The setting – including the scent of strong perfumes – reminds me of *saar* (also Tiilikainen 2003b, p. 63). And indeed, I have been told several times about weddings where women have entered trance during *buraanbur* (see also Filippi-Franz 2009). In those cases, special *saar* songs were sung for them in order to decide which spirit was behind the reaction and to give 'first aid'. I have also been told that in some weddings women may especially ask that, for example, *mingis* songs are sung. Hence, a wedding party may even work as a thera-peutic context for the treatment of spirits.

Conclusion

In this chapter, I have discussed the practice of *saar* in the midst of political, social and religious change in Somali society both in the Horn of Africa and the diaspora. Mainly as a consequence of current Islamization, but also of practical problems of organizing the ritual in the diaspora, *saar* rituals have become increasingly rare. I suggest, however, that *saar* has not disappeared, but appears in new ritual spaces such as women's religious *sitaat* rituals or wedding parties. A *sitaat* group gives women a unique female religious space where they can be the religious experts, define the rules and inter-pret Islam in a way that better takes into consideration the specific needs of women. *Sitaat* can also absorb new elements such as dancing, which may attract new women. Furthermore, *sitaat* may provide an alternative ritual setting for those women who previously used to attend *saar* rituals.

It would be an insult for the women in Sufist *sitaat* groups to equate *sitaat* and *saar*. Especially now that Islam has been highly politicized, women who take part in *sitaat* try hard to define and keep it within the category of 'Islam'. Hence, I want to emphasize that according to my female interlocu-tors who are involved either with *sitaat* or *saar*, the basic intentions of the two rituals are different. *Sitaat* is an explicitly Sufi religious practice in which women memorize and praise the distinguished women of early Islam, whereas *saar* is a cultural practice through which women try to pacify spirits that possess them, restore peaceful relationships with spirits and human beings, and thereby maintain and gain health. Interestingly, Somali women are defining new categories of 'religion' on one hand and 'culture' on the other. However, there are obvious similarities between the practice of *sitaat* and the practice of *saar* (also Boddy, personal information; Boddy 1989). Furthermore, structural similarities of the two rituals support and stimulate the bodily and cultural memory of some women to the extent that the trance may occur. The same is true with a wedding party.

The absorption of cultural and religious traditions such as *saar* and *sitaat* may be seen as an example of cultural revitalization or recreation; *sitaat* sets certain frames for the practice of *saar* but, at the same time, *saar* may change the practice of *sitaat*. Indeed, the participation of women who previously were part of *saar* cults may be a factor that enforces and gives new life to *sitaat* in Somaliland. In the diaspora, the situation is even more complicated because there the space for Sufi religious expression is even more marginal than in the Horn of Africa. A wedding party is one of the most important spaces for Somali women's cultural expression in the diaspora and, based on the data presented here, it may also be a space for women's folk religious expressions. Interestingly, today, *saar* (or traces of it), which used to accommodate both women and men – even though women were in the majority – has been marked within the boundaries of female gender; *sitaat* and wedding parties discussed here are orchestrated by and open just for women. In the midst of current political and religious change within the Somali community, the separate worlds of men and women may even help women to maintain, recreate and redefine for them meaningful cultural and religious practices.

Notes

[1] The aim of my overall study is to explore how transnationalism organizes and gives meaning to suffering, illness and healing among Somalis in exile. The study is a continuation of my PhD research on the everyday life of Somali women in Finland (Tiilikainen 2003a) and is funded by the Academy of Finland. I also want to acknowledge the financial support given by the Nordic Africa Institute and the Ella and Georg Ehrnrooth foundation for the fieldwork in Somaliland. My great thanks are due to Professor Janice Boddy, who pointed out the similarities between *sitaat* and Sudanese *zar*. I am also thankful for Ibrahim Mohamed Hassan who helped me to translate some of the Somali language material. Naturally, I am solely responsible for any errors. An earlier version of this text will be published shortly (Tiilikainen, 2010).

[2] From Arabic *sittaat*, 'ladies' (Orwin 2001, p. 81).

[3] *Sheekhad* and *sheekh* are Somali terms that refer to a learned woman and a learned man of religion, respectively.

[4] All the names are pseudonyms.

[5] *Xadra* and *dikri* mean ritual song of praising of God. The interviewed women used the term *xadra* also to signify the place where *dikri* or *sitaat* is performed.

[6] According to Janice Boddy, women in Sudan may become possessed only after they have lost their virginity (Boddy 1989, p. 166).

[7] *Halal* means permissible according to Islamic law.

Bibliography

Ahmed, A. M. (1988), 'Somali traditional healers: role and status', in A. Puglielli (ed.), *Proceedings of the Third International Congress of Somali Studies*. Roma: Il Pensiero Scientifico, pp. 240–7.

Antoniotto, A. (1984), 'Traditional medicine in Somalia: an anthropological approach to the concepts concerning disease', in T. Labahn (ed.), *Proceedings of the Second International Congress of Somali Studies*. Hamburg: Helmut Buske Verlag, pp. 155–69.

Berns McGown, R. (1999), *Muslims in the Diaspora: The Somali Communities of London and Toronto*. Toronto: University of Toronto Press.

Boddy, J. (1989), *Wombs and Alien Spirits: Women, Men, and the Zār Cult in Northern Sudan*. Madison: University of Wisconsin Press.

Declich, F. (1995), 'Identity, dance and Islam among people with Bantu origins in riverine areas of Somalia', in A. J. Ahmed (ed.), *The Invention of Somalia*. Lawrenceville, NJ: Red Sea Press, pp. 191–222.

Declich, F. (2000), 'Sufi experience in rural Somali: a focus on women', *Social Anthropology*, 8 (3), 295–318.

Filippi-Franz, M. (2009), 'Reconstituting Lives: Somali Women's Efforts to Reformulate Household and Community Values in Kansas City, Missouri'. An unpublished manuscript submitted to the graduate degree program in Anthropology and the Graduate Faculty of the University of Kansas in partial fulfilment of the requirements for the degree of Doctor of Philosophy.

Giles, L. L. (1995), 'Sociocultural change and spirit possession on the Swahili coast of East Africa', *Anthropological Quarterly*, 68 (2), 89–106.

Hassan, M-R. S. (2003), 'Islam, the Clan and the State in Somalia 1960–1991'. Unpublished PhD study, University of London.

Hiiraan (2006), 'Maxkamadda Islaamiga ah ee ridwaan aa albaabada u laabtay goob mingiska lagu tumi jira' [Union of Islamic courts has today closed the mingis ceremony houses]. Hiiraan online 21.8.2006 [read 13.2.2007]. Available at: http://www.hiiraan.com/news/2006/aug/wararka_maanta21.html.

Hoffmann, V. J. (1997), 'The role of visions in contemporary Egyptian religious life', *Religion*, 27, 45–64.

Kapteijns, L. and Ali, M. O. (1996), 'Sittaat: Somali women's songs for the "mothers of the believers"', in K. W. Harrow (ed.), *The Marabout and the Muse. New Approaches to Islam in African Literature*. Portsmouth, NH: Heinemann, pp. 124–41.

Kapteijns, L. and Omar, M. A. (2007), 'Sittaat: women's religious songs in Djibouti', *Halabuur – Journal of Somali Literature and Culture*, 2 (1 & 2), 38–48.

Kapteijns, L. and Spaulding, J. (1996), 'Women of the zar and middle-class sensibilities in colonial Aden, 1923–1932', in R. J. Hayward and I. M. Lewis (eds), *Voice and Power: The Culture of Language in North-East Africa: Essays in Honour of B. W. Andrzejewski*. African Languages and Cultures, Supplement 3. London: School of Oriental and African Studies, pp. 171–89.

Lambek, M. (1993), *Knowledge and Practice in Mayotte: Local Discourses of Islam, Sorcery, and Spirit Possession*. Toronto: University of Toronto Press.

Lewis, I. M. (1956), 'Sufism in Somaliland: a study in tribal Islam II', *Bulletin of the School of Oriental and African Studies, University of London*, 18 (1), 145–60.

Lewis, I. M. (1966), 'Spirit possession and deprivation cults', *Man*, n.s. 1 (3), 307–29.

Lewis, I. M. (1991), 'Introduction: *zar* in context: the past, the present and future of an African healing cult', in I. M. Lewis, A. Al-Safi and S. Hurreiz (eds), *Women's Medicine: The Zar-Bori Cult in Africa and Beyond*. Edinburgh: Edinburgh University Press for the International African Institute, pp. 1–16.

Lewis, I. M. (1998), *Saints and Somalis: Popular Islam in a Clan-based Society*. London: Haan Associates.

Lewis, I. M., Ahmed, A-S. and Sayyid, H. (eds) (1991), *Women's Medicine: The Zar-Bori Cult in Africa and Beyond*. Edinburgh: Edinburgh University Press for the International African Institute.

McMichael, C. (2002), 'Everywhere is Allah's place': Islam and the everyday life of Somali women in Melbourne, Australia', *Journal of Refugee Studies*, 15 (2), 171–88.

Menkhaus, K. (2002), 'Political Islam in Somalia', *Middle East Policy*, 9 (1), 109–23.

Nisula, T. (1999), *Everyday Spirits and Medical Interventions: Ethnographic and Historical Notes on Therapeutic Conventions in Zanzibar Town*. TAFAS 43. Helsinki: Finnish Anthropological Society.

Orwin, M. (2001), 'Language use in three Somali religious poems', *Journal of African Cultural Studies*, 14 (1), 69–87.

Pelizzari, E. (1997), *Possession et Thérapie dans la Corne de l'Afrique*. Paris: L'Harmattan.

Tiilikainen, M. (2003a), *Arjen Islam: Somalinaisten Elämää Suomessa [Everyday Islam: The Life of Somali Women in Finland]*. PhD Dissertation. Tampere: Vastapaino.

Tiilikainen, M. (2003b), 'Somali women and daily Islam in the diaspora', *Social Compass*, 50 (1), 59–69.

Tiilikainen, M. (2007), 'Continuity and change: Somali women and everyday Islam in the diaspora', in A. Kusow and S. Bjork (eds), *From Mogadishu to Dixon: The Somali Diaspora in a Global Context*. Trenton, NJ: Red Sea Press, pp. 207–30.

Tiilikainen, M. (forthcoming (2010)), '*Sitaat* as part of Somali women's everyday religion', in M-L. Keinänen (ed.), *Perspectives on Women's Everyday Religion*. Stockholm Studies in Comparative Religion, 35. Stockholm: Acta Universitatis Stockholmiensis.

Chapter 8

Taking Possession of Santo Daime: The Growth of Umbanda within a Brazilian New Religion[1]

Andrew Dawson

This chapter explores the growing popularity of the Afro-Brazilian religion of Umbanda within the new religious movement of Santo Daime. In so doing, the following material opens by introducing the Brazilian new religion of Santo Daime and plotting the historical trajectory of spirit possession from the movement's beginnings in 1930s' Brazil to its present-day international status as a member of the non-mainstream global religious scene. Subsequent to detailing the contemporary spirit possession repertoire of Santo Daime, the chapter offers a typology of the most prominent kinds of spirit possession practised by Santo Daime members (known emically as *daimistas*). The chapter closes by identifying the most likely factors behind the increasing popularity of Umbanda-inspired possession motifs relative to the more established forms of spirit-orientated activity traditionally practised by Santo Daime.

The Historical Trajectory of Spirit Possession in Santo Daime

Santo Daime emerged in the Amazonian state of Acre among the mixed-race, semi-rural subsistence community led by Raimundo Irineu Serra (1892–1971). Known commonly as 'Master Irineu', Irineu Serra is held by many to be the reincarnation of the spirit of Jesus. Based at the community of *Alto Santo*, Santo Daime emerged as a recognizably distinct religious entity in the late 1930s. Subsequent to Irineu Serra's death a breakaway organization known as Cefluris (Eclectic Centre of the Universal Flowing Light Raimundo Irineu Serra) was founded by Sebastião Mota de Melo (1920–1990) and his followers. Known as 'Padrinho Sebastião', Mota de Melo is believed to be the reincarnation of the spirit of John the Baptist. Headquartered at *Céu do Mapiá* in the state of Amazonas, Cefluris is now led by Alfredo Gregório de Melo and Alex Polari – regarded as the respective reincarnations of Solomon and David. On the back of the organizational expansion of Cefluris, Santo Daime reached Brazil's major conurbations (e.g. Rio de Janeiro and São Paulo) in the early 1980s before spreading to Europe, North America and Australasia (Couto 2004, pp. 385–411).

Santo Daime is the oldest and most geographically dispersed of Brazil's ayahuasca religions (the other two being Barquinha and the Vegetable Union). When applied to these religions, the generic term ayahuasca denotes the combination of the vine *Banisteriopsis caapi* and the leaves of the shrub *Psychotria viridis* (Dawson 2007, pp. 67–98). Ayahuasca is a psychotropic substance traditionally consumed by indigenous inhabitants of the Amazon which passed to non-indigenous cultures through its use among mixed-race communities and rubber-tappers in the late-nineteenth and early-twentieth centuries. Ayahuasca is regarded by *daimistas* as an 'entheogen'; that is, an agent whose properties facilitate ('catalyse') the interaction of humankind with supernatural agents or forces.

Known popularly as 'incorporation' (*incorporação*), spirit possession in Santo Daime has developed through three main phases. The first phase comprises the period of Irineu Serra's leadership from the time of the religion's birth to its founder's death in 1971. Before the founding of Santo Daime and throughout his time as its leader, Irineu Serra had a reputation as a healer (*curandeiro*) whose powers resided both in his knowledge of folk medicine and his ability to work with the spirits. Although the earlier years of Irineu's life and Santo Daime's history remain open to a degree of conjecture, there is widespread agreement upon the formative influence of what Yoshiaki Furuya calls 'Afro-Amazonian' religiosity; here, a mixture of Afro-Brazilian, popular Catholic and indigenous components (1994, p. 27). Together, these variegated ingredients combined to produce a religious-cultural worldview infused by the everyday interaction with, and ritualized appropriation of, a relatively diverse range of spiritual agencies (Galvão 1955; Maués and Villacorta 2004, pp. 11–58). A combination of oral history, narrative analysis and anthropological investigation evidences the centrality of spirit-orientated activity to the early religious repertoire of Santo Daime (Goulart 2004; Labate and Pachecho 2004, pp. 303–44). Although engagement with the spirits of deceased human beings probably occurred, available (but, self-interested) evidence indicates that interaction with nature spirits was the most important form of spirit-orientated activity undertaken by the early *daimista* community. In keeping with existing forms of popular healing (*curandeirismo*), then, early *daimista* activities involved, among other things, regular consultation with spirit guides (e.g. regarding the cause of a particular illness or run of bad luck), practical engagement with spirits (e.g. in the case of spirit infestation) and co-optation of spirit intervention (e.g. to treat illness or ward off spirit assault).

From the late 1940s onwards, the religious repertoire of Santo Daime was progressively modified as a result of Irineu Serra's increasing attraction to traditional European esotericism (e.g. Theosophy, Anthroposophy and Rosicrucianism) as mediated through the publications of the Esoteric Circle of the Communion of Thought (*Círculo Esotérico da Comunhão do Pensamento*) (Moura da Silva 2006, pp. 225–40). Among other things, trad-itional esotericism concerns itself with interior states of mind, experiences and dispositions which are awakened through access to particular forms of knowledge and practice. These interior realities are nurtured through a range of disciplines and techniques (e.g. meditation, introspection and regression) and provide access to further truths located deep within the self (Faivre 1986, pp. 156–63). Although Irineu Serra eventually severed formal relations with the Esoteric Circle, by the time of his death, the influence of European esotericism had played a significant role in reforming the religious repertoire of Santo Daime. As a result, the spirit-orientated activity which had once been so important to Santo Daime was marginalized, if not denigrated, thanks to the introduction of many of the rationalized and individualistic practices of traditional esotericism. Rather than encouraging personal well-being through the ritualized interaction with spirits, the Santo Daime repertoire now promoted the nurturing of the 'higher self' through the harnessing of impersonal cosmic energies. Although never officially repudiating the existence of spirits, by the time of Irineu Serra's death in 1971, Santo Daime embodied, at most, a kind of nominal spiritism in which spirits existed in theory but not in formal ritual practice.

Like Irineu Serra, Sebastião Mota de Melo enjoyed an established reputation as a *curandeiro*. Unlike Master Irineu, however, and somewhat indicative of his different background, the popular spiritism within which Sebastião Mota de Melo was raised had little, if anything, by way of Afro-Brazilian influence. By the time of his conversion to Santo Daime in the mid-1960s, Sebastião was a practising medium in the Brazilian Kardecist tradition – for which the disembodied spirits of deceased human beings constitutes the sole supernatural reference point (Cavalcanti 1983). Although acting as medium for some of the most exemplary spirits of Brazilian Kardecism (e.g. Bezerra de Menezes and Antônio Jorge), Sebas-tião continued to employ many of the symbolic components of the popular spiritism of *caboclo* (peasant) culture; which, by implication, involved recognition of the supernatural agency of certain animals. In addition to both his latecomer and exogamous status, Sebastião's still explicit association with spirit-orientated activity impeded his campaign for the leadership of Santo Daime subsequent to Irineu Serra's death. Upon failing to gain control of the movement, Sebastião split from the originating *daimista* community of Alto Santo and, taking a sizeable tranche of established practitioners with him, founded a separate branch of Santo Daime known today as Cefluris. As this organization is the primary focus of what follows, use of the term Santo Daime refers to Cefluris, unless otherwise stated.

By the mid-1970s, the community of Padrinho Sebastião had reestablished Kardecist-informed mediumistic activity as a formal component of the Santo Daime ritual repertoire. It did not, though, replace the esoteric framework which had become so important to Irineu Serra but rather integrated the two paradigms within a single, and self-consciously eclectic, worldview. Consequently, and while esoteric concerns with developing the 'higher self' remained to the fore, interaction with individual spiritual agents (understood now as the disembodied spirits of deceased humans) represented an increasingly legitimate mode of *daimista* activity. As indicated above, the supernatural agency of certain animals was likewise acknowledged. Interaction with these animal spirits, however, was and continues to be regarded both with a degree of suspicion and as likely to result in some form of illness or bad luck (Arruda et al. 2006, p. 146). Although the growing influx of new-age backpackers brought with it the adoption of a progressive number of alternative spiritual practices and beliefs, in terms of spirit-orientated activity the increasing appropriation of ritual components from Umbanda had most impact upon the subsequent direction of the *daimista* repertoire.

The origins of Umbanda are commonly dated to the 1920s during which the religion emerged from the fusion of elements drawn from Brazilian Kardecism and popular Afro-Brazilian religiosity (Brown 1994). Umbanda complements Brazilian Kardecism's traditional concentration upon the spirits of deceased Caucasians with a focus upon other kinds of spirits, the most important of which are those of deceased Amerindians (*caboclos*) and African slaves (*pretos-velhos*). In addition to having spread throughout the Amazonian region by the 1960s, at the time of their appropriation by Cefluris, Umbanda practices were establishing themselves among sectors of the (overwhelmingly white) urban-industrial middle classes. Indeed, it was the growing import of urban middle-class members within the now expanding movement of Cefluris that most influenced the ingression of Umbanda practices within the increasingly hybrid repertoire of Santo Daime. By the time of Sebastião's death in 1990, Umbanda-inspired possession rituals were being practised by nascent *daimista* communities throughout Brazil. It should be noted, though, that Umbanda-inspired possession rituals were not at this time considered part of the official *daimista* calendar, they were not conducted in the 'church' (*igreja*) and nor was the appearance of Umbanda spirits sanctioned outside of strictly delimited ritual contexts. All of this was to change, however, under the dual leadership of Alfredo Gregório de Melo (Sebastião's son) and Alex Polari (former political prisoner and founder of one of the Santo Daime's most important churches, *Céu da Montanha*).

Subsequent to Sebastião's death and the progressive influence of urban professionals across the ever-expanding Cefluris movement, beliefs and practices appropriated from Umbanda made their way increasingly from the ritual margins towards the repertorial core of Santo Daime (Guimarães 1992). For approximately two decades the incorporation of spirits appropriated from Umbanda practice has taken place in the church at a number of now official rituals, the most important of which are those of *São Miguel* (7th of each month) and *Mesa Branca* (27th of the month). Complementing the traditional practices of Concentration, Dance, *Feitio* and the Mass, the addition of these two rituals to the formal calendar represented a fundamental modification of the Santo Daime religion. Explicitly intended as cultic arenas for incorporation, the formalization of these two new rituals not only cemented spirit possession within the *daimista* world view but did so in a way which valorized Umbanda-inspired practices relative to the longer established, but lower profile, motifs of Brazilian Kardecism. Although of a more *ad hoc* and unofficial nature, I have also seen spirit-orientated activity occur at the long-established *daimista* rituals of Concentration, Dance and the Mass. In addition to the spirits of Brazilian Kardecism and Umbanda, and indicative of its progressive appeal to the urban middle-classes (e.g. Prandi 1991), a growing number of churches today practise the incorporation of supernatural agents venerated in the traditional Afro-Brazilian religion of Candomblé. In keeping with the Candomblé worldview, these supernatural agents are usually referred to as 'gods'. In practice, however, the incorporated agents perform the same cultic functions as their Umbanda ('spirit') counterparts.

The *Daimista* Possession Repertoire

The evolution of the *daimista* possession repertoire is characterized by the appropriation of successive spirit discourses of a variegated and often contrasting kind. Catalysed by rapid geographical and demographic shift, the trajectory of spirit possession has been further accelerated by Santo Daime's progressive insertion within the alternative cultic milieu populated by the urban middle classes and suffused by the increasingly vertiginous dynamics of the late-modern spiritual marketplace (Dawson 2007). Occurring within the relatively compressed historical framework of sixty years, Santo Daime has evolved from the Afro-Amazonian cult of a small band of impoverished, mixed-race peasants to become a globally diffused new-era religion practised by the predominantly white, urban middle classes. In between, Santo Daime has embraced traditional European esotericism, Kardecist Spiritism, New Age spirituality, and Umbanda. In respect of its contemporary repertoire Santo Daime is currently evolving thanks to the growing use of possession motifs drawn from the traditional Afro-Brazilian religion of Candomblé. Popular in Brazil for a number of decades, Japanese new religions are likewise proving influential sources of spirit-orientated practical knowledge. Albeit as yet on a small scale, extra-terrestrial discourse and attendant channelling motifs are also beginning to crop up.

Hybrid by birth and self-consciously eclectic in tenor, the Santo Daime repertoire allows for the articulation of a wide range of spirit-orientated experience. For example, and indicative of traditional Afro-Brazilian influences, some *daimistas* describe possession as a dissociative event involving suppression of the conscious self and an inability to remember anything from the point of actual possession to the moment of 'despatch'. Others, however, adopt a typically Kardecist line to describe themselves as remaining conscious throughout the possession episode. Here, some regard their subjective presence as integral to directing the possessing spirit; whereas others talk of the self as an interested but passive third party looking on to what the spirit is doing through their bodies. The *daimista* 'spirit idiom' (Crapanzano 1977, p. 11) also permits the expression of possession as an ecstatic process involving the dislocation of the self from its physical moorings. Employing esoteric notions of astral flight, some *daimistas* talk of disembodied trips across the globe or of visiting different historical periods to interact with other (usually famous) personalities. Indigenous shamanistic and popular folk motifs of soul flight are likewise employed to describe disincarnate journeys to assorted spiritual realms populated by supernatural agents of both human and non-human provenance. Others, however, eschew both enstatic and ecstatic conceptualizations of spirit-orientated activity. Instead, notions of expanded consciousness or broadened spiritual vision are employed to articulate interaction with the world of spirits. In a similar vein, some _daimistas_ describe the spirits with whom they interact as astral counterparts of the variegated aspects of the material self.

It is important to note that not all of the above modes of expressing spirit possession in Santo Daime are treated as mutually exclusive. Indeed, it is commonplace for some _daimistas_ to employ a number of motifs to describe a single possession episode. Others, however, apply different motifs to articulate what they regard as different kinds of spirit possession. It should also be noted that not every member of Santo Daime regards the incorporation of external spiritual agents as a necessary expression of _daimista_ religiosity. While the regularity of possession rituals and the incidence of individual possession events have increased markedly in recent years, there remain large numbers of practising _daimistas_ who do not incorporate spirits. Although spirit possession is accepted by the majority of these individuals as an entirely licit component of the Santo Daime repertoire, the practice of incorporation is not something they engage in on a personal level. While not gainsaying the legitimacy of the possession motifs mentioned above, nor regarding their own practices as incompatible with the prevailing spirit idiom, those who choose not to incorporate spirits express themselves religiously by employing alternative components (of a predominantly esoteric provenance) from the Santo Daime repertoire.

The pantheon of spirits lauded by Santo Daime is as hybrid and fluid as the religious repertoire through which it is manifested. As with most of the other spiritist religions in Brazil, Santo Daime acknowledges the existence of a Creator deity whose absolute status and generative cosmological activity sets the metaphysical backdrop against which spirit possession plays out. Likewise in keeping with established spiritist religions, the god of Santo Daime, called 'Father' (_Pai_), is an altogether otiose divinity who remains distant from everyday belief and cultic practice. The highest and most powerful spirits of Santo Daime are inherited principally from popular Catholic and esoteric paradigms. In addition to the popular Catholic trinity of Jesus, Mary and Joseph, the archangels Michael, Gabriel and George feature prominently in _daimista_ hymnody. The spirits of other biblical characters (e.g. John the Baptist and Solomon) and heavenly beings (e.g. Cosmo and Damien) are also praised. Except for one or two extremely rare instances I have come across, spirits from the higher echelons of the _daimista_ cosmos are not incorporated. Where they do appear in material form, the extensional syntax of reincarnation rather than the punctual language of possession is employed.

The ritual workload of incorporation is overwhelmingly borne by spirits appropriated from Brazilian Kardecism and Umbanda. Antônio Jorge, Doctor Fritz and José Bezerra de Menezes are the most famous figures of Brazilian Spiritism regularly called upon during rituals of incorporation. From the multitudinous range of the Umbanda spectrum, the mainstream spirits of deceased indigenes (*caboclos*), black slaves (*pretos velhos*) and children (*herês*) appear most frequently and are complemented by representatives of the oriental lines (*linhas do oriente* – e.g. gypsies, cowboys and European aristocrats) and street people (*povo da rua*). Although calling upon the supernatural agency of the *orixás* (Umbanda spirits regarded as gods in their original context of Candomblé), these beings are not traditionally incorporated by mainstream Santo Daime. At the lower end of the spiritual hierarchy, spirits in want of charity are known variously as 'suffering', 'disorientated' and 'inferior'. Incorporated by trained mediums as part of ritualized possession practices, these spirits also act in extra-cultic contexts attaching themselves to (*encostar*, literally 'to lean on') the spiritually unwary, ill-prepared or careless thereby causing illness, bad luck and other unwelcome effects. Although by no means shared by every community, the term *atuação* (literally, 'action' or 'performance') is often employed to distinguish involuntary possession from voluntary incorporation (*incorporação*).

As with Kardecist Spiritism, the official narrative of Santo Daime regards everyone as having mediumistic tendencies. Consequently, and irrespective of age, spiritual maturity and formal training, every human being is prone to some form of interaction with the spirit world. For many, however, this interaction is so subtle and our experience of the spiritual world so dulled that it goes unnoticed at a conscious level. This is unfortunate because a lack of awareness of the manner in and extent to which the spirit world impacts upon the material sphere at best undermines human freedom (here, self-determination) and at worst leaves the unwary self open to spiritual assault. Even for those without the aptitude or desire to become a practising medium, some degree of training in respect of managing spirit-interaction is highly recommended. For those with a greater receptivity to and desire of interacting with the spirit world, formal training is something of a necessity. To this end, communities affiliated to Santo Daime are expected to offer regular mediumistic training.

The requisites of successful mediumship in Santo Daime are varied in nature. Among the many issues and technicalities which need to be mastered in the cause of successful mediumistic activity, the following are worthy of note. First, and perhaps most importantly of all, the individual must learn to control the physical side-effects of incorporating an otherwise disincarnate spirit (e.g. shaking, expostulating and gesticulating). In addition to inducing and managing the possession event, the individual must also learn to identify and express appropriately the particular type of spirit by which he or she is being possessed. Given that different kinds of spirit execute different ritual tasks, a medium's ability to communicate the type of spirit incorporated is a vital part of her performative repertoire. As each of the various rituals of the Santo Daime calendar performs a very specific function, it is likewise important for those incorporating spirits to know in what contexts and at what juncture a particular type of possession is permitted. Although spirit possession of most kinds is actively encouraged in the rituals of *Mesa Branca* and *São Miguel*, only limited types of possession are qualifiedly permitted in some (e.g. Concentration and Dance), while other rituals tolerate no kind of possession at all (e.g. Mass).

As *daimista* rituals are tightly regimented events, a particular kind of incorporation must also occur at the correct point and for the proper duration. The incorporation of the wrong kind of spirit at an inappropriate moment both interrupts the spiritual current generated by the ritual in question and risks public censure (sometimes administered during the ritual itself) from those in authority. At the same time, the medium must also pay close attention to existing social hierarchies. For, in addition to influencing the number and cosmological status of the spirits one regularly incorporates, social standing may also determine the pecking order in which individuals get to incorporate. In the same vein, *daimista* ritual space is a highly differentiated arena with participants occupying a specific place relative to their sex, age, marital status and seniority (some communities also use height as an additional determinant). Consequently, the medium has a responsibility not only to incorporate the right kind of spirit at the right moment, but also to ensure that enactment of the possession event does not lead to assigned spatial boundaries being transgressed.

A Typology of Spirit Possession in Santo Daime

Given the practical-symbolic overlap, uneven appearance, equivocal expression and vertiginous evolution of the different forms of spirit posses-sion across the Santo Daime movement, any typology of possession prom-ises to be both a messy and provisional affair. Holding this point in mind, I offer a typology of voluntary incorporation which is informed by the nature and degree of interaction exhibited by the mode of possession in question and its relationship to the ritual context of enactment. The two types of voluntary incorporation to be examined are here labelled 'individual' and 'interactive'.

'Individual possession' is so termed because the person being possessed is the principal locus of spirit-orientated activity. There are two kinds of individual possession – 'private possession' and 'expressive possession'. 'Private possession' is the most traditional form of incorporation practised by the Santo Daime religion and tends to appear most frequently within the movement's older communities. Most commonly involving discrete interactions with less evolved (e.g. 'suffering', 'disorientated' and 'inferior') spirits, this form of incorporation accords with established *daimista* notions of 'trial' (*prova*) and 'firmness' (*firmeza*). In view of the exacting psychophysical effects of consuming *Daime*, in tandem with the numerous strictures regulating ritual participation, *daimistas* must remain firm (i.e. disciplined, resolute and focused) in the face of the trials provoked. In combination with the prevailing spirit idiom, these values engender a twofold rationale for private possession. First, the act of incorporating spirits is seen as an additional trial to that provoked by both the psychotropic effects of *Daime* and generic demands of ritual participation. Consequently, private possession likewise demands firmness which, in turn, entails restraint on the part of the possessed. A general rule regarding this form of possession (whence I take the term 'private') is that the act of incorporation should be conducted in such a way as not to distract others from remaining firm in the face of their own particular trials. Second, private possession comprises an act of charity in which the lower spirits incorporated are prayed with, instructed in the ways of *Daime* and exhorted to accept their allotted path. As with the merit earned by staying firm in the face of trial, the performance of charity towards the incorporated spirit is held to generate credit or 'karma' which is subsequently drawn upon in this life or a future incarnation. Although each of these elements tends to be present in most explanations of private possession, differences in emphasis exist within each community and across the movement as a whole.

'Expressive possession' is the most recent form of incorporation to establish itself in Santo Daime and is rapidly on the way to becoming the most popular. Although typologically distinct by virtue of its outward expression, in actuality expressive possession is a modified form of private possession. Perhaps because of its relative novelty within the Santo Daime tradition, expressive possession lacks a well-defined ritual function. Unlike both private and interactive forms, expressive possession involves only the incorporation of higher spirits appropriated from Umbanda.

Although not always the case, the higher spirits incorporated expressively tend to be the spirit guides of the possessed individual. Given their prevalence across the Santo Daime movement, this means that expressive possession usually involves the incorporation of *caboclo* and *preto velho* spirits; although the appearance of other kinds of spirits (e.g. children, cowboys and aristocrats) is on the rise.

Expressive possession is so designated because of its demonstrative and theatrical character. Similar in form to charismatic modes of worship (though less ostentatious than neo-Pentecostal forms), expressive possession appears to have no obvious ritual function other than the dramatic externalization of the incorporating spirit's presence. Clearly, the onset of the sounds and gestures associated with expressive possession serves to indicate the arrival of the spirits subsequent to having been called at the appropriate juncture by the relevant tranche of hymns. Once present, however, the spirits do little more than reassert their incorporated condition through their respective stereotypical noises and stylized gesticulations. Perhaps in view of its relative novelty, expressive possession lacks the kinds of ritual rationales offered in respect of private and interactive forms of incorporation. When asked to explain the purpose of expressive possession, the responses offered by *daimistas* most commonly include reference to: the spirit serving to protect against the unwarranted appearance of inferior spirits; the spirit's desire to enjoy the trappings of physical sensation (e.g. singing, dancing and *Daime*); the edifying benefits which the spirit's presence brings to its host; and the externalization of particular aspects of the higher self.

In contrast to individual possession, interactive possession is predicated upon ritualized interface with other human beings. Practised only by trained mediums, 'interactive possession' is thereby more restricted in scope than individualized forms of incorporation. By no means mutually exclusive, and in no order of priority, interactive possession has three principal modes of cultic expression. First, it exists as a form of charity enacted towards lesser spirits, the majority of whom are the suffering souls of deceased human beings. Here, the medium works upon lesser spirits whom she has incorporated or upon spirits possessed by others who may or may not be trained mediums. On occasion a skilled medium may relieve a less experienced colleague or untrained *daimista* by assuming responsibility for a troublesome spirit by transferring it to her body. The possessed medium then works with other mediums (possibly incorporating higher spirits for assistance) who help to instruct (*doutrinar*), enlighten (*iluminar*), reassure and guide the incorporated spirit to the end of easing its pains and aiding its passage. The administering of *Daime* to the troubled spirit is commonplace in work of this nature.

Interactive possession might also be practised as an act of charity towards one's fellow *daimistas*. Here, mediums possessed by higher spirits move among their peers to distribute astral energy by way of the 'pass' (*passe*) and other forms of gesture. A traditional practice of Kardecist Spiritism, the pass involves the incorporating medium passing her hands over the head, up and down the limbs and around the torso of another person. In so doing, the medium helps to reinforce or recalibrate the vibrational field of the pass's recipient. Third, interactive possession exists in oracular form. Restricted to the most senior mediums, this mode of interactive possession intends the edification of ritual participants through the impartation of wisdom, instruction or admonition. Although oracular possession tends to employ the traditional supernatural agents of Kardecist Spiritism, the spirits of deceased *daimista* celebrities, including Sebastião himself, are occasionally incorporated by members of Santo Daime's higher echelons. As with private possession, interactive possession (in all its forms) constitutes an act of charity said to earn cosmic merit ('karma') for its practitioners.

Taking Possession of Santo Daime

The spread of Umbanda within Santo Daime and the growing enactment of non-private forms of incorporation are directly related. Without doubt, the increasingly popular expressive possession and its interactive counterpart embody distinctly *umbandist* modes of discourse and practice. Both the growth in Umbanda-informed discourse and the increased incidence of *umbandist* forms of possession reflect a significant degree of what, in other contexts, scholars have termed the process of 'umbandization' (*umbandização*) (e.g. Furuya 1994, pp. 11–59). Although evidence of *umbandist* forms of spirit-orientated activity within Santo Daime dates back to the early 1980s (Polari 1999, pp. 109–17), it was not until the movement fully established itself in the traditional urban-industrial heartlands of Umbanda that the umbandization of its ritual repertoire commenced in earnest. It was at the beginning of this period of geographical transition that the term *umbandaime* was coined to describe the fusion of Umbanda and Santo Daime. Commencing in the late 1980s with the staging of para-liturgical rituals inspired by *umbandist* possession practices, the umbandization of the *daimista* repertoire was firmly secured by the late 1990s via the inclusion of the rituals of Saint Michael (*São Miguel*) and the White Table (*Mesa Branca*) within the formal cultic calendar of Santo Daime's mother community Céci do Mapiá. Today, the majority of *daimistas* regard both the spirits and practices appropriated from Umbanda as integral parts of the Santo Daime religion.

One would be mistaken, however, to regard the umbandization of Santo Daime as either the wholesale adoption of Umbanda discourse and practice or the simple overwriting of previously existing narratives and ritual activities. Two reasons for this can be noted here. First, and as with earlier developments which have occurred throughout the eighty-year history of Santo Daime, the continued presence of Afro-Amazonian, popular Catholic, esoteric, and Kardecist discourse and practice reflects a hybrid ritual repertoire whose practitioners are both aware of and very much at ease with its variegated nature. The appearance of 'eclectic' within the assumed name of Santo Daime Cefluris is, after all, a self-conscious affirmation of the movement's unabashed openness to the conspicuous appropriation of otherwise disparate beliefs and practices. A case in point, the co-existence of the various interpretations and ritual enactments of incorporation identified above is directly indebted to the thoroughgoingly hybrid character of the *daimista* repertoire. Although *umbandist* tropes enjoy a contemporary repertorial prominence, they are by no means the only themes in play.

Second, the umbandization of Santo Daime is a process inspired by rather than slavishly replicating Umbanda discourse and practice. The principal reason for this resides in the religious-cultural profile of the contemporary *daimista* community. More diverse than Brazil's other ayahuasca religions (i.e. Barquinha and Vegetable Union), the demographic profile of Santo Daime is nevertheless overwhelmingly white, urban middle class in nature; a far cry from the mixed-race, subsistence lifestyle of its Amazonian origins. Refashioning Santo Daime in its own image, this, now dominant, urban middle-class constituency is the principal driving force behind the umbandization of the *daimista* repertoire. Of vital importance, however, is the fact that this urban, middle-class constituency – in contrast to a poorer and predominantly mixed-race demographic – is not traditionally associated with the Umbanda religion (see Bastide 1960; Brown 1994; Camargo 1961). Rather, its historically recent association with Umbanda forms part of a rapidly evolving religious trajectory which traverses what I have elsewhere termed the 'new-era spectrum' (Dawson 2007). The new-era spectrum comprises a fluid nexus of relationships involving a highly diverse array of beliefs and practices which articulate a range of dynamics typical of late-modern, urban-industrial existence. By virtue of its late-modern ethos, the new-era spectrum embodies a typically individualized, pluralistic, consumerist and technologized world view (Bauman 2005; Beck 2002; García Canclini 1995, pp. 41–65). In effect, the appropriation of Umbanda discourse and practice by the contemporary *daimista* community is undertaken relative to a range of characteristics typical of the new-era spectrum as a whole.

In respect of the particular characteristics of the new-era spectrum through which these typically late-modern dynamics are mediated, the most relevant for our purposes are: a *holistic* world view in which a universal force underlies and unites every individual component of existence – such that particular beliefs and practices are but relative (and, thereby, inter-changeable) expressions of the cosmic whole; an *individualistic* emphasis upon the self as the ultimate arbiter of religious authority and the primary agent of spiritual transformation; an *instrumentalized* religiosity driven by the goal of absolute self-realization – to which end an eclectic range of spiritual knowledge and mystical techniques is employed; an *expressive* demeanour through which inner states of being are externalized by verbal and practical means tending towards the dramatic; a *meritocratic-egalitarianism* which is both inherently suspicious of religious hierarchy and expectant of just rewards for efforts expended; and, an *immanentist* spirituality which – alongside the avowal of transcendent transformations and rewards (e.g. reincarnation and cosmic merit) – valorizes the pragmatic implications of self-realization (e.g. psychological and material well-being).

Together, these factors combine to engender a religious world view in which the individual has the right, if not the duty, to pursue her absolute self-realization through any available means and at any possible opportunity. Such is the self-orientated nature of this pursuit that prevailing narratives and customary practices are evaluated relative to their perceived support for, or hindrance of, individual fulfilment. As a consequence, the traditional *daimista* repertoire and its established components are reviewed, revised and, at times, rejected with a view to their optimal facilitation of individual expression. Subjected to the unremitting assertion of the late-modern self, Santo Daime's traditional spirit possession repertoire is undergoing change in a variety of ways, the most important for us being the growing popularity of *umbandist* motifs. In combination, these typically new-era characteristics determine the manner in which *umbandist* discourse and practice is appropriated by the contemporary *daimista* community.

Orchestrated by aforementioned characteristics of the new-era spectrum, selected elements of *umbandist* discourse and practice are wrested from their traditional religious contexts and relocated to the *daimista* repertoire.

Excised from its original ritual domain and isolated from its customary frame of reference, selected *umbandist* discourse and practice are rendered wholly amenable to being remoulded, reintegrated and re-operationalized relative to the prevailing preoccupations of white, urban-professional *daimistas*. Whereas the practice of possession in Umbanda has traditionally revolved around the quest for cure (predominantly among the poor) or edification (chiefly among the not-so-poor), this is not the case in Santo Daime. Relocated to the *daimista* ritual repertoire, the therapeutic and instructive emphases of *umbandist* possession practices are subsumed within a broader set of concerns centred upon the self-assertive and expressive preoccupations of the late-modern individual. Although centred upon the ritualized incorporation of *umbandist* spirits, expressive possession is not a form of spirit-orientated activity traditionally found in Umbanda, just as interactive possession is of a very different ilk than its *umbandist* counterpart. Despite the ostensible centrality of Umbanda spirits, each is a thoroughgoingly *daimista* phenomenon which articulates typically new-era preoccupations centred upon the late-modern self. While much of the cast, dialogue and performance of spirit possession in Santo Daime appear distinctly *umbandist*, the orchestrating ritual direction and attendant dramatic thrust are pure urban-professional *daimista*.

The *umbandization* of the spirit possession repertoire of Santo Daime is wholly symptomatic of the demographic shift undergone by the movement over the course of the last two decades. This demographic shift has fundamentally altered the social–cultural context in which much of its ritual activity is undertaken. Refracting a very different set of social–cultural dynamics, the *daimista* ritual repertoire asserts its contemporary relevance by articulating the practical-symbolic demands of the now dominant urban-professional membership. Subjected to the unremitting assertion of the late-modern self, Santo Daime's possession repertoire assumes an increasingly expressive tenor. The established components of the traditional *daimista* repertoire, however, do not furnish sufficient practical-symbolic means to articulate these newly present expressive concerns. As a consequence, tried, trusted and readily available components of the Umbanda repertoire are appropriated for the task. The growth of Umbanda discourse and practice thereby responds to the inability of Santo Daime's traditional possession repertoire to mediate the typical new-era preoccupations of the now hegemonic urban middle classes. By way of conclusion, then, the umbandization of Santo Daime is perhaps best understood as a by-product of the movement's 'new-erization' (*nova-erização*).

Note

1 Fieldwork informing this chapter was made possible by grants from the British Academy and the Leverhulme Trust.

Bibliography

Arruda, C., Lapietra, F. and Santana, R. J. (2006), *Centro Livre: Ecletismo Cultural no Santo Daime*. São Paulo: All Print Editora.

Bastide, R. (1960), *As Religiões Africanas no Brasil: Contribuição a uma Sociologia das Interpenetrações de Civilizações*. São Paulo: Pioneira.

Bauman, Z. (2005), *Liquid Life*. Cambridge: Polity.

Beck, U. and Beck-Gernsheim, E. (2002), *Individualization: Institutionalized Individualism and its Social and Political Consequences*. London: Sage.

Brown, D. D. (1994), *Umbanda: Religion and Politics in Urban Brazil*. New York: Columbia University Press.

Camargo, C. P. F. de (1961), *Kardecismo e Umbanda: Uma Interpretação Sociológica*. São Paulo: Livraria Pioneira Editora.

Cavalcanti, M. L. V. de C. (1983), *O Mundo Invisível: Cosmologia, Sistema Ritual e Noção de Pessoa no Espiritismo*. Rio de Janeiro: Zahar Editores.

Couto, F. de La R. (2004), 'Santo daime: rito da ordem', in B. C. Labate and W. S. Araújo (eds), *O Uso Ritual da Ayahuasca* (2nd edn). Campinas: Mercado de Letras, pp. 385–411.

Crapanzano, V. (1977), 'Introduction', in V. Crapanzano and V. Garrison (eds), *Case Studies in Spirit Possession*. New York: Wiley, pp. 1–39.

Dawson, A. (2007), *New Era – New Religions: Religious Transformation in Contemporary Brazil*. Aldershot: Ashgate.

Faivre, A. (1986), 'Esotericism', in M. Eliade (ed.), *Encyclopedia of Religions*. New York: Macmillan, pp. 156–63.

Furuya, Y. (1994), 'Umbandização dos cultos populares na amazônia: a integração ao Brasil?', in H. Nakamaki and A. P. Filho (eds), *Possessão e Procissão: Religiosidade Popular no Brasil*. Osaka: National Museum of Ethnology, pp. 11–59.

Galvão, E. E. (1955), *Santos e Visagens: Um Estudo da Vida Religiosa de Itá, Amazonas*. São Paulo: Companhia Editôra Nacional.

García Canclini, N. (1995), *Hybrid Cultures: Strategies for Entering and Leaving Modernity*. Minneapolis: University of Minnesota Press.

Goulart, S. (2004), *Contrastes e Continuidades em uma Tradição Amazônica: As Religiões da Ayahuasca*. PhD Thesis. State University of Campinas.

Guimarães, M. B. L. (1992), *A 'Lua Branca' de Seu Tupinamba e de Mestre Irineu: Estudo de Caso de um Terreiro de Umbanda*. Masters Thesis. Instituto de Filosofia e Ciências Sociais da Universidade Federal do Rio de Janeiro.

Labate, B. C. and Pachecho, G. (2004), 'Matrizes maranhenses do santo daime', in B. C. Labate and W. S. Araújo (eds), *O Uso Ritual da Ayahuasca* (2nd edn). Campinas: Mercado de Letras, pp. 303–44.

Maués, R. H. and Villacorta, G. M. (2004), 'Pajelança e encantaria amazônica', in

R. Prandi (ed.), *Encantaria Brasileira: O Livro dos Mestres, Caboclos e Encantados*. Rio de Janeiro: Pallas, pp. 11–58.

Moura da Silva, E. (2006), 'Similaridades e diferenças entre estilos de espirituali-dade metafísica: O caso do círculo esotérico da comunhão do pensamento (1908–1943)', in A. C. Isaia (ed.), *Orixás e Espíritos: O Debate Interdisciplinar na Pesquisa Contemporânea*. Uberlândia: EDUFU, pp. 225–40.

Polari, A. de A. (1999), *Forest of Visions: Ayahuasca, Amazonian Spirituality and the Santo Daime Tradition*. Rochester: Park Street Press.

Prandi, R. (1991), *Os Candomblés de São Paulo: A Velha Magia na Metrópole Nova*. São Paulo: Editora Hucitec.

Chapter 9

Spirit Attacks in Northern Namibia: Interpreting a New Phenomenon in an African Lutheran Context

Kim Groop[1]

Between the years 2004 and 2007 four schools in the north of Namibia were allegedly attacked by supernatural powers. The attacks looked dramatic. Students were seen collapsing, crying, screaming or roaming around the school yard and neighbourhood. Some of the students – most of whom were females – had visions. Others feared that they would catch fire, experienced sheer panic or reacted with aggression towards all and everything. The incidents created a stir throughout Namibia and were vividly portrayed in the national newspapers and television news.

The first time a school was believed to be attacked by spirits en masse was in 1996, when Mweshipandeka Senior Secondary School in Ongwediva found itself in the limelight. Female students had hysteric outbursts, hallucinated, screamed and cried. The incidents lasted for only a short period, but touched a sensitive nerve in Namibia (*The Namibian*, 13 April 2007; Interview: Mweutota). Most of the Namibian ethnic traditions acknowledged or had, at least, vague notions of spirits and their involvement in human affairs, but what happened in the schools was beyond anything previously experienced. The Owambo, among whom all the incidents occurred, had relatively long and deeply rooted Lutheran traditions in which these incidents were not easily interpreted.

This chapter will focus on interpretations of spirit attacks[2] in schools in northern Namibia, with particular attention given to the context of the Lutheran church. The geographical area covered is commonly called Owamboland which consists of four regions: Omusati, Oshana, Ohangwena and Oshikoto. The key question is: How has the phenomenon of spirit attacks in Namibian schools been interpreted? Among those who witnessed the school drama three dominant theories were suggested for the origin of the attacks. Some believed that the students were attacked or possessed by evil spirits. Others were convinced that the students had been bewitched. A third group believed that the schools were haunted by restless ancestor spirits or *oilulu*.

Spirit possession has often been understood as a response to powerlessness, offering a possibility for individuals to vent social frustrations or to act out wishes that cannot be expressed directly. However, possession has also been seen as a means of negotiating modernity, sometimes involving elements of reaction against institutions and practices which threaten the traditional ways of living (Bourguignon 2004, pp. 557–9; Luig 1999, pp. xiii–xviii). What happened in the Namibian schools bears some resemblance to possession among Taita schoolgirls in Kenya, Maasai women in Tanzania or female factory workers in Free-Trade Zones on the east coast of the Malay Peninsula. These three examples show, in one way or another, girls and women struggling to cope with modernity and change while hoping for a brighter future (Keller 2002, pp. 105–11; Smith 2001, pp. 427–30, 442–54; Hodgson 2005, pp. 210–29; Groop 2006, pp. 297–304).

Political Events

The most visible transformation in Namibia in the twentieth century was one that took place in the political arena. When, in 1966, South Africa refused a United Nations order to withdraw from Namibia, the South West Africa People's Organization (SWAPO) began its armed struggle against South African rule. Most of the fighting took place in Owamboland, in the densely populated north, and many people fled to other countries in Africa and beyond. However, at the same time as the struggle brought division and misery to the families in the north, it had a unifying effect on the Owambo people. They all dreamed of better days ahead in an independent Namibia (Eriksen 1982, pp. 33–4, 166–82) and Namibia's independence in 1990 was greeted with seemingly limitless joy. However, along with independence a political vacuum appeared.

Post-independence Namibia offered new possibilities – to both men and women – such as a diversification of work opportunities, improved access to education, improved means of communication and so forth. Yet, despite many new opportunities, it soon became clear that success could not be granted to everyone. While some were supported by wealthier relatives, others lacked this luxury and, also, had to care for loved ones who were sick and poor. Political change in Namibia was followed by economic change and globalization. The increasing movement of people within Namibia, as well as to and from Namibia, brought a new level of awareness of (and a hunger for) the surrounding world. Television – and after the turn of the millennium the increased use of mobile phones and even the Internet – connected the people with the outside world as never before. For the young Owambo, awareness of the world around them increased and so did their awareness of growing inequalities.

At the beginning of the twenty-first century – at least when viewed through statistics – Owamboland looked like a sinking ship rather than the Promised Land for a people who had fought and won the fight against political oppression and who were aiming for a brighter future. HIV/AIDS hit hard in the densely populated north, with one woman in four testing positive for the virus (Namibia: NPC 2007a). Largely as a result of HIV/AIDS, life expectancy rates started plummeting towards the end of the 1990s. In the Omusati Region, for instance, life expectancy in 1991 was 67 for women and 63 for men. Ten years later it was expected that the average woman would only live until 51, and average man would die at the age of 47. In the Oshikoto Region, life expectancy was only around 40 years of age. With nearly 20,000 AIDS orphans in the four Owambo regions, the epidemic left few unaffected. Being orphaned became one of the key fears occupying the minds of the young (Namibia: NPC 2003 and 2007b; Interviews: Shikulo and Ondukuta Combined School students). At the same time as this reduction in life expectancy in the four Owambo regions, quite the opposite occurred with regards to violence. In 2004 the WHO Global School-Based Student Health Survey revealed grim statistics regarding violence among children and violence aimed at children. No less than 64 per cent of boys and 55 per cent of girls had been in a physical fight during the 12 months previous to the survey. The corresponding figures in southern Namibia were 56 and 29 per cent respectively. Moreover, 77 per cent of boys and 71 per cent of girls had been seriously injured at least once during the previous 12 months. The equivalent figures for southern Namibia were, again, considerably lower at 52 per cent and 34 per cent (WHO 2004). The Namibian school system was also suffering. After independence the schools were made open and equal to all (Angula 2001, pp. 8–15), but it soon became apparent that free education alone could not promote equality. While education increasingly became the key determiner of a person's future, schools in the rural areas lagged behind. Secondary schools remained few and far apart, school classes were large and the government struggled to find competent teachers (Namibia: NPC 2007a, p. 41). The harsh realities affecting the young in Owamboland, in combination with problems in the education sector, gradually became more apparent after independence, and most prominent and visible in the growing number of students who failed grade 10 examinations and were thus denied further education. In 2007 more students failed than passed grade 10 (Namibia: NPC 2007a, p. 41; *The Namibian*, 21 November 2007).

As their world became more insecure the young had an increasing need for comfort from the older generations – comfort which the older generations often failed to provide. In an increasingly international, complex and challenging world of which they knew so little, many parents had little to offer in terms of support. They felt lost in the processes of globalization, unemployment and disease, and many failed to equip their children for these challenges.[3]

The Owambo People and their Traditional World-View

It is believed that the Owambo people moved in from eastern Africa and arrived in their present location in northern Namibia and southern Angola between the sixteenth and seventeenth centuries (Tuupainen 1970, p. 12). Although the Owambo are mostly thought to consist of seven ethnic societies with closely related languages or dialects, a number of other ethnic groups are sometimes counted as belonging to the Owambo (Salokoski 2006, p. 64). The Owambo economy has, as long as they can remember, been based on farming and cattle herding. The staple food has been mahangu (or pearl millet); other crops such as sorghum, maize, durra, nuts and melon have been considered rather as substitutes. But the region of northern Namibia and southern Angola is notorious for infrequent rainfall. The Owambo economy has thus been fragile with extensive drought or too heavy rainfall often spoiling the harvests. Owambo wealth, however, has lain in their cattle. The more cattle a family possessed the wealthier it has been considered. When harvests have failed, Owambo families have depended on their cattle for survival. The Owambo have also supplemented their food reserves by other means, such as hunting, gathering and fishing (Siiskonen 1990, pp. 50–60). During the twentieth century a third source of income arrived on the Owambo scene: migrant labour. During colonial and later apartheid rule men were forced into work in distant regions. Although this detested form of employment was at the very heart of the Owambo resistance against foreign rule, it was a considerable source of employment (Kjellberg 1972, pp. 12–15). After Namibia's independence in 1990 many Owambo have continued to receive their income from work in larger towns such as Windhoek and Oshakati.

Cosmology

According to Albin Savola (one of the early Finnish missionaries in Owamboland), the traditional Owambo spirit world essentially consisted of four elements: (i) High God (Kalunga), (ii) ancestor spirits (*omuthithi*, pl. *aathithi*), (iii) witches (*omulodhi*, pl. *aalodhi*) and (iv) diviners (*onganga*, pl. *oonganga*) (Savola 1924, pp. 165–88). The Owambo conception of Kalunga was quite vague. He was the creator of the universe, and continued to create and uphold the world, but he was also considered clearly separated from the human world. Therefore, the Owambo seldom sacrificed or prayed to Kalunga (Savola 1924, pp. 167–8). The *aathithi* or ancestor spirits played a considerably more prominent role in the life of the Owambo. When a person died it was believed that the spirit lived on in a different realm. But, as the world of the *aathithi* was believed to border the world of the living, it was extremely important for the Owambo not to forget the ancestors but to nurture good relations with their spirits. Sacrifices of various kinds were therefore an inevitable part of life. If the *aathithi* were made angry they could, and would, bring misfortune to their living relatives (Aarni 1982, pp. 60–4). However, at least equally influential among the old Owambo were the *aalodhi* and *oonganga* – the witches and diviners. These were in many aspects each others' opposites. Yet, in one essential way, they had similarities: they both knew how to orientate in the unseen world. Whereas the *omulodhi* used her or his power to harm or 'eat' a victim – mostly in the protection of darkness (and this is believed to be one of the reasons why so few seemed to know who the witches were) – the *onganga* had the powers to reveal witches in order that they could be eradicated. Since it was believed that sickness and death were caused by witchcraft, the *onganga*, who had also healing powers, was held in particularly high esteem (see for instance Hiltunen 1986 or Aarni 1982). The *onganga* was typically a man, and although it appears that it was more common that women were exposed as witches than men, witchcraft was not, in practice, gender restricted.

However, as Märta Salokoski points out, Owambo cosmology was somewhat more complicated than the four personified elements already mentioned. In reality, it comprised a number of floating notions about powers and spirits. For instance, the Owambo of the early twentieth century drew no clear line between spirits associated with human beings and nature spirits (Salokoski 2006, pp. 133, 147–50). The commonly used word *ombepo* (meaning breath or wind) refers to something that the Owambo believed was a part of the human being – the soul or spirit. Savola noted that *ombepo* was 'the element in the human being which might move even outside the body' (1924, pp. 70–1, my translation). For instance, people's thoughts and imagination were considered to be *ombepo*. Finally, Veikko Munyika (2004) mentions three classes of spirits which were believed to play a role in human affairs, namely the *ounhikifa, oipumbu* and the *oilulu* (all of which are in the plural). All three were believed to be malicious spirits of deceased humans (Munyika 2004, pp. 174–8).[4] Of the three, however, it is mainly the notion of the *oilulu* (sing. *oshilulu*) which has survived the influence of Christianity.

Lutheranism and the change of Owambo conceptions

When the missionaries of the Finnish Missionary Society began sowing the seeds of Christianity among the Owambo people in 1870, they broke new ground and, with a few exceptions, they had a monopoly on the missionary work in Owamboland for the following century. The Finnish missionaries, emphasizing creed rather than speed, put considerable effort into creating a church with a strong Lutheran theology. Rather than opting for a rapid increase in numbers they taught their baptismal candidates meticulously and they were careful not to baptize catechumens whom they did not consider sincere or 'ripe'. The initial growth of the Finnish Mission Church was slow. After forty years of hard work by the Lutheran missionaries, the Christians in Owamboland hardly totalled more than two thousand. With regard to theological foundations, however, the Lutherans were more successful. When the work finally revived – and indeed the Lutherans grew twentyfold between the two world wars – the church managed to preserve its Lutheran identity. This was also, in part, due to an emphasis on the education of a future indigenous leadership. The first seven Owambo pastors were ordained in 1925, after three years of theological studies, and in 1957 the Evangelical Lutheran Ovambo-Kavango Church was registered with the South African government with its own constitution (Peltola 1958, pp. 163, 210–13, 239–42; Buys and Nambala 2003, pp. 117, 163, 169). At the end of the twentieth century more than 50 per cent of the Owambo population, roughly estimated to be 800,000, were Lutheran church members (Helminen 1991, p. 49).

The Lutheran Christianity which was brought to the Owambo was a modest one, and coloured with pietistic ideals (Löytty 1971, pp. 20–31). Regarding the local culture, the Finnish missionaries (like many of their fellow-missionaries) were interested but rather suspicious. In order to make 'good Christians' they saw it necessary to be thorough and thus condemned most 'heathen' customs which, in their view, clashed with Christianity. They were careful when preaching and translating lest their message would be (intentionally or unintentionally) misinterpreted. The same applied to the Finnish missionaries' attitudes regarding the Namibian conceptions of spirits and witches. Kari Miettinen notes that both bad and good magic (*aatikili* and *oonganga*) 'were considered to be essential carriers of heathen culture, and therefore any Christian who resorted to their [the witches', sorcerers' and diviners'] services was committing a serious offence against the Christian faith and was punished accordingly' (2005, pp. 118–24).[5]

From an Owambo perspective, the Lutheran faith not only disapproved but was also quite ignorant of the spiritual world. As far as demonology was concerned – at least according to many Owambo – becoming a Lutheran Christian was, therefore, a poor exchange. Like most contemporary Lutherans, the Finnish missionaries recognized the existence of evil personified by the devil and the demons. Yet, when these were talked about – which by African standards was quite rarely – they were done so rather theoretically. Satan, in missionary demonology, worked with the tools of temptation and deceit rather than by attacking the body. With this approach in mind it can be understood how difficult it would be for the Finnish missionaries to demonstrate spiritual evil. In contradiction to the Owambo, who preferred counter-action against evil – by consulting the *onganga*, through wearing amulets, sacrificing to the spirits, punishing, killing or chasing off witches and so on – the Lutheran missionaries emphasized prayer and restraint (Hiltunen 1993). A Christian could not escape the devil altogether, but he or she could minimize temptation by living a humble and disciplined Christian life.

Like many other Protestant missionary societies the Finnish Lutheran missionaries focused on translating the Bible. The first New Testament in the Ndonga language (or Oshindonga), largely translated by Martti Rautanen, was published in 1903. But although Rautanen had finished his translation of the Old Testament by 1923, the whole Bible was not printed before 1954 (Peltola 1958, pp. 190, 187, 241). Miettinen believes that 'concern for furnishing advocates of syncretism with arguments may have been one reason why the Oshindonga translation of the Old Testament was not published until 1954' (2005, p. 131).

Undeniably some of the words in the Bible were not easily translated into the Owambo languages, or vice versa from Owambo culture to a biblical language. Savola called it a great leap when the early Finnish missionaries (contrary to the German Lutherans working among the Herero) decided to translate God into Kalunga in their preaching (Savola 1924, p. 167). Another Owambo word which made it into the Bible was *oshilulu* (pl. *oilulu*). In Matthew 14:26 and Mark 6:49, the disciples screamed when they saw Jesus walking towards them on the surface of the water, believing him to be an '*osīlulu*' (British and Foreign Bible Society 1936). The word in the Greek New Testament is φάντασμα (fantasma), meaning phantasm, ghost or phantom. In Luke 24:39 in the Ndonga New Testament, however, Jesus, when returning to his disciples, tells them not to be afraid, he is not an '*ombepo*' (British and Foreign Bible Society 1936). The translated Greek word is πνεῦμα (pneuma), meaning spirit or breath. Controversially, in the Kwanyama translation of the New Testament, which was published as late as 1974, Jesus is believed by his disciples to be an *oshilulu*, both when walking on the lake and when appearing among them after his resurrection (Bible Society of South Africa 1974, Matthew 14:26, Mark 6:49 and Luke 24:39). In addition, in the New International Version of the New Testament Jesus appears as a 'ghost' in all three gospels. Although most people in the westernized world would probably understand the 'ghost' in all three texts in a similar way, the Owambo knew the *oilulu* and *oombepo* as dissimilar spirits. In traditional Owambo thinking *ombepo* was considered to be something quite neutral: wind or breath (including the breath which 'abandoned' the body when a person died [Salokoski 2006, pp. 144, 168]). When Christianity entered Owamboland the comprehension of *ombepo* was expanded to include also evil spirits (sing. *ombepo ja ńata*, pl. *oombepo za ńata*) and even the Holy Spirit (*Ombepo Ondjapuki*).

The *oshilulu*, by contrast, was not redefined, but continued to be strictly associated with Owambo conceptions of the ancestors and ancestor spirits. By importing the word *oshilulu* into the New Testament the Lutheran missionaries demonstrated to the Owambo Christians that Jesus and his disciples acknowledged the existence of wicked Owambo spirits (who had been denied entrance to the world of the ancestors). Despite their determination not to do so, the missionaries gave rise to a form of syncretism. This is probably also one of the main reasons why the word *oshilulu* has remained in use among the Owambo until today. With time, however, the 'original' conceptions of the *oilulu* changed. Although many Owambo, if not most, in the early years of the twenty-first century acknowledged the existence of *oilulu* in one way or another, it seems that they did not have a clear picture as to who these ghosts were. With time the understanding of the *oilulu* became blurry – especially since so few could testify that they had seen one. Mostly, however, the *oilulu* were thought of as ghosts or spirits of wicked people. These ghosts could be seen at night, especially near cemeteries. The *oilulu* were believed to be able to cause great discomfort to people, but they were seldom spoken of as killing people. *Oilulu* were considered malicious, but not as malicious as witches (Questionnaire, October 2008; Interview: Amadhila).

Witchcraft or *uulodhi* came to pose a somewhat different challenge to Lutheran Christianity in Owamboland. Early missionaries believed that the Owambo fear of witchcraft as well as witch-hunting would disappear with time as it was considered a relatively recent element in Owamboland (Hiltunen 1986, p. 31). Therefore, it was not considered a major problem that relatively little was written in the Bible about *uulodhi*. When the missionaries translated the Bible they could not – and probably saw no reason to – differentiate between good and bad magic. Where the Apostle Paul condemns 'witchcraft' in Galatians 5:20 (in the English New International Version), the word witchcraft is a translation of the word φαρμακεία (farmakeia, meaning medication, but by extension also magic, sorcery and witchcraft) in the Greek New Testament. When translating the word into the Ndonga language, Martti Rautanen – between the words *uulodhi* (bad magic) and *uunganga* (good magic) – opted for the latter (British and Foreign Bible Society 1936, Galatians 5:20). In the more recent translation, in the Kwanyama language φαρμακεία was similarly translated into *oundundu*, which is the Kwanyama equivalent to *uunganga* (Bible Society of South Africa 1974, Galatians 5:20). In Owambo tradition, *uunganga* performed by the *onganga* was (contrary to *uulodhi*) considered not only valuable but also necessary in the fight against witchcraft. In the Owambo translations of the New Testament good and bad magic were judged alike. Yet, contrary to what the missionaries had believed during the first decade of the twentieth century, the fear of witches was deeply rooted among the Owambo. The Christian church therefore managed to push belief in witchcraft to the periphery, but it did not manage to do away with it completely.

As the Finnish Mission Church gradually turned into a Namibian Lutheran Church, with an indigenous leadership, the Namibian pastors kept the legacy of the Finnish missionaries largely intact.[6] If the Finnish mission had feared that the Owambo would read the Bible in the 'wrong way' these fears did not materialize when the whole Bible finally emerged in the Ndonga language in 1954. To some extent, of course, the borderline between the African-Traditional and Western-Lutheran was reinterpreted. Where, for instance, the missionaries had been vague regarding the existence of spirits, witchcraft and ghosts, the Namibian pastors tended to read the Bible more literally. They were assured, on biblical grounds, that *oombepo*, *aalodhi* and *oilulu* existed, but they did not have much Lutheran experience in relating to or fighting them. Thus, generally speaking, the

Lutheran church in northern Namibia remained a church with a rather weak demonology.

Spirits, but of What Kind? – Interpreting Spirit Attacks in Owambo Christianity

When students in schools in Owamboland appeared to be subject to attacks by supernatural powers, the teachers did not know how to interpret the situation. They called in help from a number of people and organizations – from church and from society – and others who had not been invited arrived of their own accord (Interview: Nangombe). The active public involvement led to interaction between representatives of medical institutions, churches, traditional medicine and Owambo culture. Some of this interaction was open-minded, co-operative and ecumenical, whereas, in other cases, it was tinted by competition or simply resulted in reinforcement of already existing divides. As we will see, the school attacks were interpreted in various spiritual ways, with very few people understanding it in purely logical or medical terms.

In academic circles spirit possession is often seen as something of a vent or reaction against frustrations, stress or fears, rather than something purely spiritual. It seems reasonable, one could argue, that people in great distress at times (voluntarily or involuntarily) become detached from reality in various ways. When help was desperately needed in schools in northern Namibia, however, psychology was given little consideration by those involved. Between the medical and the spiritual explanations most Owambo opted for the latter. People in the north were in general reluctant to acknowledge medical theories such as conversion disorder or hysteria. Although it was seldom denied that the students suffered from stress – and in fact the symptoms often escalated before examinations – many people in northern Namibia found the psychological reasoning too simple, too vague or generally odd. Even if some people were ready to admit that the fits were connected with stress or panic, others found such a diagnosis shallow. In Owambo thinking it was logical to probe deeper in order to find out what or who caused the possession – or hysteria – in the first place (Interviews: Iitula and Nelumbu). Given the many biblical references to spirits and witchcraft, and the virtual lack of medical references, it was difficult for the Owambo Christians not to interpret the incidents in the schools in spiritual terms. A sole psychological interpretation would not only have sounded illogical but would have questioned biblical authority, which in turn would have made the interpretation sound even more absurd. Therefore, the moment an affected student was taken to a clinic or hospital and was declared physically normal, was the moment when people turned their backs on medical explanations and opted for spiritual solutions (Interview: Shilongo; *The Namibian*, 18 March 1998, 18 November 2005).

Although the spirit attacks in the Owambo schools did not lead to any particular interest in human behaviour under stress, it brought the relationship between the Christian and the traditional to the forefront. If the Finnish missionaries in doctrinal matters had co-operated well with western medicine, but fenced off Owambo beliefs as superstition or evil, the Owambo Christians (in quite a reverse manner) did not, theologically, feel at home with western medicine but continued to thrive in the world of Owambo traditions. Although Christians in the north, in general, considered belief in witchcraft and ancestor spirits rather shameful, many strongly believed that they existed and feared them (Interviews: Amungulu and Moses). During the school mayhem of 2005 to 2007, people were desperate for answers and looked for them both in the Bible and in Owambo folklore.

What happened in the schools fitted equally well or badly within traditional Owambo and Lutheran concepts. Both acknowledged spiritual warfare and the school attacks were interpreted according to both traditions. During the attacks in some schools many children were deliriously fighting a dark creature, carrying a garden fork or a rope, who they believed was trying to strangle them. Some students screamed at the beast to leave them alone, whereas others set off running around the school surroundings in a desperate attempt to escape violence or death. Many students collapsed (*New Era*, 17 and 22 November 2005; *The Namibian*, 18 November 2005). The beast was generally interpreted as Satan or a demon. In some other cases, however, students were believed to be attacked by an *oshilulu*. At Mumbwenge, close to Oshigambo, many believed that the old Kavango chief Mbwenge had returned in the shape of an *oshilulu* to haunt the school (*New Era*, 22 November 2005, 13 January 2006; Interview: Nampala). Mbwenge, it was believed, had left Okavango in the late-seventeenth or early-eighteenth century to settle at Oshigambo. With time his influence grew in the area, and the local chiefs became jealous and had him killed (Salokoski 2006, pp. 81–3).

At the Ondukuta Combined School children also collapsed and some woke up in hospital. Unlike the events in Mumbwenge, however, few students were harassed by the beast in black. The character in the hallucinations at Ondukuta was a woman and she was typically holding a snake. This woman was reported to call to the students, sometimes to come and swim in the *oshanas* (pools of water) and sometimes to receive gifts or fruits. The woman was cunning, trying to lure the children towards her, and when they did not take the bait she would hit them. The students' encounter with the woman was widely connected with panic and a fear of dying (Interviews: Shikulo and Ondukuta Combined School students). These testimonies convinced a large proportion of the parents that the school had been bewitched, and naturally the theory was strengthened when Christian prayer did not seem to provide a clear-cut solution. Parents, and some teachers, turned to the diviners, the *oonganga*, for help and, as expected, they pronounced that witchcraft was the reason for the school madness. Both at Mumbwenge and Ondukuta, people were singled out as witches (*New Era*, 17 November 2005, 13 January 2006; *The Namibian*, 23 January 2006; Interview: Iitula). At Etunda Combined School, near Ruacana, witchcraft was also suspected and rumours were further fuelled by the mysterious death of a number of teachers and school children (*New Era*, 5 August 2004). Some of the witch accusations were eagerly supported by parents and other adults who had little or no evidence to sustain their claims, but who had something against those accused or (in some cases) saw prospects of personal gain. It is apparent that witchcraft accusations in northern Namibia continued to be a tool for regulating social relations and frustrations. During the turmoil at Ondukuta Combined School even Queen Lisa Taapopi (the wife of King Gideon Shikongo Taapopi) was accused of witchcraft. At the time she was a teacher in the troubled school and one of the contenders for the vacant position as headmaster (Interviews: Iitula and Shihungeleni).

As far as the Ministry of Education was concerned, the diviners and other traditional practitioners were required to keep a safe distance from the Namibian schools. But at least in one case, when the Director of Education was slow to respond to the needs in a 'haunted' school, the headmaster invited not only representatives of Christian churches but also local healers. When the Director finally visited the school he suspended the principal and urged the community to 'desist from bringing unscientific and controversial practices like witchcraft into schools' (*The Namibian*, 23 January 2006). One parent called upon the Government to go to the school together with the media and 'get the "oshiluli" (Ghost) out of his hiding place and take pictures of it. [. . .] We want to see where this thing is hiding and attacking our children. We want government to assist us' (*The Namibian*, 17 November 2005). However, shortly after, when King Immanuel Elifas of Ndonga sent a delegation to inspect the school it opted not to (or had been instructed not to) use traditional medicine. Hopes had been high and some of the people were disappointed, stating that they knew that there were 'strong people in traditional matters, sciences in the Ndonga traditional community' and that they 'thought the King would send those people to Ombalayamumbwenge village to fight these demons' (*The Namibian*, 2 March 2006).

The school epidemic demonstrated that the Lutheran church had not come even close to eradicating Owambo belief in witchcraft and ancestor spirits. On the contrary, there was considerable intermingling between Christian and traditional customs and ideas. It was not unexpected by the leadership of the Evangelical Lutheran Church in Namibia (ELCIN) that many of its members – though they were baptized Christians – identified themselves more with old Owambo than Lutheran Christian belief (Interviews: T. Shivute and Henok). The Lutheran pastors had, by and large, preserved the rather dualistic and pragmatic Lutheran legacy, and old customs were therefore either seen as nonsense or devilish. While most pastors – at least officially – denied the existence of *aalodhi* and *oilulu*, some incorporated them into their Christian world-view as servants of the devil, which could easily be achieved with the help of the Bible. Some pastors maintained that what happened in the schools was the result of witchcraft, suggesting that teaching of the Bible should be reintroduced in the schools. Others not only acknowledged witchcraft but were afraid of it and wanted to move away from the alleged witches (*New Era*, 17 November 2005; Interviews: Shikongo, Shilongo and Amungulu).

Whether it was witchcraft, demons, or in some cases even *oilulu*, which caused the chaos in the schools, most Owambo Christians would (and could), without too much difficulty, interpret it within a satanic realm. Given that all three candidates could be traced in the Bible there was not too much of a conflict between Christianity and Owambo traditional understanding. The most unfortunate consequence seemed to be the conflict and the souring of relationships within Christianity itself in Namibia: between the Lutheran church and the more recent organizations, namely the predominantly Charismatic churches. While most Lutheran pastors probably felt more at home with soul care than with exorcism, some church members found the hands-on approach of the Charismatic churches more promising. The Charismatic churches had been growing during and after the 1990s and many of these were more than willing to offer their services to the tormented students (Interview: Shikongo). Many Christians were simultaneously Lutherans and active members of Charismatic churches. However, most of them were too ashamed to discuss the issue, and thus (in secret) kept dual membership in both the Lutheran and Charismatic parish. Although many of the Charismatic churches did not satisfy the needs of their 'Lutheran' members in the long run – and many apostates did return to the Lutheran church after some time – the competing churches were still numerous, ambitious and posed a real threat to Lutheran hegemony (Interview: Amutenya).

The Lutheran church, however, enjoyed the full support of the Namibian government. Most of the parliamentarians and ministers came from the rural north and were, as Lutherans, suspicious of the competing churches. One Director of Education who visited a problem school urged the community not to let some of the new churches have any dealings with the affected children, as he saw that they merely wanted 'to advertise themselves' (*The Namibian*, 23 January 2006). The Lutheran pastors had, until recently, enjoyed a virtual monopoly on Christianity in Owamboland, and at the same time as they played a decisive role in the spirit drama – and enjoyed the sense of unity and significance which it brought about – they guarded the schools anxiously. Under their personal supervision, representatives of a number of non-Lutheran churches were allowed to pray for the students (and indeed most pastors were happy to receive help from any Protestant colleague during the turmoil), but church ecumenism was persistently overshadowed by an element of (or fear of) competition (*New Era*, 5 August 2004, 17 November 2005; *The Namibian*, 18 November 2005; Interviews: G. Shivute and Nakale). Therefore, many Lutheran pastors were probably both disappointed and relieved when they saw that the Charismatic pastors were unable to drive out the demons.

Conclusions

Eventually, the situation in the schools calmed down. Views on why the situation had settled differed, however. Some Christians maintained that the students had been helped by the many prayers and the ceaseless participation of the local pastors. Some teachers and relatives, on the other hand, emphasized the importance of government intervention. Although they were sceptical about the theories that the students had suffered from hysteria, they observed that the attacks had decreased or stopped altogether after the Director of Education had paid a visit to their school and talked to the students. To most people, however, the attacks and why they ceased remained a mystery. (Interviews: Tanyanda, Shikulo, Mweutota and Nampala; *New Era*, 5 August 2004; *The Namibian*, 2 March 2006, 19 June

2006.) I claim that it is difficult to grasp the problems in the schools in Namibia without taking into account the major political, economical and sociological changes which took place in the twentieth century. Life in the north at the turn of the millennium had changed in so many aspects – not least since independence in 1990 – that some human reaction was unsurprising. Whereas migrant labour had been seen as either temporary or enforced before independence (and as something which predominantly concerned males), after independence migration and commuting became the norm for both men and women. People became aware of the world around them and there were ample opportunities for those who were lucky, or sponsored. Owamboland had turned into a smorgasbord of possibilities. But the critical issue was that the smorgasbord was available to some and denied to others. Many young people who were dreaming of a good life did not see their dreams materialize. Some were tested positive for HIV/AIDS or had to care for loved ones who were diseased. Others had lost one or both parents to the disease. Some were merely deprived of a good education because their school did not have qualified teachers. At the turn of the millennium many young people in northern Namibia were suffering from stress, frustration and anxiety and the schools held the centre stage, either as springboards or as stumbling blocks.

However, few people in northern Namibia would agree that the students in Namibian schools collapsed and hallucinated as a consequence of stress. What was happening was rather interpreted spiritually: through the Bible, through Owambo folklore or through a combination of the two. Finnish missionaries had strongly emphasized the need for Lutheran Christians to dissociate themselves from Owambo traditional thinking and many local customs had been thwarted. Against this background it might seem contra-dictory that the two Owambo Bible translations should include elements from the local spiritual world (which would, to some extent, have the opposite affect). Whereas some of the spirits that the Owambo had acknow-ledged before they converted to Christianity seem to have disappeared, others survived into the twenty-first century. Most of those who claimed that spirits were attacking the schools and their students interpreted the attackers as *oombepo ja ñata* (evil spirits). The *oombepo* were not only found in Owambo folklore, but had been incorporated in the Bible as a synonym for the *oompuizuli* (demons). Another Owambo spirit which made it into the Bible was the *oshilulu*. This restless ghost was generally not taken as seriously as the *ombepo za ñata*. When spoken about, it was often done so in a rather good-humoured way (similarly to how westerners talk about ghosts). The *oilulu* were generally not believed to kill. Therefore, when it was suspected that an *oshilulu* was haunting a school, people were concerned about the health of the students, and their examinations, but they did not expect anyone's life to be in jeopardy.

In terms of witchcraft the early Lutheran missionaries had not expected much conflict. At the time when Christianity came to northern Namibia the Owambo (at least in the Ndonga kingdom) were considered as having a very weak notion of witches and the belief in witches was expected to die out soon. More than a decade later, however, when students in the north saw frightful visions of women or beasts it was commonly believed that the students were subject to attacks by witches. Moreover the belief in (or fear of) witchcraft was not exclusive to church members, but included also pastors. It is possible that the early missionaries had misinterpreted the situation and that belief in witchcraft had been more deeply rooted among the Owambo than assumed. It is also likely, however, that this belief had spread from other regions with a stronger belief in witchcraft. When witchcraft and sorcery occurs in the Bible it largely does so in a rather disapproving way. When the Bible was translated to the Ndonga and later Kwanyama languages, however, some negative notions regarding witchcraft were translated into *uunganga* which was seen by the Owambo as good or even inevitable magic. This translation reflected the opinion of the missionaries regarding local medicine, but above all it placed traditional healers in an unfavourable position and on a par with the witches whom they were actually trying to fight.

Interpreting what was happening in the schools in Namibia seemed far from simple and many people were unconvinced by the opinions of those who were supposed to be experts. The medical institutions mostly found nothing wrong with the affected students, local medicine was considered outdated, destructive or sinful and when pastors from the local congregations conducted prayers in a school it was not long before the students suffered from new attacks. Perhaps the Namibian cases, rather than bringing forth new interpretations of spirit possession, brought forth interpretations of a new phenomenon. What was happening in some schools in Owamboland made people desperate for *any* interpretation regarding a phenomenon which had never before been heard of. In fact, most people – even those who suffered from attacks – did not even have a clear idea regarding whether they were attacked or possessed by spirits. Here it seems that Owambo traditional belief and Christian comprehensions intertwine. Evil spirits in the Bible usually possessed their victims, but witches and spirits in Owambo tradition were not usually believed to dwell in the person whom they wished to harm or harass.

It is difficult to assess to what extent people in northern Namibia interpreted the attacks through Owambo tradition or through Christianity. If people already felt ashamed to admit that they attended Charismatic church services, parallel with the Lutheran, it would be even more embarrassing to admit that they had consulted local healers. But two things appear to be clear: Owambo people were reading the Bible with great respect and there was a tendency towards fusion between Owambo folklore and Christianity – or perhaps, rather, people interpreted Owambo spirituality through the Bible. The attackers could be spirits (in a classical Owambo sense), witches, or a combination of the two, but they were predominantly seen as satanic. Over the years parts of Owambo and Christian thought had been amalgamated – in a sense Owambo institutions had been Christianized. This included the spirits (the *oombepo* and the *oilulu*), the witches (the *aalodhi*), and to some extent also the diviners (the *oonganga*). They had all been incorporated into the Christian thought process; it was predominantly in their (semi)Christian 'suit' that they (re)appeared and were interpreted as attacking students in northern Namibia.

Notes

[1] This research is part of the project 'African Christian Identity: Construction of African Christian Identity as a Dialogue between the Local and the Global' funded by the University of Helsinki and the Academy of Finland. I thank Dr Doc. Mika Vähäkangas, Dr Päivi Hasu, Mrs Mari Pöntinen and Ms Elina Hankela for their generous comments on earlier versions of this chapter. My curiosity in this topic started in 2003–6 when my wife and I lived in Windhoek and occasionally read in the newspapers about spirits attacking schools in the north. The actual research for this chapter was done in February–March and November 2008. During two research trips I made interviews with twenty-four individuals who had in one way or another been involved in the school attacks or who possessed particular knowledge regarding the themes covered in this chapter. A comprehensive group interview was done with six of the worst affected children in the Ondukuta Combined School on 10 March 2008. Finally a questionnaire (in Oshiwambo) was distributed in and around Outapi, Nakayale and Ondukuta in October and November 2008. The informants were asked to provide information regarding *oilulu, aalodhi* and the school attacks. Out of 150 distributed questionnaires 116 were returned. I thank Rev. Kleopas Nakale for being my right hand in Owamboland and Aini Niinkoti for helping me with translations.
[2] Instead of the commonly used term 'spirit possession' I will, in this study, utilize the expression 'spirit attacks'. Both expressions are valid and could correctly be used, but I feel that the latter is more appropriate in the Namibian cases where many felt that they were attacked but claims of actual possession were scarce.

³ In fact clinical psychologists in Namibia questioned Namibian parenting, claiming that parents tended to give too little freedom of choice to their children, and took the responsibility for decisions upon themselves. Many Namibian young, as a result of autocratic parenting, were not given enough space to develop their own identity and therefore lacked the necessary skills when making decisions (Whittaker 2005, p. 7).

⁴ Probably the belief in *oipumbu* and *ounhifika* was stronger among the Kwanyama people than among other ethnic groups. When asked today what an *oipumbu* is, most people, apart from the Kwanyama, have never heard of it.

⁵ It should be noted that missionary understanding of Owambo culture and medicine became more affirmative during the course of the twentieth century.

⁶ In 1992 almost 50 Finnish missionaries were still serving in northern Namibia (Pinola 1993, p. 105).

Bibliography

Interviews (some of the names have been changed).

Amadhila, Mark (farmer), 12 November 2008.
Amungulu, Thomas (pastor), 14 November 2008.
Amutenya, Matthew (pastor), 4 March, 14 November 2008.
Henok, Philippus (ELCIN Education and Training Secretary), 3 March 2008.
Iitula, Maria (teacher), 6 and 10 March 2008.
Moses, Albin (pastor), 11 November 2008.
Mweutota, Jonas (pastor), 4 March 2008.
Nakale, Eric (pastor), 4 March 2008.
Nampala, Hosea (pastor), 4 March 2008.
Nangombe, Matthew (pastor), 8 March 2008.
Nelumbu, Martin (Dr Th., lecturer), 6 November 2008.
Ondukuta Combined School: six students, 10 March 2008.
Shihungeleni, Martti (businessman), 11 November 2008.
Shikongo, Peter (pastor), 7 March 2008.
Shikulo, Loide (deputy headmaster), 6 March 2008.
Shilongo, John (pastor), 3 March 2008.
Shivute, Gideon (farmer, evangelist), 15 November 2008.
Shivute, Thomas (Dr Th., Presiding Bishop), 11 November 2008.
Tanyanda, Tylväs (pastor), 12 November 2008.

Questionnaire on religious beliefs (2008), Omapulo Paitaalo lya pashiwambo. October 2008. Outapi, Nakayale, Ondukuta. 106 replies out of 150.

Aarni, T. (1982), *The Kalunga Concept in Ovambo Religion from 1870 Onwards.* Stockholm: Almqvist & Wiksell.
Angula, N. (2001), 'Education for all: the Namibian experience', in K. Zeichner and L. Dahlström (eds), *Democratic Teacher Education Reform in Africa: The Case of Namibia.* Windhoek: Gamsberg Macmillan.

The Bible Society of South Africa (1974), *Ombibeli*. Cape Town: National Book Printers.

Bourguignon, E. (2004), 'Suffering and healing, subordination and power: women and possession trance', *Ethos*, 32, 557–9.

British and Foreign Bible Society (1936), *Etestamenti Epe: Lj'Omũua Guetu Jesus Kristus*. Sortavala: Raamattutalo.

Buys, G. L. and Nambala, S. V. V. (2003), *History of the Church in Namibia 1805–1990: An Introduction*. Windhoek: Gamsberg Macmillan.

Eriksen, T. L. (1982), *Namibia: Kolonialisme, apartheid og frigjøringskamp i det sørlige Afrika*. Uppsala: Nordic Africa Institute.

Groop, K. (2006), *With the Gospel to Maasailand: Lutheran Mission Work among the Arusha and Maasai in Northern Tanzania 1904–1973*. Åbo: Åbo Akademi University Press.

Helminen, L. (1991), *Suomen Lähetysseuran viides viisivuotissuunnitelma 1991–1995*. Helsinki: Finnish Missionary Society.

Hiltunen, M. (1986), *Witchcraft and Sorcery in Ovambo*. Helsinki: The Finnish Anthropological Society.

Hiltunen, M. (1993), *Good Magic in Ovambo*. Helsinki: The Finnish Anthropological Society.

Hodgson, D. (2005), *The Church of Women: Gendered Encounters between Maasai and Missionaries*. Bloomington: Indiana University Press.

Keller, M. (2002), *The Hammer and the Flute: Women, Power and Spirit Possession*. Baltimore: Johns Hopkins University Press.

Kjellberg, S. (1972), *Finsk mission och apartheid i Namibia: En översikt av Finska Missionssällskapets inställning till rassegregationen I Sydvästafrika*. Åbo: Institutet för ekumenik och socialetik vid Åbo Akademi.

Löytty, S. (1971), *The Ovambo Sermon: A Study of the Preaching of the Evangelical Lutheran Ovambo-Kavango Church in South West Africa*. Helsinki: Publications of the Luther-Agricola Society B 7.

Luig, U. (1999), 'Introduction', in H. Behrend and U. Luig (eds), *Spirit Possession: Modernity and Power in Africa*. Oxford: James Currey.

Miettinen, K. (2005), *On the Way to Whiteness: Christianization, Conflict and Change in Colonial Ovamboland, 1910–1965*. Helsinki: Suomen Kirjallisuuden Seura.

Munyika, V. (2004), *A Holistic Soteriology in an African Context: Utilising Luther's theology and the Owambo Traditions to Overcome a Spiritualised and Privatised Concept of Salvation in the Evangelical Lutheran Church in Namibia (ELCIN)*. Pietermaritzburg: Cluster Publications.

Namibia: NPC (2003), *2001 Population and Housing Census*. Windhoek: Central Bureau of Statistics, National Planning Commission. Available at: http://www.npc.gov.na/census/index.htm.

Namibia: NPC (2007a), *Omusati: Regional Poverty Profile*. Windhoek: National Planning Commission.

Namibia: NPC (2007b), *Oshikoto: Regional Poverty Profile*. Windhoek: National Planning Commission.

Peltola, M. (1958), *Sata vuotta suomalaista lähetystyötä 1859–1959. 2, Suomen lähetysseuran Afrikan työn historia*. Helsinki: Suomen Lähetysseura.

Pinola, S. (1993), *Suomen Lähetysseuran vuosikirja 1993 – Finska Missionssällskapets årsbok 1993*. Helsinki: Finnish Missionary Society.

Salokoski, M. (2006), *How Kings are Made – How Kingship Changes: A study of ritual change in pre-colonial and colonial Owamboland, Namibia*. Helsinki: University of Helsinki.

Savola, A. (1924), *Ambomaa ja sen Kansa* (2nd edn). Helsinki: Suomen Lähetysseura.

Siiskonen, H. (1990), *Trade and Socioeconomic Change in Ovamboland 1850–1906*. Helsinki: Societas Historica Fennica.

Smith, J. (2001), 'Of spirit possession and structural adjustment programs: government downsizing, education and their enchantments in neo-liberal Kenya', *Journal of Religion in Africa*, 31 (4), 427–54.

Tuupainen, M. (1970), *Marriage in a Matrilineal African Tribe: A Social Anthropological Study of Marriage in the Ondonga Tribe in Ovamboland*. Helsinki: Academic Bookstore.

Whittaker, S. (2005), 'Psychologically speaking: What is democratic parenting?', *The Big Issue*, 7.

World Health Organization (WHO) (2004), *Global School-based Student Health Survey (GSHS)*. World Health Organization.

Chapter 10

Divine Possession and Divination in the Graeco-Roman World: The Evidence from Iamblichus's *On the Mysteries*[1]

Crystal Addey

Their actions are in no way human, because what is inaccessible becomes accessible under divine possession: they cast themselves into fire and they walk through fire, and they walk over rivers like the priestess at Kastabala. (Iamblichus 2003)[2]

Introduction

Possession by the gods, or 'divine inspiration', was an important phenomenon in ancient, polytheistic Graeco-Roman religion. Divine possession formed one of the most significant elements of certain divination rituals. One of the most ubiquitous and widespread types of divination was the Oracle.[3] Oracle centres were specific temples of deities which both individuals and state delegations frequently visited to ask for guidance. This oracle was obtained through a prophet or prophetess who was thought to be 'inspired' or 'possessed' by a god or goddess or by a *daimon*, a type of semi-divine spirit. The god Apollo was particularly popular. He was considered to be the god of oracles and of truth and also had many other functions. The most famous Oracle of Apollo was the Oracle at Delphi; however, by the second century CE the Oracles of Apollo at Claros and Didyma in Asia Minor (modern-day Turkey) had become influential centres of oracular activity, and Apollo had many other, smaller Oracles throughout the Mediterranean world. Other popular oracular temples include the Oracle at Dodona dedicated to the god Zeus and the goddess Dione in northern Greece. There were many debates in the ancient Graeco-Roman world as to how oracles worked and where the divine possession affecting the prophet or prophetess came from.[4] Many people thought that oracles came from a *daimon*.[5] Many others, particularly philosophers, argued that this *daimon* acted on behalf of the deity in an intermediary role, conveying divine wisdom to humans from the divine realm.[6] Others saw the divine inspiration or possession as coming directly from a deity (cf. especially Iamblichus, *Mysteries*, 3.7 [114.5–8]).

This chapter will consider the views of the philosopher Iamblichus on the nature of divine possession and its effects on certain kinds of divination. His detailed philosophical account remains one of the few, extant explanations of this phenomenon from Graeco-Roman Antiquity. Iamblichus lived in the third century CE (c. 240–325 CE), a period of the late Roman Empire referred to as 'Late Antiquity.' He lived in Syria but wrote in Greek. Iamblichus was a Neoplatonist philosopher, a modern term usually used to describe philosophers of this period who followed and interpreted Plato's philosophy. His treatise, which is now called *On the Mysteries*,[7] is one of the most extensive surviving works on Graeco-Roman polytheistic religious practices. This treatise answers the questions posed by the philosopher Porphyry on the nature of various kinds of religious phenomena. In this sense, the work functions as a kind of dialogue. This chapter will examine Book 3 of this work in order to consider Iamblichus's views of the nature of divine inspiration, possession and divination (*mantikê*). Iamblichus uses various terms to denote divine possession and inspiration: these include *enthusiasmos, epipnoia* and *theophoria*, which are generally translated as 'divine inspiration', while *katachos* in the passive sense means 'held' or 'owned'; and is akin to the English term 'possessed.' Iamblichus uses these terms interchangeably and does not treat 'divine possession' and 'inspiration' as distinct states (cf. Sheppard 1993, pp. 138–9; Clarke 2001, pp. 70, 86, n.1): although he makes it clear that there are different types of divine possession – which are often dependent on the particular deity who is considered to possess the individual – the differences between the 'possessed' states of individuals are generally relocated within the realm of the individual's receptivity to the divine, a concept which will be considered in the course of this exploration. This chapter also seeks to evaluate Iamblichus's views on divine inspiration, possession and divination in the light of a long-standing anthropological debate concerning the relationship between two varieties of ecstatic experience: shamanism (soul-flight) and possession.

Anthropological Debates: Shamanism vs. Possession

Mircea Eliade's dichotomy categorizes possession and shamanism as two different kinds of religious behaviour: shamanism has men rising to the gods while possession sees the gods descend to man (Eliade 1964 [1951], pp. 3–4, 434–8). This theory has been further developed and expanded by Luc de Heusch (1962, pp. 136–37), who solidified this schema into a formalistic structure of religious states, viewing possession and shamanism as mutually exclusive. This approach has been influential on studies of ecstasy in the ancient world: the seminal work of E. R. Dodds applied similar concepts to the religious cults of the ancient world (Dodds 1951, pp. 139–42; 1965, pp. 7, 72). He views philosophers such as Pythagoras as shamans who rise to the gods during mystical soul flights; while characterizing prophetesses such as the Pythia at Delphi as possessed 'victims' who are totally overcome by the descent of the gods (Dodds 1951, p. 140; 1965, p. 72). Ioan Lewis has argued against viewing shamanism and possession as mutually exclusive. He sees these two kinds of ecstatic experience as extremes on the same continuum rather than as products of different cosmologies (Lewis 2003 [1971], pp. 43–51; 1986, pp. 85–91). He characterizes them as separate stages in the career of the shaman, who is afflicted with involuntary possession and becomes a fully fledged shaman when he learns to master the spirits who possess him or her (Lewis 2003 [1971], pp. 50, 51). Iamblichus's discussion of divine possession seems to offer a different perspective on this issue which dissolves this dichotomy.

Divine Inspiration and Possession in Iamblichus's
On the Mysteries

Iamblichus claims that there are many different kinds of divine possession: he goes on to explain that this is because the gods and goddesses who inspire human beings are different and therefore produce diverse kinds of inspiration (*Mysteries*, 3.5 [111.3–7]). Thus, cults of different deities were viewed as producing different kinds of possession states and experiences. Later, Iamblichus includes a detailed discussion of the different types of possession produced in initiates by the god Dionysus, the god Pan and the goddess Cybele, often referred to as the 'Mother of the gods' (cf. *Mysteries*, 3.9–10; Iamblichus uses the cults of these specific deities as key examples of different types of possession, rather than postulating that these examples constitute an exhaustive account). He claims, too, that the nature of the possession is also dependent upon the manner of the inspiration, a point to which I shall return shortly.

The philosopher Porphyry had questioned whether those who are divinely possessed have an inferior state of consciousness to their everyday, waking consciousness (*Mysteries*, 3.4 [109.6–9]). In response to this inquiry, Iamblichus asserts very strongly that those who are truly possessed by the gods do not act according to sense-perception, and they are not conscious of themselves in the sense of using their personal knowledge or experience (*Mysteries*, 3.4 [109.9–110.3]). To prove his point, Iamblichus gives a list of 'evidence' or 'characteristic signs' (*ta tekmêria*) which demonstrate that those who are possessed do not utilize normal human consciousness or sensation. These signs involve anaesthesia and resistance to injury.[8] For example, many of them are not burned even when fire is applied to them on account of their divine inspiration; those who are burned do not react, 'because at this time they are not living the life of an animate being' (*Mysteries*, 3.4 [110.4–7]).[9] He ends his list of examples as follows:

> From these examples it is clear that those who are inspired have no consciousness of themselves, and they lead neither the life of a human being nor of a living animal so far as concerns sensation or appetite, but they exchange their life for another more divine life, by which they are inspired, and by which they are completely possessed. (*Mysteries*, 3.4 [110.12–111.2])

Iamblichus's concept of divine possession rests on two central points. First, the recipient is wholly possessed by the gods. Secondly, and as a consequence of the first point, he or she does not act or experience in a human manner using sense perception. Does this mean that the inspired individual has no consciousness at all, according to Iamblichus? A common conception of possession in anthropological scholarship is that all cases of possession necessitate the complete expulsion of the host individual out of their own body (De Heusch 1962, pp. 129–33; Lewis 2003 [1971], p. 40). According to Iamblichus, it is not the case that the recipient has no consciousness at all, though: the central point is that the inspired individual is not conscious of anything else except the gods. As Emma Clarke has noted, 'the human individual is eclipsed, not annihilated, by the divine force' (2001, p. 83). Iamblichus emphasizes the fact that those who are possessed exchange their human life for a divine life, 'For if they have subjected their entire life as a vehicle or instrument to the gods who inspire them, either they exchange their human life for the divine, or they direct their own life towards the god' (*Mysteries*, 3.4 [109.10–13]; cf. also 8.7 [270.10–14]; 8.8 [272.1–4]; Shaw 1998, p. 248). According to Iamblichus, inspiration is emphatically not a transport of the mind, for the mind is not carried or swept away during the experience of true possession. Rather, the human individual consciousness is replaced or enhanced by a kind of super-consciousness. This idea underlies Iamblichus's explanation of how divination works:

> But if the soul weaves together its intellectual and its divine part with higher powers, then its own visions will be purer, whether of the gods, or of essentially incorporeal beings, or, generally speaking, of whatever contributes to the truth about intelligible things. If, however, it refers accounts of things happening to their causes, that is, to the gods, it receives from them a power and knowledge embracing things that were and will be, and takes a view of all time, and surveys events happening in time (*Mysteries*, 3.3 [107.7–108.1])

Here Iamblichus postulates a theory of divination whereby the prophet or prophetess takes on a type of divine consciousness which entails a complete and transcendent perspective of all events and phenomena. This type of divine consciousness is envisioned as being non-spatial and non-temporal.

It is clear that Iamblichus's conceptions rest firmly on his broadly Platonic view of the nature of the human being: for him, the human being is composed of the body and the soul. It is the soul that is *primarily* linked with the intelligible, divine realm and which can therefore perceive intelligible or 'divine' truth. In possession states, the soul of the human being becomes illuminated by the specific deity. Iamblichus explicitly states this when he describes the operation of the Oracle at Claros in Asia Minor. After describing the ritual preparations of the prophet of the Oracle, which include fasting, seclusion and drinking the water from the sacred spring of the oracle site, Iamblichus states 'through these means, he has the inspiration of the god illuminating the pure sanctuary of his own soul, and providing for it an unhindered divine possession, and a perfect and unimpeded presence' (*Mysteries*, 3.11 [126.1–3]). According to Iamblichus, the possession of the god affects and 'illuminates' the prophet's soul. Yet it is important to note that, as is the case with ancient philosophical views of the soul generally, Iamblichus's view of the nature of the human soul is very different from modern, Western conceptions of 'self,' generally conceived as an autonomous and independent entity. In Iamblichus's philosophy, the soul bears an imprint or reflection of divinity: in his commentary on Plato's *Phaedrus* he referred to the 'One in the soul', maintaining that 'it is the essential nature of the One of the soul to be united with the gods' (Iamblichus, *In Phaedrum*, Fragment 6); elsewhere Iamblichus refers to 'that element in us which is divine and intellectual and one' (*Mysteries*, 1.15 [46.9]; cf. also 1.3 [7.11–8.2; 9.7–9; 10.4–10]; Shaw 1998, pp. 237–8). Iamblichus conceptualizes the soul as intrinsically and constantly connected with the divine in an ontological sense. Thus, the possessing deity is simultaneously and paradoxically seen as 'other' and 'not-other'. This ancient view of possession suggests the importance of considering philosophical, metaphysical and cosmological frameworks when attempting to evaluate the role of divine possession in different cultural contexts.

Possession and Ecstatic Trance

Many scholars now associate possession states with ecstatic trance. Indeed, this was often thought to be the case in Graeco-Roman traditional religion, but Iamblichus is keen to emphasize that divine possession is not the same as ecstasy (*ekstasis*):

> Yet it [i.e. divine possession] is not even ecstasy pure and simple, but an exaltation and transference to what is superior, whereas frenzy and ecstasy actually reveal a perversion toward what is inferior. Still more, the one who represents this ecstasy says something about the incidental feature of those who are inspired, but does not put his finger on the main point. That is, they themselves are wholly possessed by the divine, the consequence of which is ecstasy. (*Mysteries*, 3.7 [114.8–13])

Iamblichus is not simply opposing inspiration to ecstasy, but rather saying that ecstasy is only a symptom and consequence of possession, not proof of its occurrence, and may sometimes occur through human actions (Shaw 1998, pp. 249–50; Clarke 2001, p. 75). Thus, in Iamblichus's schema, an individual exhibiting the traits commonly conceived as 'ecstasy' (*ekstasis*) could be in a state of divine possession, but they could alternatively be experiencing a state such as drunkenness or madness. Ecstasy is thus not a defining characteristic of possession, but only a symptom of possession in some cases. This is reinforced by Iamblichus's comments later, where he explicitly rejects the idea that possession is identical or similar to the ecstatic state caused by drunkenness or madness. He argues that the latter states are purely human. They divert the human to inferior states which are contrary to nature, whereas divine possession is superior to nature and leads the human being to be united with divine entities which are superior (*Mysteries*, 3.25 [158.6–159.4]).

Simultaneous Divine Descent and Human Ascent

Iamblichus's discussion dissolves the shamanism–possession dichotomy: the human soul rises to the gods while *simultaneously* the gods descend to the human soul to possess it. Iamblichus argues that divine possession involves the human agent subsuming his or her consciousness to that of the gods, so that his or her soul is possessed by the divine. Thus the human soul, while possessed, sees through the eyes of a deity. Crucially, however, this is only possible because the soul contains a reflection of the divine, as Iamblichus states 'earthly things . . . whenever they come to be ready for participation in the divine, straight away find the gods pre-existing in it prior to their own proper essence' (*Mysteries*, 1.8 [29.1–3]). Iamblichus is not generally explicit regarding the simultaneous ascent of the soul with the descent of the gods in possession rituals. This is because he is so concerned to emphasize the divine as the ultimate and primary cause of divine possession.[10] However, when Iamblichus compares divine possession to other states which provoke ecstasy in the recipient, he explicitly delineates some of the key features of possession in an explicit comparison with ecstatic states caused by drunkenness and madness. He maintains that divine possession provides benefits which are more precious than human sense, it unites the human being with beings who are superior, it is unchangeable, superior to nature and causes the ascent of the soul:

> It is thus necessary initially to distinguish two forms of ecstasy . . . one is contrary to nature [i.e. ecstatic states caused by drunkenness and madness], the other superior to nature [i.e. divine possession]; one causes the descent of the soul, *the other its ascent; and one separates it [i.e. the soul] wholly apart from participation in the divine, while the other unites it to it* [my italics] (*Mysteries*, 3.25 [158.8–9; 159.2–4])

It may be instructive to examine how this paradoxical situation occurs, according to Iamblichus. The philosopher describes states of divine possession which occur in cults where musical instruments (such as pipes, cymbals, tambourines, etc.) are used to encourage or induce a state of receptivity in the human being. He then explains why music is used in these possession rituals:

> But one should not even claim this, that the soul primarily consists of harmony and rhythm; for in that case divine possession would belong to the soul alone. It is better, then, to bring our discourse back to this

assertion: before it gave itself to the body, the soul heard the divine harmony. And accordingly even when it entered the body, such tunes as it hears which especially preserve the divine trace of harmony, to these it clings fondly and is reminded by them of the divine harmony; it is also borne along with and closely allied to this harmony, *and shares as much as can be shared of it* [my italics]. (*Mysteries*, 3.9 [120.3–10])

Here, Iamblichus states that the harmony and rhythm of the music which induce the state of possession do not primarily belong to the soul. Rather, they are a reflection of the divine harmony: the rhythm and harmony are infused and permeated with divinity. This idea is based on the Neoplatonic view of a hierarchically structured universe and the ancient concept of cosmic sympathy (*sympatheia*), where every ontological level of reality is connected through 'chains' of things which bear the imprint of the divine.

The soul bears a memory and trace of the divine harmony which it heard before incarnating in a human body; in this sense, the soul bears a trace of this 'divine harmony' and is closely allied with it. Iamblichus's theory is heavily based on the Platonic theory of recollection: Plato had discussed the way in which the human soul travelled in the train of the gods and glimpsed the divine realm before descending into a body in the physical world (Plato 1982 [1914] [*Phaedrus*, 250b–251a]; cf. Plato 1963 [1935] [*Republic*, 402a]). While Iamblichus is concerned to emphasize the ultimate importance of the divine as the primary cause of the possession, the soul's memory and trace of the divine harmony, and their receptivity to this trace of the divine, act as an 'ascent' allowing the soul to receive the inspiration of the deity.

Divine descent and illumination

It is clear that Iamblichus's conception of the 'descent' of the divine is not to be taken literally as implying a descent in physical, spatial terms. Rather, he conceptualizes the divine as giving off emanations which illuminate the whole of the physical world with no diminution. This idea of divine emanation was common to the Neoplatonist philosophers writing in the same philosophical milieu as Iamblichus. They compared this process to the light of the sun whose rays light up external phenomena without any kind of detraction. This idea clarifies Iamblichus's frequent descriptions of divine manifestation and power in terms of illumination.[11] As John Finamore (1999, p. 87) has pointed out, 'Iamblichus defends the view that although the gods are superior to us and exist separately, they illuminate this realm with their light. It is this light that allows the gods' presence in this lower world'. For Iamblichus then, the divine illuminates the whole world perpetually. The divine is primarily located in the divine realm but simultaneously is manifested throughout the physical cosmos. Within his cosmology, the divine is both transcendent and immanent:

> For neither is it the case that the gods are confined to certain parts of the cosmos, nor is the earthly realm devoid of them. On the contrary, it is true of the superior beings in it that, even as they are not contained by anything, so they contain everything within themselves (*Mysteries*, 1.8 [28.11–29.1])

The idea of the simultaneous transcendence and immanence of the gods forms the central foundation of Iamblichus's religious conceptions. According to the philosopher, the gods are transcendent in a causal and essential sense: they exist in a superior, eternal realm and so do not 'move' from one location to another, as a more partial and temporal being such as a human soul does. However, through their causal superiority and power, the gods are also immanent throughout the lower world, the material cosmos, through their divine illumination which permeates all things, even material objects (*Mysteries*, 3.12 [128.8–129.11]). This notion of divine illumination and emanation is dependent upon the concept of *sympatheia* and encapsulates the idea of an animated cosmos, permeated by divinity. The 'descent' of the divine refers to this process of emanation or illumination and also implicitly refers to the superiority of the divine in a causal sense.

Human ascent and receptivity

In a similar sense to divine descent, the 'ascent' of the soul was clearly not conceptualized by Iamblichus as an ascent in spatial, physical terms but an abstract ascent of the soul to its own causal origins through its receptivity (*epitedeiotes*). Speaking of the divinatory power of the gods, Iamblichus maintains that 'existing itself prior to the totality of things, it is sufficient, by its own separateness, to fill all things to the extent that each is able to share in it' (*Mysteries*, 3.12 [129.9–11]). The first part of this statement emphasizes the causal superiority and power of the gods, while the latter part ('the extent that each is able to share in it') refers to the 'receptivity' or 'suitability' (*epitedeiotes*) which enables the prophet or prophetess to share in divine power. Through ritual, intellectual and moral means, the human being can increase the receptivity of his or her soul to these illuminations so that he or she can become possessed by a deity.[12] Iamblichus's account of oracles includes an examination of the ritual preparations and procedures which the prophet or prophetess undergoes in order to increase his or her receptivity to divine illumination so that he or she can become possessed and utter the oracles of the god: the prophet at the Oracle at Claros purifies himself through withdrawal to solitary places, meditation and fasting (*Mysteries*, 3.11 [125.11–126.3]), while the prophetess at the Oracle of the Branchidae (another name for the Oracle at Didyma) undergoes ritual bathing, fasting for three days and withdrawal and meditation in the innermost sanctuaries of the temple (*Mysteries*, 3.11 [127.10–13]). Elsewhere, Iamblichus seems to suggest that different levels of ascent are involved in different cases of divine possession, which varies according to the manner of inspiration:

> For either the god possesses us, or we become wholly the god's property, or we exercise our activity in common with him. And sometimes we share in the god's lowest power, sometimes in his intermediate, and sometimes in his primary power. And sometimes there is a mere participation, sometimes a communion, and sometimes even a union. (*Mysteries*, 3.5 [111.7–11])

According to Iamblichus's schema, different states of divine possession can involve participation sharing in the god's lowest power, communion sharing in the god's intermediate power and union sharing in the god's primary power. The level of ascent involved in these types of possession seems to be dependent upon the receptivity of the possessed human being: the greater the capacity or receptivity of the human being, the greater the level of ascent is. However, all are conceived as a type of ascent to the divine, conceptualized philosophically as reversion to the causal origin of the human being.

The soul is seen as the receptacle of the gods, a conception which seems similar to Mary Keller's notion of the *instrumental agency* of the possessed. Keller maintains that instrumentality refers to the power of receptivity, comparable metaphorically to a hammer, flute or horse that is wielded, played or mounted and agency implies *action* as well as *a place where exchanges occur* (2002, pp. 9–10). Iamblichus too focuses on the receptivity of the possessed, describing them as an 'instrument' and 'vehicle' of the gods. Divine possession for Iamblichus is not a matter of a totally alien agency overcoming its human victim. Rather, divine possession is conceptualized as a phenomenon involving a transcendent and simultaneously immanent deity working *through* the soul of the possessed. The deity is conceived as being already linked to the human soul causally and ontologically and so the possession experience is seen as enhancing the soul. Thus, receptivity to the divine is seen as enhancing the human being and is a source of power. This conceptualization of divine possession can be more fully explored using Keller's notion of instrumental agency, since the notion of instrumentality entails a far more subtle conception of the agency of the possessed individual: 'the instrumental designation indicates that the subject exercises a unique type of agency that is neither autonomous nor passive' (Keller 2002, p. 77). Keller maintains that:

> the concept of instrumental agency serves to highlight the way that receptivity has often been evaluated as an extremely powerful capacity among possession traditions. Rather than coding receptivity negatively as a type of passivity, instrumental agency accounts for this revaluation; one's receptivity marks a developable sacred space. (Keller 2002, p. 82)

Thus this notion of instrumental agency allows us to appreciate the nuances of Iamblichus's account of divine possession and to reassess his conceptualization of the receptivity of the possessed as an area where the individual uses intellectual, ritual and moral means to develop and to increase his or her capacity to receive the divine. Thus possession is reassessed as a sacred space which necessarily entails the involvement of both divine and human agency.

Conclusion

Iamblichus's discussion of possession states offers an alternative perspective to the dualistic dichotomies proposed by anthropologists such as Luc de Heusch and Ioan Lewis and Classicists such as E. R. Dodds. Iamblichus, a philosopher and ritual practitioner who himself calls into question the dichotomy we so often apply to religion and philosophy, suggests that the possessed prophet(ess) or initiate and the shaman are one: the mystical ascent of the soul is assimilated with divine descent. His view dissolves a rigid dichotomy between active possessing agent and the possessed, passive victim. It suggests the possibility of a more subtle and complex view of the relationship between deity and possessed human, since the human soul is viewed as being causally and ontologically connected with the deity. Thus, the divine possession does not annihilate the human consciousness but replaces it with divine consciousness, representing an enhancement of the human being's power and perception. This view seems to bear some resemblance to Mary Keller's view of possession as involving instrumental agency, a category which also dissolves the dichotomy between subject/ agent and object/passive victim. Iamblichus uses the idea of divine reflections patterned and contained within the soul as the link which connects god and mortal unceasingly. Thus, according to Iamblichus, states of divine possession enable the human soul to participate in, commune with or unite with its own ultimate causal origin, the divine, to a greater or lesser extent. The extent of participation, communion and union are conceptualized as being directly linked with the receptivity (*epitedeiotes*) of the human being. Thus, Iamblichus's account delineates receptivity as a vital element of possession rituals and divination; in this sense, divine possession involves a subtle yet complex blend of human and divine agency.

Through this exploration of the Neoplatonist philosopher Iamblichus's views of divine possession in traditional Graeco-Roman religion, this discussion has attempted to show the importance of reflecting on cultural and philosophical notions of soul, self and agency when examining ritual phenomena, particularly possession states and divination. In a wider sense, this suggests the relevance of cosmology, metaphysics and philosophy in approaches towards understanding and interpreting possession within different cultural contexts and frameworks.

Notes

[1] I wish to thank the trustees of the Thomas Wiedemann Memorial Fund and the Classics Section of the Higher Education Academy for generous funding to attend the conference on 'New Interpretations of Spirit Possession' at which this paper (chapter) was originally presented. I also wish to thank Dr Bettina Schmidt, who organized the above mentioned conference at Bangor University, Wales, and all of the speakers and attendees of the conference for their challenging questions and stimulating discussion during the conference. I also wish to thank my supervisor, Professor Gillian Clark, for her assistance with preparing this paper, and Professor Geoffrey Samuel, Tim Addey, Dr Louise Child and Leigh Almey for reading and commenting on drafts of this paper.

[2] Iamblichus 2003 (hereafter referred to in the text as *Mysteries*), 3.4 (110.9–15). All quotations and translations of this work are from this edition, unless otherwise specified. The ancient geographer Strabo says that the priestesses of Artemis Perasia ('the one crossing over') at Castabalis walked barefoot on burning coals without pain. (Cf. Strabo 1928, 12.2.7).

[3] Throughout this chapter, I use the term 'Oracle' (with capitalization) to refer to an oracular temple or sanctuary where oracular practices were located and I use the term 'oracle' (without capitalization) to refer to the oracular response or utterance given by a prophet or prophetess to an enquirer.

[4] The philosopher and Prophet of Delphi, Plutarch of Chaeronea, wrote a whole dialogue which explicitly addresses this question in relation to the Delphic Oracle. (Cf. Plutarch 2003 [1936].)

[5] In particular, the view that pagan oracles were the work of evil *daimones* can be attributed to, and may even have been developed by, Christian apologists of Late Antiquity, who frequently advance this view in their polemic against the oracles of traditional Graeco-Roman religion. For an important example see Eusebius 1981 [1903], Books 4 and 5.

[6] Plutarch 2003 [1936], 415a1–3; Plato 1975 [1925], 202b–203b. Cf. also Plato 1962 [1924], 99b–c; 99d–100b. Porphyry 2000, 2.38.3, refers to *daimones* as 'carrying back to us their [i.e. the gods] advice and warnings through oracles.' The Plotinian version of the intellectual categorization of *daimon* as a god and a spirit and thus a hypostasis is constructed so that the *daimon* as a true lover constantly and eternally looks upwards at the Intellectual Principle whose off-spring Aphrodite or Soul is his parent. (Cf. Plotinus 1967, 3.5.3.)

[7] The original title of the work is: *The Reply of the Master Abamon to the Letter of Porphyry to Anebo and the Solutions to the Questions It Contains*. The modern title by which the work is now commonly known, *On the Mysteries of the Egyptians, Chaldae-ans and Assyrians (De mysteriis Aegyptiorum, Chaldaeorum, Assyriorum)*, was coined by Marsilio Ficino in the fifteenth century.

[8] Cf. Clarke 2001, p. 77, who includes references to modern psychological reports which detail similar phenomena; Eliade 1957, p. 96, views resistance to injury and 'mastery of fire' as 'the proof that the shaman participates in the condition of the "spirits" while still continuing to exist in the flesh: the proof that the "sensibility" can be transmuted without being abolished; that the human con-dition has been surpassed without being destroyed, that is, that it has been "restored" to its primordial perfection'.

[9] Cf. Euripides 2002, pp. 757–5, which describes the Bacchic revellers (women inspired by the god Dionysus) as unharmed by the fire on their heads. Cf. Clarke 2001, p. 77, who refers to Theophrastus's *De Igne*, 57–8, which records the actions of fire-eaters and men that walk across burning coals. Cf. also Eliade 1957, pp. 92–5, for a comprehensive discussion of the perennial theme of 'mastery of fire' in diverse, worldwide religious cults and shamanic practices.

[10] I have argued elsewhere that one of the central agendas of Iamblichus's *On the Mysteries* is to show the divine as the ultimate and primary cause of divine posses-sion and divination, but that this argument has to be considered within the schema of simultaneous and multiple levels or grades of causation. In other words, in Iamblichus's view the divine *ultimately* causes these religious phenom-ena, but this does not nullify the vital, lower, auxiliary causes such as the receptiv-ity of the prophet(ess)'s soul. Cf. Addey 2007, pp. 73–87. Cf. also *Mysteries*, 3.1; Shaw 1998, p. 235.

[11] For a detailed analysis of the role of light within the philosophy of Iamblichus and other Neoplatonist philosophers, cf. Finamore 1993, pp. 55–64.

[12] Cf. Shaw 1995, pp. 84–87, for a discussion of the importance of receptivity/ fitness (*epitedeiotes*) in Iamblichus's account of divine possession: 'Following the Neoplatonic principle that like can only be joined to like, the theurgist had to purify the future vehicle of the god in order to receive its power, for the presence of the god was always in proportion to the purity of its receptacle.'

Bibliography

Primary texts

Euripides (2002), *Bacchae*, trans. D. Kovacs, in *Euripides: Bacchae, Iphigenia at Aulis, Rhesus*, Loeb Classical Library Volume 6. Cambridge, MA and London: Harvard University Press.

Eusebius (1981 [1903]), *Preparation for the Gospel (Praeparatio Evangelica)*, trans. E. H. Gifford, 2 vols (reprinted edn). Grand Rapids, MI: Baker Book House.

Iamblichus (1973), *Fragments = Iamblichi Chalcidensis In Platonis Dialogos Commentariorum Fragmenta*, ed. and trans. J. M. Dillon. Leiden: Brill.

Iamblichus (2003), *On the Mysteries (De mysteriis)*, ed. and trans. E. C. Clarke, J. M. Dillon and J. P. Hershbell. Atlanta: Society of Biblical Literature.

Plato (1962 [1924]), *Meno*, trans. W. R. M. Lamb, in *Plato: Laches, Protagoras, Meno, Euthydemus*, Loeb Classical Library (reprinted edn). London and Cambridge, MA: Heinemann and Harvard University Press.

Plato (1963 [1935]), *Republic*, trans. P. Shorey, Loeb Classical Library Volume 2 (reprinted edn). London and Cambridge, MA: Heinemann and Harvard University Press.

Plato (1975 [1925]), *Symposium*, trans. W. R. M. Lamb, *Plato: Lysis, Symposium, Gorgias*, Loeb Classical Library (reprinted edn). London and Cambridge, MA: Heinemann and Harvard University Press.

Plato (1982 [1914]), *Phaedrus*, trans. H. N. Fowler, in *Plato: Euthyphro, Apology, Crito, Phaedo, Phaedrus*, Loeb Classical Library (reprinted edn). London and Cambridge, MA: Heinemann and Harvard University Press.

Plotinus (1967), *Enneads*, trans. A. H. Armstrong, Loeb Classical Library Volume 3, London and Cambridge, MA: Heinemann and Harvard University Press.

Plutarch (2003 [1936]), *On the Decline of Oracles (De Defectu Oraculorum)*, trans. F. C. Babbit, Loeb Classical Library (reprinted edn). Cambridge, MA and London: Heinemann and Harvard University Press.

Porphyry (2000), *On Abstinence from Killing Animals (De abstinentia)*, trans. G. Clark. London: Duckworth.

Strabo (1928), *Geography*, trans. H. L. Jones, Loeb Classical Library (8 vols). London: Heinemann.

Secondary works

Addey, C. (2007), 'Consulting the oracle: the mantic art and its causation in Iamblichus' *De Mysteriis*', in J. F. Finamore and R. M. Berchman (eds), *Metaphysical Patterns in Platonism: Ancient, Medieval, Renaissance and Modern Times*. New Orleans, LA: University Press of the South, pp. 73–87.

Arnott, G. (1989), 'Nechung: a modern parallel to the Delphic oracle?' *Greece and Rome*, 36 (2), 152–7.

Clarke, E. C. (2001), *Iamblichus' De Mysteriis: A Manifesto of the Miraculous*. Aldershot: Ashgate.

De Heusch, L. (1962), 'Cultes de possession et religions initiatiques de salut en Afrique', *Annales du Centre d'Etudes des Religions: Vol. 2*. Brussels, pp. 136–7.

Dodds, E. R. (1951), *The Greeks and the Irrational*. Berkeley and Los Angeles: University of California Press.

Dodds, E. R. (1965), *Pagan and Christian in an Age of Anxiety: Some Aspects of Religious Experience from Marcus Aurelius to Constantine*. Cambridge: Cambridge University Press.

Eliade, M. (1957), *Myths, Dreams and Mysteries: The Encounter between Contemporary Faiths and Archaic Realities*. trans. P. Mairet. London: Harvill Press.

Eliade, M. (1964 [1951]), *Shamanism: Archaic Techniques of Ecstasy*. London: Routledge, trans. W. R. Trask from the original French edition: (1951), *Le Chamanisme et les techniques archaïqies de l' exstase*, Paris: Librairie Payot.

Finamore, J. F. (1993), 'Iamblichus on light and the transparent', in H. J. Blumenthal and E. G. Clark (eds), *The Divine Iamblichus: Philosopher and Man of Gods*. Bristol: Bristol Classical Press, pp. 55–64.

Finamore, J. F. (1999), 'Plotinus and Iamblichus on magic and theurgy', *Dionysius*, 17, 83–94.

Goodman, F. D. (1990), *Where the Spirits ride the Wind: Trance Journeys and other Ecstatic Experiences*. Indianapolis: Indiana University Press.

Keller, M. (2002), *The Hammer and the Flute: Women, Power, and Spirit Possession*. Baltimore and London: Johns Hopkins University Press.

Lewis, I. M. (1986), *Religion in Context: Cults and Charisma*. Cambridge: Cambridge University Press.

Lewis, I. M. (2003 [1971]), *Ecstatic Religion: A Study of Shamanism and Spirit Possession* (3rd edn). London: Routledge.

Maurizio, L. (1995), 'Anthropology and spirit possession: a reconsideration of the Pythia's role at Delphi', *Journal of Hellenic Studies*, 115, 69–86.

Shaw, G. (1995), *Theurgy and the Soul: The Neoplatonism of Iamblichus*. University Park: Pennsylvania State University Press.

Shaw, G. (1998), 'Divination in the Neoplatonism of Iamblichus', in R. M. Berchman (ed.), *Mediators of the Divine: Horizons of Prophecy, Divination, Dreams and Theurgy in Mediterranean Antiquity*. Atlanta: Scholars Press, pp. 225–67.

Shaw, G. (2003), 'Containing ecstasy: the strategies of Iambichean theurgy', *Dionysius*, 21, 53–88.

Sheppard, A. (1993), 'Iamblichus on inspiration: *De Mysteriis* 3.4–8', in H. J. Blumenthal and E. G. Clark (eds), *The Divine Iamblichus: Philosopher and Man of Gods*. Bristol: Bristol Classical Press, pp. 138–43.

Chapter 11

Waking the Entranced: Reassessing Spiritualist Mediumship Through a Comparison of Spiritualist and Shamanic Spirit Possession Practices

David Gordon Wilson

Spiritualism is a movement that fosters mediumistic communication with the dead; as such, it reminds us that possession practices are found in contemporary Western culture. Furthermore, Spiritualism is not an import but is an indigenous practice – indigenous in the sense that it originated and established itself in the modern Anglo-American world and cannot properly be said to belong anywhere else.[1] In Britain, Spiritualism has had periods of mass appeal but in popular accounts of Spiritualism there is often the sense of a movement that belongs to the past. In addition, academic research into Spiritualism has tended to examine the Spiritualist movement and mediumistic practice during the nineteenth century and the first half of the twentieth century. Jay Winter tells us that after the Second World War, Spiritualism 'faded into the margins of cultural history, where it has remained to this day' (1995, p. 77). While it may be true that Spiritualism does not noticeably inform public discourse at a political level, it is important to examine Spiritualist activity at a more popular or demotic level. It cannot be taken for granted that public discourse accurately reflects actual private practice and there is little doubt that the British Spiritualist movement is still an active one. For example, in the United Kingdom, there are approximately 350 churches affiliated to the Spiritualists' National Union, the largest Spiritualist organization to be found in Britain. The principal activity in nearly all Spiritualist churches is to provide regular 'platform demonstrations' of mediumship.[2]

Spiritualism persists as a form of religious observance in modern Britain and, on that basis alone, it merits examination. However, if Spiritualism is to be (re)introduced to public or, at least, academic discourse, it is helpful to identify an appropriate language with which to do so, and to show that the study of Spiritualism can contribute to contemporary attempts to understand spirit or possession phenomena. During the course of my own mediumistic development, I have been interested in shamanism, and, in particular, in attempts to develop cross-cultural models of shamanism, because of the parallels that seem to be apparent in Spiritualism. The field of shamanic studies has often seemed to me to offer an academically familiar language with which to describe Spiritualism.

Several thinkers (e.g. Geoffrey Nelson and Bernice Martin) argue that Spiritualist mediumship is comparable to shamanism, and I shall evaluate their claims. Despite this suggestion, a contrast has often been drawn between the 'passive' mediumship of Spiritualism and the 'active' journeying of shamanism. In order to maintain this contrast, some writers on shamanism adhere to a typology of either passive or active attitudes that is itself a product of Western patriarchal attitudes, and which have also been evident in the history of Spiritualism.

I will argue that active or passive characterizations of mediumship have hindered a full appreciation of Spiritualist mediumship and possibly also of shamanism. To support my argument I will examine insider accounts of Spiritualist mediumship in order to reveal an understanding of mediumship as a learned craft that enables the practitioner to use trance states for the purpose of communicating between this world and the spirit world.

Using Participant-Observation to Test other Insider Accounts

A notable feature of the academic literature on shamanism and neo-shamanism is that it contains a significant proportion of works by authors who are themselves practitioners: a useful example is *Shamans/Neo-Shamans* by Robert Wallis. As a neo-shamanic practitioner, Wallis acknowledges the need to 'develop, refine and apply a careful and well-considered interpretative framework' (2003, p. 2). Wallis argues that his first-hand experience is crucial in researching neo-shamanism and in developing 'well-rounded perspectives on the various interest-groups considered here' (2003, p. 7). Although Wallis acknowledges a wide range of methodological concerns, it is not obvious that that awareness of itself constitutes a clear methodology. Insider experience is undoubtedly valuable but it is inevitably particular, one narrative among many others. However wide that experience, it cannot be regarded as definitive. In drawing upon my own role as a Spiritualist medium, I adopt the more limited approach of using examples from my experience to illustrate, or to test, other insider accounts drawn from

Spiritualist literature.[3] In this way, this chapter exemplifies how participant-observation can be used to re-engage with relevant sources so as to develop a deeper understanding of the practice(s) under examination, and, more particularly, to show that there are difficulties with the characterization of Spiritualist mediumship as 'passive'.

Literature on Spiritualism

Although Spiritualism makes use of Christian forms of worship (e.g. in the format of its services), it has no recognized scripture or other equivalent to the Bible. However, Spiritualism is a literary movement in the sense that it has given rise to a considerable body of emic literature, including mediums' (auto)biographies, histories of the movement and philosophical scripts that are regarded as being 'guided' or 'inspired' (that is to say, the product of mediumistic activity). By contrast, the body of etic literature dealing with Spiritualism is much more limited (for instance, published examples of participant-observation are particularly rare). Two notable examples of participant-observation are *Intimacy and Ritual* (1974) by Vieda Skultans (who was a member of a Spiritualist development circle in south Wales), and that of Burke Forrest, whose membership of the two development circles, in southern California and southern England in the 1970s, provided material for her article 'Apprentice-Participation' (1986).

For Skultans one of the central issues raised by her book is that of cross-cultural comparisons, the challenge being that of 'establishing whether spirit possession has a core of critical characteristics, on the basis of which one can compare, for example, spirit possession cults in South Wales with spirit possession cults in Africa' (Skultans 1974, p. 5). In 'The Spiritualist Meeting', Bernice Martin claims that the 'most appropriate analogues' of Spiritualist mediumship are to be found in 'shamanism, spirit possession and divination' (1971, p. 146). At a later point in the article, Martin refers again to mediumship as comparable to 'shamanism, spirit mediumship and divination in small-scale societies, and in some historic cultures such as classical Greece and Rome', and goes on to suggest that the closest comparison is with ancestor worship in China and Japan (1971, pp. 155, 158). That particular comparison needs to be treated with care: to suggest that Spiritualists worship their forebears is misleading. Examples of worship or reverence towards 'people in spirit' are rare, as is the sense that people in spirit should be feared or that they need to be placated. That said, Martin does prompt us to ask whether there is, as Skultans puts it, a 'core of critical characteristics' that enables us to compare possession practices found in different parts of the world. It is in order to make some progress in answering this question that I explore the comparison between Spiritualism and shamanism.

Nelson's sociological work *Spiritualism and Society* (1969) remains the only comprehensive treatment of the Spiritualist movement in the United States and Britain. Nelson sees Spiritualism as a developed form of shamanism, which he regards as existing 'in the simplest forms of society' (Nelson 1969, p. 269). Nelson's principal source on shamanism is Mircea Eliade's *Shamanism* (1964). In Nelson's bibliography Eliade's work is listed under typologies of 'Authority and Leadership' (Nelson 1969, p. 301) and Nelson clearly draws attention to shamanism as a form of charismatic leadership. This characterization of shamanism is used by Nelson to support his argument that Spiritualism became established as a religious movement in part because of its ability to provide a succession or lineage of charismatic leaders. For Nelson (following Eliade) it is the exercise of control of the ecstatic state that characterizes shamanism and therefore mediumship (Nelson 1969, p. 240). By contrast, if we consider more recent publications on shamanism, there is often a tendency to emphasize differences between shamanism and mediumship. In particular, one finds a perceived contrast between the active travelling of the shaman (that enables interaction with, if not mastery or control of, spirits) in contradistinction to a passive characterization of the medium as one who is impressed upon and used as an instrument by spirits.

This is a contrast that is drawn in Nevill Drury's work *The Shaman and the Magician* (1982), in which Drury uses Eliade's description of the shaman as one who 'specializes in a trance during which his soul is believed to leave his body and ascend to the sky or descend to the underworld' (Drury 1982, p. 3). For Drury, the special skill of the shaman is the ability to control the trance state, which 'contrast[s] with the spirit medium who in trance becomes possessed by inhabiting spirits and is often unable when recovering consciousness to recall anything that has transpired' (1982, p. 17). This particular work by Drury is a semi-popular one in which we might expect to find sharply drawn contrasts, but it is still important to examine whether or not Drury has characterized mediumship correctly.

The characterization of Spiritualist mediumship as passive has a long history in Anglo-American culture and within the Spiritualist movement itself. In *The Darkened Room* (1989) Alex Owen examines power and gender relationships in late-Victorian England and the ways in which Spiritualism and understandings of mediumship were shaped by patriarchal attitudes of the time. Spiritualism gave rise to medical debate not merely because of the practice of spiritual healing within the movement but also because a number of influential figures in the medical profession perceived a connection between the mediumistic state (regarded as passive and involving a failure to maintain self-control) and mental illness. For Owen, early experts in the field of lunacy 'regarded with distaste and suspicion the close involvement of women in spiritualist practice, likening female mediumship to hysteria – a condition which had unsavoury sexual and expressive connotations' (1989, p. 139). In a movement where female mediums seemed to predominate, normative conceptions of womanhood (as articulated by men) became closely bound up with debates over the nature of mediumistic practice. Owen observes that 'The trance state, so central to effective mediumship, was tied in to medicine's conception of morbid behaviour' (1989, p. 143).

Owen considers in some detail the attitudes and influence of the Victorian psychologist, Dr Henry Maudsley, whom Owen describes as being 'of central importance in the development of medical psychology' and as epitomizing its approach during the latter half of the nineteenth century (1989, p. 144). Maudsley was an opponent of religion in general and of Spiritualism in particular, and argued for the connection between Spiritualist mediumship and insanity as a way of undermining Spiritualist claims. In particular, as Owen claims, 'he linked ecstatic religious experience with the clinical condition of epilepsy' (1989, p. 145). Indeed, for Owen, 'The issue here is not whether some ecstatics were epileptic, cataleptic, or unbalanced, but that Maudsley and others like him assumed that ecstatic or seemingly uncontrolled religious experience was to be equated with abnormalcy and sickness' (1989, p. 146).

Characterizations of mediumship became closely bound up with patriarchal attitudes involving the perceived weakness or vulnerability of women. Mediums, whether female or male, came to be described as passive, receptive, vulnerable, or otherwise not in control; in turn, this led to perceptions of psychological instability or weakness. This attitude continues to underlie understandings of mediumship. For example, Skultans argues that spirit possession always relates first to illness and secondly to what she terms the 'mystically sanctioned' 'assumption of roles which in the ordinary way lie beyond the social repertoire of the possessed person' (1974, p. 5). The implication here is that the ability to engage in a possession practice allows the practitioner to step outside their everyday social role or position so as to adopt a more interesting and fulfilling role. Skultans proposes that illness is relevant because it justifies setting aside existing roles and responsibilities, creating an opportunity to assume the role of medium.

Yet a number of writers have expressed the view that mediumship is a more complex phenomenon than this. For example, Jenny Hazelgrove draws attention to the ambiguous nature of mediumship, which she describes as 'situated between conscious and unconscious processes, activity and passivity, psychosis and revelation' (Hazelgrove 2000, p. 110). This is a theme found in much of the emic literature and which I now go on to consider in greater detail.

Insider Accounts of Mediumship

Published spiritualist literature

The ambiguous nature of mediumship, and the difficulties of determining what is happening when a medium is working, are subjects actively debated within Spiritualism. Maurice Barbanell's book *This is Spiritualism* (originally published in 1959) is one that is often recommended by Spiritualists. Both Barbanell and his wife, Sylvia, were prominent Spiritualist writers during the mid-twentieth century. In addition, Barbanell was the medium through whom a lengthy series of books attributed to a spirit guide called Silver Birch were produced.[4] Barbanell poses, and goes on to answer, the question,

> What happens when a medium enters the trance state and willingly surrenders control of her body to a spirit guide? The action is always a voluntary one, for the essence of mediumship is that the medium is the mistress of her own physical being. (2001 [1959], p. 77)

Spiritualist practice seeks to prevent uninvited or uncontrolled possession. Indeed the word 'possession' itself is rarely in use in Spiritualist discourse and seems to be resisted, possibly because of the often negative connotations that it has carried in Western culture.[5] Despite this, it seems to be widely accepted within Spiritualism that mediumship involves some form of spirit 'control', which is often termed 'overshadowing'. Speaking of a well-known mid-twentieth-century medium, Barbanell goes on to tell us that

> I asked Helen Hughes to describe her reactions as she went into trance and came out of it. The process is akin to falling asleep, she said. As a preparation, she relaxes physically and mentally; she becomes aware of a

gradual drugging of her consciousness which reminds her of the sensations accompanying the inhalation of chloroform. (2001 [1959], p. 77)

This description contains an implicit suggestion that mediumistic communication involves achieving some form of trance state. Through my participation at Portobello Spiritualist Church, I have learnt that the nature of 'trance' mediumship is a topic of continuing interest to Spiritualists and a frequent subject of conversation. It is often acknowledged that trance states can vary widely in their 'depth' or 'completeness', so that the deeper or more complete the trance state is, the less likely it is that the medium will be aware of what occurs while that state is maintained. So is Drury correct to depict mediumship as an unconscious activity that the medium has no memory of? Barbanell goes on to tell us that the medium 'returns to normality with the feeling of having travelled from some distant place' (2001 [1959], p. 77). Furthermore, Barbanell maintains that

The number of mediums who are completely unconscious while under spirit control is comparatively small. . . . Some say they listen to the communication coming through them, but they seem to be standing some distance away from themselves. . . . A few are conscious of experiencing 'out-of-the-body' travels and are able to narrate what they have seen and heard in distant places. (2001 [1959], pp. 78–9)

We have here a wide variation in what is often said to be the 'degree' or 'level' of trance achieved. As mentioned, this is also referred to as the degree of overshadowing or of control, descriptions which appear to indicate variation in the degree of awareness maintained by the medium.

A very influential figure in the Spiritualist movement of the mid-twentieth century was the healer Harry Edwards. In his *Guide for the Development of Mediumship*, Edwards tells us that 'trance states can vary from 1 per cent to 99 per cent' (2003, p. 10), by which he appears to indicate the maintenance of some degree of awareness during a trance state. The reference to 99 per cent as being the fullest possible extent of a trance state suggests that Edwards took the view that the trance state, at least as practised within Spiritualism, is never characterized by a complete lack of awareness on the part of the medium. For this reason, both Barbanell and Edwards maintain that 'pure' spirit communication is not possible because it is a human 'instrument' that is being used, the nature and identity of which cannot be entirely displaced.

In a 2009 work by a well-known contemporary British medium, Gordon Smith, entitled *Developing Mediumship*, we find a heavy emphasis on the need to develop and maintain awareness:

> The first thing to be aware of when trying to link with Spirit are the same set of sensations that will occur each time you sit. For me it was the feeling of having a fine wispy beard, the sense of wearing a robe type of garment, and also my hands would move slowly, as if performing some type of Tai Chi. . . . The deeper a medium can allow him or herself to go into trance, the more receptive they become to the feelings of the personality of the Spirit people who overshadow them and wish to come through. (Smith 2009, p. 31)

However trance might be defined, it implies more than a simple loss of consciousness and is, I argue, a heightened state of awareness. Whatever the attraction of past stereotypes, there are strong indications that the medium is never entirely unconscious and, indeed, cannot be. There are many accounts by insiders in which they claim they do not fully remember what transpired while working mediumistically, but claims to remember nothing at all are very rare. It is also important to note that within Spiritualism I have often come across mediums using the term 'trance' to refer in a casual way to a mediumistic state that involves limited or partial recall. It cannot be assumed that references to trance are intended to indicate a lack of awareness. Thus I contend that references to trance in Spiritualist literature need to be treated with care.

There is support for this view in Harry Boddington's *The University of Spiritualism* (1947).[6] Boddington observes that 'during early development, the sensations induced often lead to widely divergent conclusions' (1947, p. 191). In my own experience of giving platform demonstrations in Spiritualist churches, the information I communicate to members of the congregation is not recalled in the same way as I recall my own memories. What happens during a demonstration of mediumship can afterwards seem more difficult to recall, and yet, during the demonstration, the experience is brighter and more vivid in the mind. I can therefore sympathize with those mediums who say that their memory of what happened while working is patchy, but I resist the suggestion that trance necessarily entails a lack of consciousness. What we have instead might be said to be degrees of trance, or degrees of depth in the mediumistic state. This may be better represented as a spectrum across which particular examples of mediumship can be ranged, according to how slight or complete the degree of trance is.

This is consistent with a view I have repeatedly encountered in Spiritualism, which is that every medium works differently. The understanding appears to be that because every medium is a unique personality, she or he represents an 'instrument' that differs in its inherent qualities and attributes from any other. Furthermore, mediumship is understood as a collaborative effort between spirit and medium, so that information from the spirit world can be passed into the physical or natural world. This information is said to be mediated or even limited by the characteristics of the particular medium. In this connection, there is a sense that maintaining a fuller degree of trance will allow 'spirit' to be expressed more fully, and consequently, to some extent overcome the limitations of the medium.

For Boddington, the 'ideal' mode of mediumistic communication that developing mediums should seek to achieve is to 'pass through unconscious control to conscious co-operation', on the basis that 'entrancement by . . . spirit guides is a frequent preliminary to general unfoldment of psychic powers' (1947, pp. 192, 196). Boddington's suggestion is that differences of interpretation in how mediumship works can be made sense of by understanding the process of mediumistic development as one that proceeds in stages. The line of development Boddington proposes is one that begins with unconscious control or overshadowing and which progresses to conscious co-operation or participation:

> We must not therefore misunderstand the peculiar meaning attached to the word 'passive'. It is your own subconscious interference that has to be subordinated or 'passified'. Hence, there are stages in passive development which would be better defined as 'well-regulated activity'. It is by no means mental laziness or stupor. You actually become 'selective' and distinguish your own creations from extraneous thought. Consciousness is active, though apparently quiescent. (Boddington 1947, p. 202)

So what is the nature of this participation? What is the Spiritualist understanding of the craft or mechanism that enables mediumistic communication as a collaborative effort? Are there sources we might draw upon to overcome the difficulty in identifying what is going on in the process of mediumistic development and/or demonstration?

James Padgett's 'inspired' explanation of mediumship

It is at this point that I wish to consider the work of the medium James Padgett, which contains the most detailed account of the workings of

Spiritualist mediumship that I have found in the emic literature. To my knowledge, Padgett is not widely known within the British Spiritualist movement outside Spiritualist circles in southern England, but there has been interest in his writings at Portobello Spiritualist Church in Edinburgh. There are many other examples of this kind of material, but I use Padgett because it articulates particularly well the understanding taught in the development circle I attended at Portobello Spiritualist Church during the period 2003 to 2007. Appropriately perhaps for an attorney (patent lawyer), Padgett's mediumistic activity took the form of what is often termed 'automatic' or trance writing, rather than any form of verbal demonstration. His mediumistic writings began in 1914, continued until his death in 1923, and were published in a series of four volumes from 1958 to 1972.

Padgett's writings take the form of letters or messages to Padgett from various individuals 'in spirit', including deceased relatives, friends, historical figures, and others unknown either to history or to Padgett. A great many of the messages stress the need for Padgett to get himself into what is referred to as 'the right condition' so as to enable these messages to come through more clearly and to enable messages of a more spiritual nature to be given. But what is meant by 'the right condition'? This seems to be meant as an encouragement for Padgett to develop his own spiritual nature by seeking divine love through prayer, thereby becoming at one with God. Indeed, there is a highly developed theology based upon this theme that comes through from the material, and which maintains a high degree of internal consistency over the period during which the letters were written.

I have identified three messages which describe in more detail what are termed the 'laws of rapport and communication' (Padgett 1965, p. 216). These letters support the view that the mind of each medium is a particular instrument with inherent characteristics, and is not simply a blank slate upon which anything may be written. In one letter, the explanation given is that 'a high thought cannot be transmitted through a human brain which is not in the condition that qualifies it to receive the thought' (Padgett 1965, p. 220). The suggestion is that there is variation in the nature of the information it is possible to express mediumistically, because of the individual character of each medium. Thus we are told that

The rapport of the spirit with the human is determined by the development of the brain and the moral qualities of the human at the time the rapport is attempted . . . The possibility of rapport, and the kind thereof, lie at the foundation of mediumship, and determines and limits the power of the spirit to convey its thoughts and the capacity of the mortal to receive them. . . . Hence, you will in a way understand why so few of the higher spiritual truths have ever been delivered to the world through . . . mediumship. . . . And this . . . will explain to you why the same spirit may communicate through several mediums, and yet the communications be of a dissimilar character; (Padgett 1965, p. 221)

Mediums, then, are highly variable instruments of communication, through whom communications are transmitted in a way that is always, in a sense, partial. My experience as a member of a Spiritualist development circle is that trainees are actively discouraged from copying other mediums, even those whose mediumship is highly regarded. There is active encouragement to develop one's own 'link' or rapport with one's own guides or spirit helpers and this limits what can be taught explicitly by existing mediums. There is, however, a high degree of both express and implicit tutoring; in particular, normality and ordinariness are emphasized, in contrast to some of the more flamboyant forms of mediumship of the past (which were in themselves often excused on the basis of 'spirit control').[7]

An example of participant-observation

According to the guidance given at Portobello Spiritualist Church, sitting 'in circle'[8] involves sitting quietly in a meditative state, with or without music (according to the circle leader's preference), and in maintaining an internal focus and being attentive to what one might be 'shown' by spirit. Characteristic of the early stages of development is the sitters' inability to distinguish between that which they are being shown and thoughts or images that are the product of their own imagination. Gradually, however, there develops a sense of a difference in 'feeling tone' between the two. If the information seems to be intended for another person in the circle, it is shared with that person in order to obtain feedback. Gradually, the developing medium becomes more confident in their ability to discern information of a spiritual origin. As the developing medium becomes more confident in their ability to maintain that state of awareness over an extended period, opportunities to work in public are arranged, usually under the guidance of a more experienced medium.

Whether drawing upon my own experience, or that of other Spiritualists I have had discussions with, or the literary sources available within Spiritualism, what is made clear to me is that mediumship is not simply a matter of surrendering one's conscious control. At Portobello Spiritualist Church the process of development as a medium involves regular reminders that the medium is stronger than spirit, always has the ability to bring proceedings to an end, and must not abdicate responsibility for what occurs when working as a medium. It is a truism in the Spiritualist movement that there is no such thing as a fully developed medium, and that the process of development continues for as long as the medium continues working. It is widely acknowledged that 'every one is an original', that different mediums are instruments suited to different purposes. Although it is one spirit world, it will be glimpsed differently through the different openings offered by different mediums.

The suggestion that the nature of the medium's mind is relevant, and that the medium is, in some degree, always 'present', whatever the degree of overshadowing achieved, is consistent with my experience of Spiritualist practice. Broadly, I argue that Spiritualism can be defined as a shamanism in which an altered state of awareness is used to communicate with spirits, specifically for the purpose of demonstrating personal survival beyond death. That particular purpose to which Spiritualists put mediumship, along with other aspects such as its modern, Western, urban cultural setting and relative disregard of animal or elemental spirits, makes Spiritualism appear more different from (other) shamanism(s) than it actually is. The Spiritualist understanding of mediumship is that the medium is an active participant as well as an instrument. Mediumship is an activity in which the practitioner chooses whether or not to engage, and during which the practitioner not only remains aware, in varying degree, of what is happening but must actively achieve the 'link' or rapport that will enable communication. Thus one comes across expressions such as 'getting the link', 'making the connection', 'working with spirit' and 'blending with spirit'.

Within Spiritualism, this link can be used in a variety of ways. The two forms of mediumship most commonly encountered when visiting Spiritualist churches are public or 'platform' demonstrations, which involve the medium giving a personal message from someone in spirit, and spiritual or 'hands-on' healing. However, there is a much wider range of applications of mediumship. If we look at a 1938 account of mediumship by the well-known medium Horace Leaf, we find a wide variety of 'forms' of mediumship, including psychometry, telepathy, clairvoyance, clairaudience, healing, telekinesis, direct voice,[9] materializations, automatic and impressional writing, controlled speaking, and astral projection or travelling. To the list of particular applications of mediumship, we might also add psychic art (of which Coral Polge was a noted exponent[10]) and clairsentience, a term that seems to have come into use to indicate an awareness of sensations, rather than visual or auditory information.

In terms of my experience of Spiritualism, this is a classic exposition of the applications of mediumship, from which it becomes apparent that journeying (or astral projection, as it is usually referred to in Spiritualism) is simply one option among many. From the Spiritualist perspective, journeying is simply one available means of bringing useful information back into this world from the world of spirit.

Spiritualism and Shamanism: Similarities in Place of Differences

The mediumistic repertoire is well established and widely written about in emic literature. Although the forms of mediumistic activity may seem varied, Spiritualist mediumship retains a focus on the goal of demonstrating personal survival beyond death.[11] This is why mediums are encouraged to use their mediumship to obtain information about the dead, rather than about the living. The process of entering the mediumistic state is less well documented. Many examples of shamanism involve elaborate ritual preparations, which may involve drumming, dance or the performance of other repetitive actions, perhaps combined with the consumption of alcohol or other entheogens.[12] In Spiritualism, by contrast, preparation for entering the mediumistic state is more akin to meditation, with very little in the way of external signifiers that can be described objectively. Spiritualist mediumship is characterized by the practice of a controlled, meditative state of awareness, and many of the outwardly visible signs of entering trance to be found in other shamanic settings are, to all intents and purposes, absent.

Observing such outward differences can divert attention from the similarities that are to be found in insider accounts of the inner experience of shamanic and Spiritualist practice. In order to demonstrate that similarity, I draw upon MaryCatherine Burgess's 2008 work *A New Paradigm of Spirituality and Religion: Contemporary Shamanic Practice in Scotland*. Burgess states that:

I define spirit possession for a shaman as a conscious and voluntary choice to enter a trance-like state in order to unite with a spirit in a type of role-taking experience of intimate partnership that facilitates communication with the spirit . . . In this, the shaman is not completely overtaken or controlled, but retains choice and consciousness. (2008, p. 97)

On the basis of both my experience of Spiritualism and other insider accounts, this is an accurate description of mediumship. In February 2009, I attended a demonstration of mediumship given at Portobello Spiritualist Church by a well-known Scottish medium during which she gave a brief explanation of mediumship. The medium explained that 'I shift my awareness so as to be able to perceive spirit.' One aspect of the characterization of shamans as controlling, and mediums as controlled, has been the view that shamans control spirits whereas spirits control mediums. Burgess reminds us that in shamanism, as in Spiritualism, the issue of control is one for the practitioner because it is fundamentally an issue of self-control, not self-surrender.

Two things that appear different about Spiritualism are its persistent use of mediumship in the effort to demonstrate the continuing life of the soul (of personal survival beyond death) and a singularly undemonstrative approach to entering the trance or mediumistic state. Beyond that, and other more obvious characteristics of different cultural settings, it becomes increasingly difficult to distinguish Spiritualism and shamanism. Any claim that the difference lies in the fact that shamans (in the Eliadean model) typically go travelling, whereas mediums allow spirits to express themselves through them, seems difficult to sustain. There has, moreover, often been a sense of some connection between shamanic practice and mediumship. For instance, for Eliade, oracular mediumistic activity is an occasional feature of shamanic practice (1964, pp. 347, 370), and a recent example of a more inclusive approach is Roger Walsh's *The World of Shamanism* (2007), which includes a chapter on mediums as 'channels for the spirits' as part of his exploration of shamanic cosmology.

In support of this approach, I again draw attention to Burgess's work in which she develops a cross-cultural model of shamanism. The elements of her model are (1) vocation and initiation, (2) cosmology, (3) soul flight/ journeying, (4) shamanic consciousness, (5) spiritual allies, (6) soul healing and (7) community support. It is significant that each of these is found, in some form, in Spiritualism, and a comprehensive discussion of these elements would certainly provide a useful account of Spiritualism. But in order to develop a comprehensive account of contemporary Spiritualism by using such a model, there are additional elements that need to be taken into account, and which I shall now explain.

In Spiritualism, initiation is not so much an event but a process of apprenticeship or development, which can be lengthy indeed, and depends upon the particular application of mediumship sought. However, there do seem to be 'phases' in the process of development that can seem to be almost initiatory in their significance or difficulty. One aspect of medium-istic development is managing painful feelings of vulnerability or exposure that arise as a result of heightened awareness. Developing mediums often describe feeling as though they are being pulled apart and remade. The Rev. Bernice Winstanley, former Minister of Portobello Church, expressed the opinion in conversation with me that every developing medium goes through a phase where they feel exposed and sensitive, as though (in her words) 'your nerves are on the outside of your skin'.

As we have seen, the practice of 'soul flight' or 'journeying' has achieved particular prominence in shamanic studies as a result of Eliade's represen-tation of shamanic practice. As I have shown, the Spiritualist understanding is that this is simply one possible characterization of mediumistic ability. The Spiritualist movement places priority on the demonstration of per-sonal survival beyond death and is willing to use mediumship in such ways as will serve that purpose. The expectation that Spiritualist mediums primarily 'talk to spirit people' on behalf of the living leads to a collaborative understanding of mediumship that is, like any conversation, both passive and active.

Spiritual healing is a significant activity within Spiritualism, yet it is often overlooked. Many mediums choose to work as healers in preference to practising other forms of mediumship. Soul healing gives a certain specificity to shamanism: by contrast, spiritual healing, as practised within Spiritualism, may variously be directed at the physical and spiritual bodies as well as the soul or spirit.[13] The element of community support is also a crucial one within Spiritualism. It is, in my experience, extremely rare (but not unknown) for an individual to develop mediumistic abilities other than in a development circle. Thereafter, Spiritualist congregations or other groups become the significant 'places' where a mediumistic career can be pursued.

As I have explored the Spiritualist–shamanic comparison, commonality of practice becomes increasingly obvious, just as it has become apparent that the traditional, 'passive' characterization of Spiritualist mediumship is partial and misleading. It is arguably significant that the language of sham-anism should lend itself so well to an exposition of Spiritualism: significant because it challenges the tendency to perceive shamanic and mediumistic practices as fundamentally different. Indeed, there are those who question whether it is possible to maintain clear boundaries, not only between mediumship and shamanism, also but between mediumship and other possession practices. In *The Self Possessed* (2006) Frederick Smith makes use of Peter Claus's distinction between spirit possession and spirit mediumship, the latter being 'the legitimate expected possession of a specialist by a spirit' (Smith 2006, p. 65): this description comes some way towards the Spiritualist self-understanding. However, I hope I have shown enough to indicate why Spiritualists resist the idea that the medium is controlled during his or her possession, and why they prefer instead to explain the practice in terms of the medium seeking to achieve a connection or rapport (so that the medium enters a particular state of consciousness in order to enable communication).

For Boddington, 'The majority of our best mediums pass through [unaware] trance states to inspiration of a higher order' (1947, p. 240). In Spiritualism, modern Anglo-American culture has given rise to a religious movement that regards itself as having developed skills in the use of trance that are specifically intended to prevent outright possession, by maintaining throughout some level of awareness or continuing presence on the part of the practitioner. Not only does this assist in our understanding of Spiritualist mediumship but it should also encourage us to look again at the trance-like aspects of shamanic initiations, encourage us to explore initiation as a process rather than an event, and to reassess the full extent of the 'passive' skills and practices available to shamanic practitioners.

Notes

[1] That is not to overlook the importance of Spiritualism in other European countries such as Iceland (e.g. Swatos and Gissurarson 1997); nor is it to overlook the importance of Spiritism, particularly in Brazil. Spiritism is a term that has become associated with a spiritual healing movement comprising lodges or spiritual communities whose activities are based upon principles derived from automatic writings produced by the Frenchman Allan Kardec (1804–69). Unlike Spiritualism, Spiritism maintains the formal teaching of reincarnation, claiming that it was once a key element of Christian belief; also, Spiritism has a clear focus on spiritual healing as its principal form of mediumship. The public and private use of mediumship to demonstrate personal survival beyond death and to maintain personal relationships between the living and those who have 'passed over', which is a characteristic feature of Spiritualism, is not evident in Spiritism. Although Spiritualism and Spiritism have settled into two distinct movements, there remains considerable similarity between the two.

[2] The phrase 'platform demonstration' derives from the tendency in Spiritualist churches to have a raised platform or dais from which the service is conducted,

and from which readings, addresses and demonstrations of mediumship are given. Thus a medium might be said to be 'a platform worker' or 'on the platform' as a way of indicating that she gives public demonstrations of mediumship in Spiritualist churches. Similarly, even in churches where there is no actual platform, figurative reference might still be made to 'the platform' or 'the platform party' as a way of indicating those involved in the conduct of the service.

3 In January 2003, I began attending the development circle at Portobello Spiritualist Church in Edinburgh and remained a member until June 2007 (the development circle is essentially the church's teaching forum). Since September 2005, I have undertaken platform demonstrations across Scotland. In October 2008, I was invited to lead the development circle at a church in Perth and have thus become one of the Spiritualist movement's teachers. My participation in the movement has exposed me to a range of unwritten teachings, personal histories and opinions that constitute an additional set of insider texts to draw upon, in addition to published memoirs of mediums and other accounts of involvement in the Spiritualist movement, such as the histories and reflections of officials of Spiritualist churches and other organizations.

4 The writings attributed to Silver Birch are extensive and have been very influential within the British Spiritualist movement from the mid-twentieth century onwards.

5 An interesting account of the preoccupation with distinguishing demonic possession is Moshe Sluhovsky's 2007 work on the changing European concept of possession in the early modern period, *Believe Not Every Spirit*.

6 Married to a famous medium, Harry Boddington was a very influential writer on Spiritualism during the middle of the twentieth century.

7 Owen describes female mediums of the 1870s as introducing 'new, thrilling, and daring phenomena and a theatrical style of mediumship which emphasised visual spectacle and display' (1989, p. 41). Even into the 1940s, the mediumship of mediums such as Helen Duncan was known for the physical manifestations that were claimed, even though much of her work involved the 'giving of messages from spirit' and was much more akin to the more routine nature of much twenty-first century mediumship.

8 It is standard usage within Spiritualism to refer to 'sitting in circle', as a way of referring to the fact that someone is a member of a development group. The reference derives from the established practice of arranging members of the group in a circle but the group may still be referred to as a 'circle' regardless of the activity undertaken at any particular meeting.

9 'Direct voice' is a shorthand reference to a form of oracular mediumship where the medium is overshadowed by spirit to the point where the sound of the medium's voice changes. In Spiritualist practice, it is generally assumed the changed voice is that of the spirit communicant and that this indicates a closer 'link', often leading to the further assumption that information can more readily be relied upon as being the 'authentic' voice of spirit. This form of mediumship is often explained in terms of a fuller or deeper form of trance that allows spirit to come through more clearly, the idea being that the psychological characteristics of the medium cause less distortion because the medium is much less aware and, therefore, less 'present'.

[10] See, for example, her biography, *Living Images* (Polge 1985).

[11] On the basis of her participation in Spiritualist development circles in England and California, Burke Forrest felt this focus to be more evident in British practice than in American.

[12] Eliade noted the use of alcohol and tobacco among Siberian shamans but regarded their use as 'a recent innovation' that indicated 'a decadence in shamanic technique' (1964, p. 401). Jakobsen feels that other drug use is primarily a feature of (North and South) American shamanism and also notes the use of alcohol by female shamans in South Korea (1999, p. 12).

[13] In Spiritualist thinking, the soul is regarded as retaining a spiritual body or aura when separated from the physical body at death. For example, Barbanell tells us, of the dead, that 'In their new state they express themselves through the spirit bodies that they always possessed' (2001, p. 16).

Bibliography

Anderson, R. (2005), *The Ghosts of Iceland*. Belmont, CA: Thomson Wadsworth.

Barbanell, M. (2001 [1959]), *This is Spiritualism* (revised edn). Oxshott: Spiritual Truth Press.

Boddington, H. (1947), *The University of Spiritualism*. London: Spiritualist Press.

Burgess, M. (2008), *A New Paradigm of Spirituality and Religion: Contemporary Shamanic Practice in Scotland*. London: Continuum.

Drury, N. (1982), *The Shaman and the Magician*. London: Arkana.

Edwards, H. (2003), *A Guide for the Development of Mediumship* (revised edn). Greenford: Con-Psy Publications.

Eliade, M. (1964), *Shamanism: Archaic Techniques of Ecstasy*. London: Routledge.

Forrest, B. (1986), 'Apprentice-Participation: "Methodology and the Study of Subjective Reality"', *Urban Life*, 14 (4), 431–53.

Hazelgrove, J. (2000), *Spiritualism and British Society between the Wars*. Manchester: Manchester University Press.

Jakobsen, M. D. (1999), *Shamanism: Traditional and Contemporary Approaches to the Mastery of Spirits and Healing*. Oxford: Berghahn Books.

Leaf, H. (1937), *What Mediumship Is*. London: Spiritualist Press.

Lewis, I. M. (2003), *Ecstatic Religion: A Study of Shamanism and Spirit Possession* (3rd edn). London: Routledge.

Martin, B. (1970), 'The Spiritualist Meeting', *Sociological Yearbook of Religion in Britain*, 146–61. SCM Press, London.

Nelson, G. K. (1969), *Spiritualism and Society*. London: Routledge & Kegan Paul.

Owen, A. (1989), *The Darkened Room: Women, Power, and Spiritualism in Late Victorian England*. Chicago: University of Chicago Press.

Padgett, J. (1965), *True Gospel Revealed Anew by Jesus, Vol. II*. Washington, DC: Foundation Church of the New Birth.

Polge, C. (1985), *Living Images: The Story of a Psychic Artist*. London: Regency Press.

Skultans, V. (1974), *Intimacy and Ritual: A Study of Spiritualism, Mediums and Groups*. London: Routledge.

Sluhovsky, M. (2007), *Believe Not Every Spirit: Possession, Mysticism, & Discernment in Early Modern Catholicism.* Chicago: University of Chicago Press.

Smith, F. (2006), *The Self Possessed: Deity and Spirit Possession in South Asian Literature and Civilization.* New York: Columbia University Press.

Smith, G. (2009), *Developing Mediumship: Transforming Self.* London: Hay House.

Swatos, W. H. and Gissurarson, L. R. (1997), *Icelandic Spiritualism: Mediumship and Modernity in Iceland.* New Brunswick, NJ: Transaction Publishers.

Wallis, R. J. (2003), *Shamans/Neo-Shamans: Ecstasy, Alternative Archaeologies and Contemporary Pagans.* London: Routledge.

Walsh, R. (2007), *The World of Shamanism: New Views of an Ancient Tradition.* Woodbury, MN: Llewellyn Publications.

Winter, J. (1995), *Sites of Memory, Sites of Mourning.* Cambridge: Cambridge University Press.

Chapter 12

To Perform Possession and to be Possessed in Performance: The Actor, the Medium and an 'Other'

Sarah Goldingay

I know I'm here, sitting on this sofa, but I'm also there – drowning. My eyes are closed here, but I can see through her [the dead person's] eyes too.

J., Medium
(Goldingay 2006a)

I felt as if it was the energy of Mrs. Hardcastle that was leading me, and that all I had to do was get out of the way.

B., Actor
(Goldingay 2006b)

Since the 1970s performance studies scholars – usually from the USA and Europe – have been conducting *inter*cultural performance ethnographies of rites involving spirit possession.[1] They have drawn on analytical frameworks developed initially for the investigation of explicitly theatrical or dramatic performances – considering the event's creation, enactment, delivery and reception – in order to understand better the context in which they witnessed the spirit possession event. Here, however, rather than taking a similarly *inter*cultural approach, I am going to take an *intra*cultural approach by considering some of the findings of a six-month study I conducted into the work of a UK-based group of psychic mediums, the Soul Rescue Group, who, by working with states of full- and partial-trance at their bi-weekly séances, became channels for the dead. They performed these altruistic interventions in order to facilitate the transition of 'trapped souls' from a postulated 'limbo' onto the 'Realms of Spirit'. The soul-rescue process, which the group has been following since its 1991 foundation in response to the Gulf War, is described by the group's convenor Michael Evans in *Billy Grows up in Spirit: A Cockney Lad Returns After Death To Tell His Story* (1997).

[F]or me, the evidence that there is Life after Death [. . .] is overwhelming. Yet I have found that some people do get stuck after death and remain 'earth bound' until they are rescued, whether by helpers on the other side [the realm of spirits] or by a rescue group on earth. Because, after death, people find themselves in a spirit body which is exactly like the earth body they have just left, some do not realise that they have died and they try to go on living as before. [. . .] Our mediums go into trance so that the spirit can speak to us through him and in quite a short time he [the spirit] agrees to move on to his proper place in the next world. (Evans 1997, p. 1)

Evans is describing how the medium enters a state of trance to become the vessel of communication by which the 'stuck' dead soul can speak with the living rescue-group. The group then facilitate the soul's acceptance of the death of their physical body thereby enabling them to move on into the Realm of Spirit.

As an actor myself, this *intracultural* study gave me a further avenue for research beyond working with the Soul Rescue Group. It presented me with an opportunity to reverse the traditional premise of a performance ethnography that asks, what might be revealed about this event and its context if it were analysed *as if* it were a performance?[2] It enabled me to investigate, with my colleagues as respondents, what might be revealed about acting if it were analysed as a process more akin to mediumship. That is to say, one that uses trance-based processes to allow its practitioners to become a vessel for an 'other' in order to enable this 'other' to communicate with those who watch. I wondered, is acting in part a process of possession and possession in part a performance, and moreover, what it is to perform possession and to be possessed in a performance?

In order to begin to answer these questions in a contemporary British context, I established a dialectic of interviews; the first of these being with J., one of the Soul Rescue Group's partial-trance mediums, and the second with professional actor B. I found strong resonances in J.'s description of channelling as a medium with the way the actor B. explained her embodied, 'transcendent' performances. In their interviews, the respondents described their non-ordinary experiences of channelling an 'other' and identified the importance of their own continuing self-development.

For both of them this took the form of embodied, imaginative and non-ordinary consciousness skills training. In this chapter, I will examine how they used these skills during a performance in order to sustain the conditions that enable an audience to perceive an otherwise unseen entity, the 'other'. Both respondents described this state as being an 'optimal state', which, I suggest, contains within it three distinct, but overlapping, states of consciousness. In the second half of the chapter, I will explore these states in detail; describing how they are constructed of elements I will term 'the pedestrian-self', 'the technical-self' and 'the self-as-other'. But, before we go on to consider these constituent parts of an optimum state of performance, I would like first to clarify my position on some of the ethical and methodological issues raised by placing performance and mediumship in a dialectic.

Truth and Authenticity: 'He's a Good Medium, but Frankly . . . He's a Bit of a Showman'

The process of comparing mediumship and acting is immediately problematic: the threads of belief, fraud and authenticity are intimately interwoven. Traditionally, the interrelationship of actors and mediums has been described in polar ways. On the one hand, those who are cynical of a medium's ability to communicate with the dead refer to the clairvoyant's public performances of psychic skill as merely 'acting'.[3] Here, the term is taken to be equivalent with fraudulence and pretence; ostensibly a means of extorting money from the gullible. On the other hand, those who believe in the psychic's ability to communicate with the dead describe mediums, who are for them less skilled or perhaps less 'authentic' than other psychics, as 'overly theatrical'. This second position was exemplified for me by one of the Soul Rescue Group's regular séance sitters. She explained – as we were discussing the work of a platform medium I had seen in the previous week – 'He's a good medium, but frankly . . . he's a bit of a showman' (Goldingay 2006c). In this statement the apparent binary of truth and fraudulence collapses, as authenticity and inauthenticity are simultaneously embodied by the fallible, but gifted, psychic.

Actors too continue to be treated with suspicion, perhaps because they also necessarily embody two states simultaneously – the real and the pretend. Beyond a historical (and perhaps continuing) reputation for being mystic, mysterious and morally lax, Michael Mangan suggests they test the 'boundaries of the human' by intentionally shifting between the real and the pretend, the natural and the supernatural (2007, pp. 76–96). This testing of the boundaries of the human is something both respondents identified in their interviews, and in acknowledgement of this resonance, I will be describing both actor and medium as performers.[4] This is not in order to undermine their roles or beliefs, or to make universal claims for the processes at work, but to highlight the connections in their practices of embodied communication.

Actors, like mediums, carry out a complex negotiation between performance events and belief-structures. B. describes her optimal performances in metaphysical terms. But not all actors would describe their experiences of training, rehearsal and performance as spiritual. Many of us train in practices like yoga and tai chi, which were originally developed in an apparently religious context, but do not, necessarily, adhere to the sacred qualities attributed to these practices. This removal of performer training methods from their religious context is problematic for some, who argue that without this spiritual framework the training is misunderstood, and therefore its efficacy diluted. As a consequence there is a complex range of vocabulary and practice at the interface where spirituality meets the acting profession and its associated academic discourses: terms like trance, the shamanic actor and finding transcendence have become mainstream terminology.[5]

Both performers enable the audience to perceive an 'other', but they understand the term in different ways. For J., as a medium, the 'other' is the energy of a trapped soul that is, for her, very real. For B. the 'other' is a character. In earlier theatre or drama scholarship 'character' might have been seen as merely a fiction, a product of the author. However, for more recent performance theorists, this term forms the catalytic centre of complex discussion. Character is interpreted differently across different performance genres and cultures. The distance between actor and character is no longer fixed in a binary opposition, but placed along a shifting continuum. Performances require different things from their actors: sometimes that they should perform themselves, sometimes that they should 'empty' themselves and become 'neutral' in order to fully embody their character – or to allow their character to fully embody them. (And here it is interesting to note a resonance with classic descriptions of the female medium as an empty vessel.) Increasingly, theatre events require actors to perform both themselves as 'actor' (or perhaps their everyday, pedestrian-self) and an 'other' in the same performance. Thus, the relationship between where the actor ends and character begins is not fixed but porous.[6]

I am not suggesting that B. perceives her character to be 'real' in the same way that J. experiences the trapped soul: their individual frameworks of contextualizing beliefs and understandings are different. But, in B.'s case, character is not as prosaic as the traditional view of the term might suggest. She describes her 'other' as an energetic construction that is formed of elements of the self, of the text, and of direct spiritual intervention, or inspiration. And therefore, although J.'s description of the trapped soul is not directly interchangeable with B.'s description of character, there are significant points of resonance between the experiences of both respondents.

Performance too is an ambiguous term. Its definition and usage continues to be a significant topic for discussion in theatre, drama and performance studies scholarship. And these discourses are, at times, at odds with the way the term is used in social sciences or anthropology. I will be using it in two ways. First, in a narrow sense, to describe an event and a process, rather than a fixed object of analysis; that is to say, the respondent's enactments of embodied processes set apart in space and time where the audience and actor directly interact. But these processes can only be fully understood in the context of a second, broader sense of the word. Therefore, I will also be using 'performance' as an organizing concept that includes the performers' expectations and personal narratives, their pre-performance training and emotional responses, in addition to the events' surrounding and constructing ideological contexts. This is in order to utilize the term's ability to describe something that is not inside or outside a given temporal boundary, but a continuum of creative exchange and influence.

Ephemerality and ambiguity, belief and make-believe, exist at the very heart of the performer–audience dialogue. This is because performers ask the audience to suspend disbelief, at least for a time, in order to treat what they experience as being provisionally 'authentic'.[7] Audiences at performances of mediumship bring different expectations with them to their reading of the event. Believers, who are performing or watching, are sure that what the audience experiences is not make-believe, but belief at work; while for audience members who are certain that they are witnessing a fiction, what takes place on stage is only make-believe. This dialectic suggests that demonstrations of psychic mediumship are on one level – at the level of the spectator – either real or pretend depending on the audience members' existing belief-structures. However, this clarity of binary conviction does not exist for many of those who watch. For these uncertain spectators, potentially, both cases are simultaneously true. As a colleague put it to me:

'I don't believe what they do, but I'd still hope for a message from my Mum.' Moreover, in a further challenge to this binary, some theatres too ask audiences to believe that what they see on stage is not make-believe but, in fact, an accurate recreation of the words of a real person – a verbatim account of a real event. All performance is a complex of change between the performance's construction and intended purpose, the actions of the performer, and the expectations of the audience. Through their relationship to the supernatural, performances of trance and possession highlight these mechanisms at work.

In the next section of this chapter, I am going to introduce the interviews I held with B. and J. into this fluid network of belief and make-believe, performer and other, real and pretend. This is in order to understand how during their performances, which by testing the boundaries of the human enable the audience to perceive an otherwise invisible other, they actively intervene into their non-ordinary states of consciousness. They do this in order to create and sustain the conditions for an optimal performance which are constituted of elements I will be terming the 'pedestrian-self', 'the technical-self' and 'the self-as-other'.

Optimum States: True-Trance and Transcendence

Both respondents describe how their 'sense of self' is simultaneously unified and fragmented within the performance process, that the success of their performance is predicated on their ability to sustain a unity of self in response to this potential fragmentation and, moreover, that their sense of self contains multiple and multi-faceted plural-selves which have different purposes and motivations. This multiplicity is identified by both B. and J., who explain that during a performance event they have a simultaneous awareness of different 'selves': their 'pedestrian-self', 'technical-self', and 'self-as-other'.

In this model the 'pedestrian' characterizes a residual awareness of the quotidian in the performer, their sense of a continuing everyday, ordinary world and body beyond the boundaries of the performance, whereas the 'other' is the performer's awareness of a non-ordinary, heightened-self that is closely connected to a supernatural force. These selves compete for finite cognitive resources and therefore need to be prioritized and managed through the application of a series of pre-performance training approaches and pre-performance preparation practices. The technical-self, the third element of the performer's sense of self, makes these interventions during the performance in an attempt to prevent fracture. Such a fracture does not lead to a permanent schism in the performer's unified self; it simply means that conditions in the performance which sustain the more fragile, transient 'other' are lost. However, if the technical-self is successful, these interventions enable the respondent to reach, and sustain, a particular state of sought-after perfection; optimal performance. For J. this perfection is being in a state of 'full-trance', and for B. it is being in a state of 'transcendent performance' (Goldingay 2006a; 2006b).

These utopian states have two key outcomes for the performer. First, to achieve them is an expression of the performer's virtuosic skill. And second, they provide fixed points of control around which the fluid performance can continue to evolve and change over time. However, these states are unstable and both respondents have only glimpsed or had fleeting experiences of them in the past: B. has reached her optimal transcendent state, whereas J. has only seen full-trance in others. But J. has achieved a stable state of partial-trance where she simultaneously sustains an awareness of her pedestrian-self as well as her self-as-other. And, although this means she is able to explain her experiences with greater clarity after the event, this partial-state remains problematic because, for her, full-trance is the utopian optimal. She explains:

> the true trance medium sits there and just goes, they blank out completely and someone takes them over, their features, their body (Goldingay 2006a)

J. is describing, via the bodies and narratives of other full-trance mediums, her optimal state, which requires that the pedestrian-self is fully removed in order that the self-as-other can fully manifest. Yet, she describes herself as a partial-trance medium who, because of fear and, as of yet, undeveloped potential, is unable to reach 'true' trance. She continues:

> I have this thing with letting go. I know I do. It's been the bugbear. I've had messages from my guides – I've had automatic writing – saying we know the problem . . . and it's this thing of not wanting to loose control (I will one day: I know I will). [. . .] I said [to my guides], 'Just zap me!'. And they said, 'We do not zap. We want full, willing participation of the medium.' So, I'm still trying, I mean so far it's been about eighteen years, so give me another twenty-five! [laughter]. (Goldingay 2006a)

In this extract, J. is describing her attempts to surrender her body fully by removing her pedestrian-self in order to make space for another force and achieve the optimum state of full-trance. But, as a partial-trance medium, her pedestrian-self remains in her consciousness while she is channelling a trapped soul. Therefore she needs to manage the relationship of her pedestrian-self and self-as-other throughout the performance.

B. identifies a similar experience and process, but uses different terminology to quantify her two experiences of optimum performance. She explained to me that they were

> [. . .] transcendent. I could tell you the two times I felt it very acutely. [. . .] One was when I was understudying the part of Mrs. Hardcastle. I knew at some point that once we got to the National [Theatre] we would have understudy rehearsals and that sort of thing, but we were not there yet. We were still on tour. [. . . O]ne night I got a 'phone call saying that the actress playing the part would be off, and would I go on the next night?

> [. . .] I knew that evening [of the performance] the only way I would be able to get through the performance, on no rehearsal – you know, no bedded in rehearsal – with less than twenty-four hours notice, was if I completely surrendered ego; if I did not allow fear, self-judgement, desire for approval, or anything like that; I had to be a completely empty vessel into which the words would flow. (Goldingay 2006b)

B.'s description, like J.'s, describes a perceived need for the willing surrender of the pedestrian-self. However, here the language takes a psychological turn where it is the 'ego'-driven self that is removed in order that B. could be a 'completely empty vessel into which the words [given by the playwright to the character] would flow'. As she continued to speak, she contextualized her experiences by attributing the cause of her feeling of transcendence to a supernatural force.

> I can't remember in absolute detail what I experienced in the process of the performance, but I know the overall feeling was, I wasn't quite sure I was in three dimensions, I couldn't quite sense if this was real or not – it was like flying [. . .] I felt very strongly that I had to plug into – this is going to sound so pretentious – a cosmic energy. [. . .] I'm not overly religious though I do believe in something, and before I went on stage that evening I did . . . well, I suppose, pray is the closest thing you can call

it – I said 'please just service me tonight, I'm going to surrender myself to you and please just get me though it'. (Goldingay 2006b)

For B. then – sharing similarities with the practices and pre-performance preparation process of J. – this transcendence is brought about by a process of prayer, surrender and connection to a controlling, yet nurturing, 'cosmic energy'. For both respondents these experiences are ephemeral and unstable, infrequent and hard to create. B. utilizes a set of technical skills in order to come close, at least for some moments of the performance, to transcendence, whereas, for J., although her ability to reach partial-trance is relatively consistent, it is not optimum. I would suggest, then, that for these two respondents, at least, their experience of trance states are – rather than a single, fixed journey from their pedestrian-self to a self-as-other – in fact, a two-phase process of 'trance' and then 'possession' that allows both senses of self to be simultaneously present.

Geoffrey Samuel in his article, 'Possession and self-possession: spirit healing, tantric meditation and āveśa' (2008, p. 2), makes a useful distinction between these two terms by examining their etymology. He explains that 'trance' comes from the Old French, *transir*, 'to die', whereas 'possession' owes its etymological roots to the Latin, *pooidere*, 'to be occupied'. For both B. and J. their process might be described as the 'death' of the pedestrian-self in order to create an 'empty vessel', followed by the 'occupation' of another force enabling the creation of a self-as-other; that is to say, they intentionally enter 'trance' in order to become 'possessed'. But, in this case, two critical points of clarification are required. First, trance – the death of the pedestrian-self – is neither negative nor absolute: for both respondents a strong presence of the pedestrian-self remains. Although, as we will explore in the next section, managing this aspect of the self in order to make space for the occupying force is a difficult process that requires rigorous training. Secondly, possession is welcomed. J. does – with her pre-performance prayers of protection – acknowledge that malevolent forces exist for her, but broadly speaking the occupying force is seen to be nurturing and beneficial.

This two-stage trance/possession process is neither full nor fixed, directly incremental or linear. Both respondents explain that they have an awareness of their pedestrian-selves throughout. For J. her awareness of her pedestrian-self means that she remains a partial-trance medium, someone who has not attained the perfection of 'true' trance. This pedestrian-self is negative, something to be eradicated. Whereas, for B., it is an inevitable, although differently problematic, part of the acting process;

that is to say, an aspect of self that needs to be managed rather than removed.

Both respondents are able to articulate this sense of retaining the pedestrian-self during the shift in consciousness. As J. explains:

> I know I'm here, sitting on this sofa, but I'm also there – drowning. My eyes are closed here, but I can see through her [the trapped soul's] eyes too. (Goldingay 2006a)

In this extract, J. is describing a stable state of dual consciousness with her pedestrian-self and self-as-other existing simultaneously – of being both 'here' and 'there'. However, this binary model becomes problematic when we attempt to quantify the complex and fluid experiences of B. She explains that during a performance she makes active interventions in order to overcome the ongoing difficulty of maintaining a stable relationship between her-selves.

A state of crisis, of not knowing what to do next, often occurs on stage when things go wrong; we forget our lines, other actors forget theirs, or the gun you are about to shoot your adversary with is not in the desk drawer where it should be. This challenges the actor's ability to sustain his or her self-as-other because too much cognitive resource is being demanded by the pedestrian-self's need to resolve the problem. As an experienced actor, B. explains that, when potential fractures do occur, she finds opportunities in the text, something intended for the self-as-other, to placate the demands of the pedestrian-self and sustain the performance.

> [W]ith the part of Masher, my first line was 'I dunno, I dunno' and often, when I was having moments when I thought, 'I don't know what I'm doing' and I thought, just use that line, 'I dunno, I dunno'. I was consciously blurring the boundary between being in the scene and doing the negotiation of the scene to . . . erm, hide the fracture? To divert the fracture? Not to make a thing out of the fracture?' (Goldingay 2006b)

Here B. is describing how she is blurring the two realms she is simultaneously occupying. Whereas the expectation would be that the actor would use her experience of reality to generate the imagined world of the performance, she explains that, in fact, in a moment of difficulty – of not knowing what to do next as an actor – the words of her character became inspiration. Because the character's line, was 'I dunno' she could intentionally use those words to express the confusion she was feeling as her pedestrian-self, rather than herself-as-other. This enabled her to articulate her difficulty without interrupting the audience's perception of the world of the performance.

Thus, B. is making a distinction between herself-as-other and her pedestrian-self. These states are not binary and oppositional, but synchronous and intentionally sustained. She manages both states simultaneously to avoid 'fractures': moments when the stable state of optimum performance is challenged, or worse is lost. This occurs because the balance between her plural selves is too heavily weighted towards her pedestrian-self, necessitating, as we will explore in the next section, an intervention on the part of the 'technical-self'.

Three in One: Multiple States of Consciousness

As an actor, B.'s awareness of these multiple states, and how they might be manipulated, is not uncommon. Double or dual consciousness is a well-established discourse in acting theory; this was identified by enlightenment philosopher Diderot (1713–84) in his classic 1751 text, *Encyclopédie, ou dictionnaire raisonné des sciences, des arts et des metiers.*[8] This discourse suggests that during a performance actors do not fully become the characters they are playing,[9] but that they necessarily sustain another sense of self; one that enables them, among other things, to modulate their voice correctly so they can be heard at the back of the theatre, to find their light on stage and to remember their lines. However, through an examination of B.'s and J.'s experiences of optimum performance, a development of this position has become possible. Thus, I suggest, rather than these performances being an embodiment of dual consciousness, that they are, in fact, embodiments of three overlapping states of consciousness. These are the pedestrian-self, the self-as-other, and the 'manager' of these selves during the performance, the technical-self.

Understanding how consciousness works, or 'the hard problem',[10] is an ongoing discussion for science, social science and the humanities. It identifies that a binary model, whether a description of two simultaneously occurring states of consciousness embodied in the 'here' and 'there' approach, or simply a description of a drug-induced altered state of consciousness, does not fully account for the complexities of consciousness. This informs an evolving discourse in theatre, drama and performance studies, which is intimately interwoven with an increasingly popular rejection of Cartesian mind–body dualism, where the 'theatre of consciousness' is no longer seen as a material absolute. In acting theory the traditional model of dual consciousness accounts for the pedestrian-self and the self-as-other. It also explains the necessary shift in focus from, or quieting of, the pedestrian-self in order to create space for the self-as-other – a process where one enters into 'trance' and 'dies' in order to become 'possessed' and 'occupied'. The binary model also supports well-established narratives in Spiritualism which suggests the performers, even if they are intentionally entering the state of trance, are only active at its inception and become passive at the point of occupation. This contradicts what B. explicitly, and J. implicitly, describe – the selves' continually active role during a performance.

In development of this position, I suggest that another self is also at work here: the technical-self – the self who manages the relationship between the pedestrian-self and the self-as-other by intentionally carrying out specific tasks, informed by pre-performance training, in order to manage the stability of the performers' performance. This is exemplified by J.'s explanation of how she mitigated for tiredness in order to 'tune-in' (Goldingay 2006a), and B.'s description of using the text to allow her pedestrian-self to express its anxiety while her self-as-other was simultaneously able to continue communicating with the audience.

Clinical neurologist and Zen practitioner, James Austin, in *Zen and the Brain* (1999) and its companion book *Zen-Brain Reflections* (2006), following Charles Tart, offers an intriguing alternative model to the problematic binary. He describes a model where multiple overlapping states of consciousness operate simultaneously as a

> conglomerate of subsystems, functioning in many separate, but interacting, dynamic configurations. [. . .] Each subsystem might be operating at a high, normal, or low level. And each might be invested with attention to a greater or lesser degree. Given all these permutations, any single one of our discrete states of consciousness would seem to be a mere temporary aggregation of substates, a 'temporal clustering of the content and organization of consciousness'. (Austin 1999, pp. 306–8)

This is a useful model if we think about the performer as a 'conglomerate of subsystems' or, in this case, a conglomerate of selves, and recognize that the performers are investing different selves with different levels of attention. During a performance, however, this conglomerate of selves is not a discrete fixed state: the performers reflexively and proactively manage their selves – controlling the demands of the pedestrian-self in order to protect the needs of the self-as-other. They are, metaphorically, applying a method of volume control. They do this by using techniques learnt during pre-performance training in order to sustain an optimum state.

Both B. and J. explain that they make interventions during performances; that is to say, they change the volume of their competing selves. This process of volume control requires another self to operate it: the technical-self. This is the reflexive aspect of the performer that identifies when a 'fracture' is going to take place and takes action to prevent it. Once equilibrium is restored, the technical-self can operate, almost silently, until it is needed again at the next point of fracture. The multiple selves work harmoniously to sustain an optimal state, to making an 'other' perceptible to an audience, by operating at differing volumes at different times during a performance. This requires a proactive trance-performer, an active empty vessel.

The Active Empty Vessel and Sustaining the 'other'

Pre-performance training, for J., took the form of psychic development circles and individual practice that centred on meditation, automatic writing and a participatory apprenticeship, where she learnt through séance-based experience. For B., like J., the training process was both practice and archive driven. Embodied knowledge, gained through psychophysical training practices, was of equal importance to cognitive/imagined processes and experience gained from live performance. The unpredictability of live performance creates the stressful conditions where this pre-performance training is applied and tested. In this final section, I will explore how both B. and J. describe the role their technical-self takes during difficult performances.

In the following extract J. describes a performance that is not optimum: the self-as-other is not heard by the audience. In this performance the technical-self is unable to make a sufficient intervention to turn down the pedestrian-self's volume.

> I was seeing someone Scuba Diving – sort of in my mind. I had a feeling that there was a need somewhere but I wasn't able to relax enough and I wasn't able to pick up. And I was told [by Spirit] that my batteries were very low – I've been tired since we got back from holiday. And, although I was physically feeling the energy, I couldn't at that point change it, and use it to channel, which was interesting because it highlighted for me how different it is when I do. (Goldingay 2006a)

Here then, when J. cannot channel and cannot achieve a state of partial-trance, she is *via-negativa*, able to articulate the intrinsic processes at work because much of her attention is invested in her pedestrian-self. Without the physical demands placed on her pedestrian-self when she is channelling she has more space to perceive and reflexively consider the processes at work.

She went on to explain how she feels, by comparison, when a performance is successful; that is to say, when she 'picks up' and 'changes' the energy and begins to channel.

> I sit there and can feel the general hum and all of a sudden it's as if my aura's being pressed on, it's almost like a hum – I mean I don't hear a hum, but it's sort of like that vibrational (*sic*) feeling [. . .] My heart rate accelerates and I feel my breathing start to change. If it's quite a traumatic rescue then it's sometimes quite an emotional and physically difficult thing. [. . .] I know that I'm still on the chair but I am that person as well. First, they start talking to me, and then, I'm almost seeing what happened, well, I *am* seeing what's happened – living through it. They see through my eyes and I through theirs. It's a sort of take over. (Goldingay 2006a)

Throughout her interview J. described her relationship with her body as a difficult one. It was an incompliant instrument that would not fully submit to the will of Spirit, one that resonated with an increased heart rate and breathing caused by her fear of 'letting go'. And this fear of letting go, this retention of her pedestrian-self, caused an even greater awareness of her body. She explained what happened when she described her experience of a particularly traumatic rescue at the post-séance debrief to another circle member.

> Afterwards she said to me, 'Do you know where she was?' and I'll say 'Oh yes' I mean the one who was buried alive – that was really scary and I knew exactly what had happened, you know I couldn't breathe. Once I was actually drowning and I could actually feel it, actually feel it! P. was next to me once and she thought I was going to have a heart attack – I'm absolutely gasping for breath and yet I know I'm me. Now that's the strange thing, how can you be you and know you are safe, but I'm there and I know that someone is still using me. (Goldingay 2006a)

After such a graphic explanation it is easier to understand why, for J., to be in full trance – and not to remember what had taken place during a channelling – is preferable to 'living' through it. But as a partial-trance medium, she does not follow the classic form and become a passive empty vessel that is occupied by another. She is, in fact, active throughout the performance. Her technical-self uses pre-performance training techniques to manage the almost overwhelming sensations in her pedestrian-body so that the trapped soul, expressed through herself-as-other, can be perceived by the watching audience. She is testing the boundaries of the human.

The active intervention of the technical-self is something B. is able to articulate explicitly. She too is testing the boundaries of the human by balancing the relationship of active intervention while being an empty vessel for the 'other' to fill. But, for her, this experience is less physically distressing, although not physically or psychologically easy. For B., to be in an optimal state is to have her technical-self engage pre-performance training and preparation in order to enable her 'to fly' in close relationship to a cosmic energy.

Conclusions

These optimal states – states of partial-trance for J. and transcendence for B. – are not snapshots, fixed in time, where the performance freezes. They are continuously active negotiations between the conglomerate of pedestrian-self, technical-self and self-as-other. These negotiations seek to sustain a state of optimum performance in order to avoid fractures where both the performers' and the audiences' perception of the 'other' are interrupted. Both B. and J. identified with the concept of becoming an empty vessel for the energy of the 'others' to fill. But this did not follow a traditional model of active-trance followed by passive-possession (where they simply abdicated their pedestrian-self) as a binary, full-trance model of being 'here' or 'there' might suggest. Instead they used a portfolio of psycho-physical pre-performance techniques to manage the competing volumes of the pedestrian-self and self-as-other. This process was facilitated by the monitoring and managing technical-self. The optimal state where, by testing the boundaries of the human, the audience could perceive an 'other', was, for these two performers, a process undertaken by an active empty vessel.

For all their rich similarities there were two key distinctions in the respondents' explanations of what was taking place. The first, unsurprising from the outset, was that both respondents perceived the source of their 'other' differently. For J. this was a trapped soul who was brought to her attention by Spirit. For B. this was a character, but a creation that was a combination of her, the text, and divine intervention/inspiration. The second distinction is more complex and involves the relationship between the pedestrian-self and the body. For B. her body was a biddable vessel she could proactively control and enjoy. Her ability to reach its full potential was only challenged by the ego. For J. the role of the pedestrian-self was also significant, but in relationship to her body. The body itself was a faulty device that would not fully yield, was exhausted by the channelling and, potentially, could be taken over by unwanted energy. For her, her body – until she was able to lose her pedestrian-self completely and become a 'true' trance medium – was an unreliable ally.

We might then see this divergence in terms of a postmodern versus late-modern reading of spirit-possession. A postmodern reading suggests that texts, and many experiences, are unreliable truths for performers like B., and the only source of 'real' truth lies in the somatic experience of living breathing flesh. Whereas a late-modern reading – where the residue of the past is carried forward into a new present – might suggest that it is the body that is at fault for its unwillingness to surrender to a higher residual meta-narrative. Yet here – where belief and make-believe, life narratives and the construction of personal identity, altruism and performance meet – perhaps, both readings are true.

Notes

1   For an interesting early anthology that includes the work of noted performance ethnographers, Schechner and Zarrilli, who are still conducting research, see Schechner and Appel (1990).
2   This is a method posited by Schechner (2002) as a useful means of examining something that is not explicitly performance in order to reveal new information about it and its processes.
3   For an interesting exploration of the cultural and historical interweavings of theatre and mediumship see Owen's excellent books (1989, pp. 54–5, 73; 2004, pp. 1–16, 63–6).
4   I am using the term performer, rather than actor, in order to make a clear distinction from the way the term 'actor' is used in some types of social sciences writing, that is to say, to indicate someone who is undertaking an embodied action, rather than it being a term to denote someone's profession or a politicized participant demonstrating agency.
5   Notions of the sacred in theatre have been re-emphasized recently in the work of Yarrow et al. (2007) and Innes (1984). See Bates (1986) for how 'the way of the actor' is claimed as a path towards enlightenment. For information on how yoga, vedic breath techniques, shamanic journeying and martial arts have

been appropriated into pre-performance training techniques, see Zarrilli (2002), Karafistan (2003), and training courses and workshops by COSmino (*sic*) (http://www.cosmino.org/en/strony/shaman.htm) and J. O. Hughes (http://spiritualpsychologyofacting.com/).

[6] For an excellent overview of the negotiations at work in the actor/character relationship see Kirby (2002).

[7] For a fuller discussion of the relationship between the medium and the audience in demonstrations of platform mediumship see Goldingay (2009).

[8] For a clear discussion of the relationship of Diderot to the development of the discourse and practice of acting, see Roach (1993).

[9] This position appears to be counter intuitive, particularly when it is compared to how the media, and popular actors themselves, describe 'method-actors' living and 'becoming' their characters for weeks at a time in order to deliver a convincing performance.

[10] For a detailed discussion see Blackmore (2003) and O'Shea (2005).

Bibliography

Austin, J. (1999), *Zen and the Brain*. Massachusetts: MIT Press.

Austin, J. (2006), *Zen-Brain Reflections*. Massachusetts: MIT Press.

Bates, B. (1986), *The Way of the Actor: A Path to Knowledge and Power*. Boston: Shambhala.

Blackmore, S. (2003), *Consciousness: An Introduction*. Abingdon: Hodder and Stoughton.

COSmino (sic) 'From the Shaman to the Actor'. Available at: http://www.cosmino.org/en/strony/shaman.htm (accessed 30 March 2009).

Diderot, D. (1967 [1751]), *Encyclopédie, ou dictionnaire raisonné des sciences, des arts et des metiers*. Stuttgart: Friedrich Frommann.

Evans, M. (1997), *Billy Grows up in Spirit: A Cockney Lad Returns After Death to Tell His Story*. Exeter: Whole Being Centre.

Goldingay, S. (2006a), 'Interview with partial-trance medium, J.: May 2006'. Exeter: Unpublished.

Goldingay, S. (2006b), 'Interview with actor, B.: July 2006'. Pangbourne: Unpublished.

Goldingay, S. (2006c), 'Interview with sitter, L: March 2006'. Exeter: Unpublished.

Goldingay, S. (2009), 'Watching the Dead Speak: the role of the audience, imagination, and belief in Late Modern Spiritualism', in *Scripta Instituti Donneriani Aboensis*, vol. 21. Abo, Finland: Donner Insitute, 25–43.

Hughes, J. O. 'The Spiritual Psychology of Acting.' Available at: http://spiritual psychologyofacting.com/ (accessed 30 March 2009).

Innes, C. (1984), *Holy Theatre, Ritual and the Avant Garde*. Cambridge: Cambridge University Press.

Karafistan, R. (2003), '"The spirits wouldn't let me be anything else": shamanic dimensions in theatre practice today', *New Theatre Quarterly*, 19 (2), 150–68.

Kirby, M. (2002), 'On Acting and Not-Acting', in P. Zarrilli (ed.), *Acting Re-Considered*. London: Routledge, pp. 40–52.

Mangan, M. (2007), *Performing Dark Arts: A Cultural History of Conjuring*. Bristol: Intellect Books.

O'Shea, M. (2005), *The Brain: A Very Short Introduction*. Oxford: Oxford University Press.

Owen, A. (1989), *The Darkened Room: Women, Power and Spiritualism in Late Victorian England*. Chicago: University of Chicago Press.

Owen, A. (2004), *The Place of Enchantment: British Occultism and the Culture of the Modern*. Chicago: University of Chicago Press.

Roach, J. R. (1993), *The Player's Passion: Studies in the Science of Acting*. Michigan: University of Michigan Press.

Samuel, G. (2008), 'Possession and self-possession: spirit healing, tantric meditation and āveśa', *Diskus*, 9. Available at: http://www.basr.ac.uk/diskus/diskus9/samuel.htm (accessed 30 March 2009).

Schechner, R. (2002), *Performance Studies: An Introduction*. London: Routledge.

Schechner, R. and Appel, W. (1990), *By Means of Performance: Intercultural Studies of Theatre and Ritual*. Cambridge: Cambridge University Press.

Yarrow, R. with Chamberlain, F., Haney, W. S., II, Lavery, C. and Malekin, P. (2007), *Sacred Theatre*. Bristol: Intellect Books.

Zarrilli, P. (ed.) (2002), *Acting Re-Considered*. London: Routledge.

Chapter 13

On the Transformation of the Spirit Possession Film: Towards Rouch as 'Emergent Method'

Saër Maty Bâ

Like anthropologists, ethnographic filmmakers must beware of a certain arrogance which amount to a more intellectualized form of the 'white man's burden'. Film is a product of industrial civilization, but this does not mean that it cannot be employed effectively by people in transitional societies. One sometimes feels that Jean Rouch has tried to make the kinds of films about West Africans that West Africans might have made had they had the means. Some, like Ousmane Sembène, have now found the means and are skilful filmmakers. (MacDougall 1976 [1969], p. 149)[1]

The representation of trance serves as a referential core for the study of ritual and transgression that has been a touchstone of the French sociological method since [Émile] Durkheim. (Bloom 2008, p. 32)

Recognizing that the presumption that realistic cinema somehow achieves a greater degree of accuracy and/or authenticity is naïve, and should at least inspire anthropologically trained filmmakers to look towards other filmic forms (the experimental, the performative) in order to explore the freedoms of narrative and stylistic unorthodoxy. (Anderson 2003, p. 74)[2]

French engineer turned ethnographer-cineaste Jean Rouch (1918–2004) was always 'in-between'. From his collaborators' interviews to academic publications drawn on in this chapter, Rouch comes across as a liminal, fluid and elusive figure. The same can be said of his prolific and complex cinema.[3]

This chapter focuses on two of the most discussed films within Rouch's impressive oeuvre – *Les Maîtres fous / The Mad Masters* (1955, hereafter *Maîtres fous*) and *Les Tambours d'avant: Tourou et Bitti* (1972, hereafter

Tambours d'avant), both set in Africa – and selected British academic perceptions of Rouch's cinema; it has two interconnected aims. First, I will give
a brief account of the fierce competition taking place between, across/
through disciplines and practices about how past, present and future meanings of Rouch's cinema should be interpreted and defined. This contest
and rivalry is born out of the Anglophone world's (read 'Britain and the
USA') so-called renewed interest in Rouch's cinema. Rouch's 'method'/
méthode Rouch (to be analysed shortly) and our own methods of perceiving
his cinema (i.e. as writers, readers, viewers and/or critics) are crucial to my
second aim in this chapter, which is to argue that, in order to find new/
viable points of entry into Rouch's cinema, we need to use its recurrent
themes (e.g. 'African' spirit possession) as thinking tools because they
answer questions crucial to this cinema's foundations and legacies.

In other words, with transforming the spirit-possession film in mind, I
will suggest that scholars more recently drawn to Rouch's cinema and not
arguing that they 'deserve', let alone need, 'the legacy, the Rouchian birth-
right' (Renov 2007, p. xv) have to start, through selected Rouch films, a
series of modest enquiries on Rouch's cinema. Inasmuch as such enquiries
may be polemical from the outset, the approach from which they spring is
currently the only way Rouch's cinema may be problematized anew and
modestly. In this line of thinking, in addition to indentifying problems with
discussions of Rouch's films, this chapter is divided into the following three
parts: 'Rouch's "African" films: transformation of the spirit-possession film',
'A question of Method 1: of themes and bases in *méthode Rouch*' and 'A
question of Method 2: *ciné-dialogue* and *ciné-transe*'.

Rouch's death found Anglophones lagging behind Francophones in
awareness, and serious consideration, of an innovative and prolific filmmaker and his cinema. Joram ten Brink's highly successful conference
Building Bridges: The Cinema of Jean Rouch (*Institut Français*, London: October
2004) was an attempt to remedy this situation by juxtaposing and inter-
facing past and current perspectives on Rouch as well as screening most of
his films. However, there is a clear sense in which this conference and the
book of the same name (Wallflower Press, 2007) are part of the above-
mentioned contest. As cases in point, both have attempted to create endur-
ing reference texts about Rouch's meanings for the Anglophone world,
while the book contains complaints like 'it is appalling how under-
appreciated Rouch remains in the Anglophone world' and 'It has long
been a scandal that so few of Rouch's films can be seen outside of France'
(Renov 2007, pp. xiii–xiv, xv). Moreover, inasmuch as ten Brink's multidisciplinary publication is very useful, its overall approach seems not to

have found new/viable points of entry into Rouch's cinema and its connections to the idea of cinematic 'method'. This is because ten Brink allows overwritten, pretentious and/or non-groundbreaking pieces to creep in and undermine the 'Foundations and Legacies' section of his book, while submerging potentially groundbreaking contributions in another section given the bland and vague title of 'The Films'. This situation is unfortunate due to the interesting historical moment the Anglophone world is currently experiencing vis-à-vis Rouch and his cinema. Nonetheless, what seems more useful than assessing this moment is spelling out what overall perspective the scholarship on Rouch tends to adopt while pointing out exceptions to this dominant outlook. Thus, if we take the book *Building Bridges* as example, Paul Henley (social anthropologist and ethnographic filmmaker), Brice Ahounou (anthropologist and journalist) and Réda Bensmaïa (Professor of French) are, among others, the very few exceptions within a scholarship on Rouch generally involved in 'projective appropriation', 'ventriloquist identification' or a combination of both (to be analysed shortly). As we shall see through Rouch's cinematic method, these latter perspectives are unsuited for grasping connections between Rouch's cinema and spirit possession.[4]

Rouch's 'African' Films: Transformation of the Spirit-Possession Film

Possession/spirit-possession ceremony/ritual is the subject matter of as many as forty of Rouch's films. These films are predominantly about the *Songhay* and the *Zarma*, two closely related peoples living in Western Niger, Mali and Burkina Faso, and whose traditional life and rituals involve no masks (unlike most African traditional life and rituals such as the *Dogon*'s whom Rouch filmed too).

In the context of spirit-possession filming, the themes and bases of Rouch's cinematic method, as well as filmic examples to be discussed below, lead to two questions: 'what can we learn about "African" spirit possession from Rouch's "African" films?' and 'How has *méthode Rouch* transformed the filming of spirit possession (in Africa, and from a European's perspective), if at all?'

Regarding the first question, we shall see that Rouch's 'African' films teach us three main lessons about 'African' spirit possession. First, interpretations of 'African' spirit possessions need to stay away from Émile Durkheim's *Elementary Forms of Religious Life* (1912) and the Durkeimian legacy that both cultivate and perpetuate a 'philosophy of conquest' granting Europeans the preposterous responsibility of 'shaping Africa's knowledge' (Mudimbe 1988, pp. 69, 68), among other fallacies. Stated differently, and signifying on Peter J. Bloom's quotation at the beginning of this chapter, Rouch's 'African' films are less about studying ritual and transgression than transgressing traditional studies of possession ritual; they are not so much about perpetuating a standard of French (sociological) method than mocking and smashing it in order to re-shape/re-invent (cinematic) method with different tools. Secondly, we shall learn from Rouch's 'African' films that 'African' spirit possessions seem ungraspable through the traditional Western-ethnographic-cinema perspective. In this chapter's context, we will need to heed Réda Bensmaïa's and Kevin Taylor Anderson's respective suggestions that distance and the fuzzy concept of objectivity need to be abandoned (Bensmaïa 2007, p. 77) while we 'look towards other filmic forms (the experimental, the performative) in order to explore the freedoms of narrative and stylistic unorthodoxy' (Anderson 2003, p. 82). Thirdly, we shall see that Rouch's 'African' films teach us that, 'in the field of "shared anthropology", Rouch has the reputation of "seeing gods" via his camera, so say those who embody the gods for the ethnographer' (Ahounou 2007, p. 66). This is because Rouch's handheld camera technique enabled him 'to penetrate into the reality, rather than leaving it to unroll itself in front of the observer' (Rouch 2003 [1973], p. 38).

Concerning the second question, we shall see that *méthode Rouch* has transformed spirit-possession filming through its own ontology, that is, the refining and embodiment of participatory camerawork, shared anthropology, *ciné-transe* and *ciné-dialogue*. Simultaneously, Rouch resembles the *Dogon* people's sky-god/spirit of thunder *Dongo*. In effect, when Rouch accidently broke his tripod in Africa, he decided to work without tripods, thus creating a strange if not unprecedented relationship between capturing possession images and camera movement.[5] While contemporary research in agronomy shows that lightning can release nitrogen, the *Dogon* believe that *Acacia Albida* (a tree also known as *Gao Beri*) attracts *Dongo*'s attention and can be struck repeatedly by lightening but carries on living. Brice Ahounou who makes this connection between agronomy and the spirit world goes on to suggest that '*Dongo* could be fertilising the earth, a fascinating avenue by which to establish [. . .] the fertilising power of this god, the paradoxical liberator of nitrogen' (Ahounou 2007, p. 64). Consequently, should Rouch's own liberation of the camera in Africa not lead us to ask – at least – if Rouch could be the paradoxical liberator of ethnographic film? I shall come back to this question in the conclusion of this chapter. Meanwhile, I will establish how Rouch's cinematic method transforms the spirit-possession film through the method's themes and bases, as well as examples from Rouch's films.

A Question of Method 1: Of Themes and Bases in
Méthode Rouch

Projective appropriation

> happens when the reader/viewer projects him or herself, his or her belief world, onto the texts. The most common example of this practice happens when a theoretical or interpretive framework elaborated for and within one cultural sphere is projected onto the signifying practices of another cultural sphere [. . .] Projective appropriation accompanies efforts to internationalise a restrictive regime of making sense. (Willemen 1994, pp. 212–13)

Ventriloquist identification, the obverse of projective appropriation,

> happens when someone presents him or herself as the mouthpiece for others, as if the speaker were immersed in some ecstatic fusion with the others' voices and were speaking from within that other social or cultural space. (Willemen 1994, p. 213)

As stated at the beginning of this chapter, Rouch's method/*méthode Rouch* and our own methods of perceiving his cinema are crucial to the current historical moment of Anglophone Rouch appreciation. Thus, while avoiding projective appropriation and ventriloquist identification, I will approach Rouch's cinema as a tapestry of recurrent themes (such as ethno-fiction, psychodrama-migration and possession) and bases in order to unpick his cinematic method. In so doing, I will suggest answers to the questions on this cinema's foundations and legacies asked above. Incidentally, it seems crucial to focus on the period 1950s–1970s, from *Maîtres fous* (1955) to *Tambours d'avant* (1972) and Rouch's seminal essay 'Man and Camera' (1973), in order to begin problematizing Rouch anew. This is because *Maîtres fous* is one of the most divisive films in old and new interpretations of Rouch, *Tambours d'Avant* and 'Man and Camera' are standard texts illustrating Rouch's trademark camerawork, while the 1950s–1970s period is suited to the thematic approach of Rouch's cinema I am suggesting in this chapter.[6] I will now turn to the themes and bases of *méthode Rouch*.

As a visual anthropologist based in Niger, Rouch had informants. *Moi, un Noir / Me, a Black Man* (1959) depicts his *Nigériens* (Niger national) informants' staged lives in a ghetto of Abidjan (Treichville, Ivory Coast) where they act out fantasies linked to Western icons like boxer Sugar Ray Robinson and Hollywood actor Edward G. Robinson, as well as recount their daily joys and pains. As a result, *Moi, un Noir* was unprecedented in visual anthropology, and to some extent in cinema for it brought 'a brand new cinematic method . . . [that] fused documentary, fiction, improvisation and feedback techniques' (ten Brink 2007b, p. 3). Yet, more important than both fusion in *Moi, un Noir* and Rouch's ethno-fictional films is the fact that Rouch made 'fiction' ethnographic, as David MacDougall (1976 [1969], p. 137) incisively argued forty years ago: these films 'have had much success in defying that automatic association of fictional techniques with falsehood and due to [Rouch] having introduced fiction into documentary rather than the other way round'. A further illustration of fiction as ethnography can be found in *La Pyramide humaine* (1959, hereafter *pyramide humaine*) in which Rouch gathers black and white High School students in Abidjan to explore issues like 'race' and colonization: Rouch invented a situation, provoked the participants and, from the outset, revealed the film's formal structure. Thus, *pyramide humaine* was a prequel to Rouch's *Chronique d'un été / Chronicle of a Summer* (1961), co-directed with Edgar Morin, *Jaguar* (1967), a feature film about the eventful daily adventures of young *Nigériens* men's journey to the Gold Coast (Ghana), and *Petit à petit / Little by Little* (1971) in which three Africans go to Paris to conduct a fake(d) anthropological study on unsuspecting white Parisians.

As can be seen from the above-mentioned films, Rouch's ethno-fiction is in turn closely linked to psychodrama (a form of participation in filmmaking) and migration. Psychodrama led *Moi, un Noir*'s 'Eddie Constantine', also known as Federal Agent Lemmi Caution, to (con)fuse reel life and real life to the point of being jailed for three months, while making a number of students from *pyramide humaine* to fail their examinations.[7] Regarding migration, *Moi, un Noir* features migrants from Niger; *pyramide humaine* mixes French and (rural and urban) Ivorian students; *Petit à petit* reverses playfully the white Western anthropological gaze; while *Maîtres fous* features the *Haouka*, a Haousa-language word meaning 'crazy' (Stoller 1992, p. 145), representing 'Songhay spirits that burlesque European colonial personages' (Stoller 1995, p. 5) in a cult whose exclusively *Nigériens* members are migrant workers to Accra, Gold Coast. Interestingly, *Maîtres fous* is also about a spirit-possession ceremony/ritual, the theme in Rouch's method to which I will now turn.

As already mentioned, possession/spirit-possession ceremony/ritual is the subject matter of as many as forty Rouch films predominantly about the *Songhay*, the *Zarma*, and the *Dogon*. At their most basic, the possession ceremonies/rituals Rouch filmed were dedicated to rainmaking (e.g. *Tambours d'Avant*), new gods of power (*Maîtres fous*) or, more generally, to what Michael Chanan (2007, p. 93) calls connections between the 'real' world and its double.

I have suggested that Rouch's cinematic method is made of interconnected themes and bases. Before discussing this method, it is worth laying out its foundations first, not least because they are useful in appreciating *méthode Rouch*'s originality vis-à-vis and relevance to 'new' interpretations of spirit possession. These foundations are: explorer and geologist turned filmmaker Robert Flaherty's film *Nanook of the North* (1915), Soviet experimental cinema filmmaker Dziga Vertov, and Rouch's interaction with various schools of thought, colonial projects, and black art.

The young Rouch was passionate about Flaherty's *Nanook of the North*, 'conventionally the first documentary' (Winston 2000, p. 19), 'probably the first true ethnographic film, for it was both a film and inherently ethnographic [. . .] despite certain fabrications which ethnographic film-makers would now probably avoid' (MacDougall 1976 [1969], p. 138).[8] It is no accident, therefore, that aspects of Flaherty's method such as intimate knowledge of his subjects, including their customs and language, spending years filming them, and seeking out 'their reactions to their own representation on film' (MacDougall 1976 [1969], p. 138), would be found, nuanced, in Rouch's own approach, as we shall see.

From Vertov came the idea of *cinéma vérité* in which one edits the film as it is shot.

> For Vertov, body and camera are one; the machine-body acquires consciousness as it cine-records. But the camera does not record objective reality; it creates a cine-reality. In this way the camera, an extension of the filmmaker's body-mind, participates consciously in filming life. (Stoller 1992, pp. 102–3)

Only Vertovian corporeal fusion of man and machine and man-machine's conscious participation in filming would be found, nuanced, in Rouch's film practice.

In terms of various schools of thought, colonial projects and black art, Rouch interacted with: Surrealism and its dialogue with anthropology and ethnography in the 1930s; the *Dogon* world that ethnographer Marcel

Griaule, an active supporter of the Nazi-controlled Vichy regime, opened to Rouch in the 1940s;[9] European (i.e. French and British) colonial projects; and Paris's pre-World War II Modern, primitivist craze for *L'art nègre* / Negro Art, from Louis Armstrong's Jazz to the sumptuous body of Josephine Baker (Henley 2007, p. 43). Baker was the Empress of the French Music Hall and an uncontested Star in French cinema, despite being cast repeatedly in stereotypical roles, among other racist visualizations of her black body at play within French popular and visual cultures. For example, in Edmond T. Gréville's film *Princesse Tam-Tam* / *Princess Tam-Tam* (1935), Baker is Tunisian shepherd girl Alwina who, despite a white male aristocrat's attempts to present her to Parisian high society as an Indian Princess, rejects 'Civilization' so as to revert to her primitive lifestyle and simple nature. Such return is epitomized by Alwina's inability to resist tom-toms (*tam-tams*) to whose beats she responds by dancing in trance/as if possessed.[10]

In summary then, *méthode Rouch* is made of a tapestry of themes and sprung from very problematic foundations. Rouch interacted with these foundations through the mediation of visual culture, hence the need to connect these problematic issues to both his cinematic method of filming contentious issues like 'African' possession and my main focus within this method: camerawork.

A Question of Method 2: *Ciné-dialogue* and *Ciné-transe*

Rouch's cinematic method draws from and connects the above-mentioned themes and bases. This method is striking because of ways in which Rouch crafted it not only from these disparate themes and problematic bases, but also through minimal cinematic influences. In 'The Camera and Man' (Rouch 2003 [1973], p. 32), Rouch borrows a phrase from Luc de Heusch to name one of the main characteristics of this method, that is, 'participatory camera'. Equally referred to as 'participating camera' (2003 [1973], p. 39) and 'participant' camera, it was an idea inspired by Flaherty's own filmmaking style and ethos, although it must be pointed out that Rouch did not copy/adopt blindly this or any other aspects of *Nanook of the North*'s director's work (or Vertov's, for that matter). As a case in point, rather than imitate Flaherty's mere search for his film subjects' reactions to their representation, Rouch invited the people he filmed into the actual making of such a representation/the film. In so doing, simultaneously, Rouch's method seems to achieve four things: it grants the people he filmed a self-expression devoid of (Rouch's) projective appropriation or ventriloquist identification interference; it reveals their wish-fulfilment, or how they would like to come across to film audiences; it 'enables us [read "Western audiences"] to approach aspects of their culture of which they [might be] unconscious'; and may help the people Rouch filmed to 'come to view themselves and their culture with new eyes' (MacDougall 1976 [1969], p. 140). Similarly, while Flaherty's cinema stressed the poetic and the exotic over 'ethnographic content' (Anderson 2003, p. 76), Rouch's did not.

Thus, 'participating camera' actively involves the filmed people in the filmmaking process and creates a *ciné-dialogue*/cine-dialogue within which 'knowledge is no longer a stolen secret' to be used later 'in another place, at another time, by another culture' (see Cowie 2007, p. 208). Instead, the film being shaped 'is judged not by a thesis committee but by the very people the anthropologist went out to observe. This extraordinary technique of "feedback", which I would translate as "audiovisual reciprocity" ',[11] is taken seriously by 'participating camera' to the point of becoming a two-way exchange between the filmmaker and the people filmed for the reason that 'Serious visual anthropology is not possible without restoring "the Other" 's image to him or her, without making them share in the film that has been shot', but also without practising a reciprocal approach that shares 'the risk and, for the first time in ethnology, [. . .] the rights of the auteur' (Ahounou 2007, p. 66). In this line of thinking then, while participating camera avoids projective appropriation and ventriloquist identification, it and Rouch are not mere observers either for, while guiding Rouch towards 'cinematographic creativity' and places he would 'otherwise never risk going', 'the [participating] camera becomes a magic object that can unleash or accelerate the phenomenon of possession', a phenomenon from which Rouch is not exempt. In fact, participating camera puts Rouch in a state of cinematic trance, hence his notion of *ciné-transe*/cine-trance:

Leading or following a dancer, priest, or craftsman, [the cameraman-director] is no longer himself, but a mechanical eye accompanied by an electronic ear. I is this strange state of transformation that takes place in the filmmaker that I have called, analogously to possession phenomena, 'ciné-trance'. (Rouch 2003 [1973], p. 39)

According to Elisabeth Cowie (2007, p. 9), *ciné-transe* draws from the *Songhay-Zarma*'s notion of double or *bia* (shadow, reflection and spirit, all at once) within a person. *bia* exists in a parallel world, is attached to the human body but may leave it when this body experiences states like sleeping, dreaming, imagination and meditation. Thus, in a possession situation, a disembodied *bia*, replaced by the spirit, is 'preserved in a protective fresh skin'; this process of disembodiment-preservation is synonymous with a voluntary projection of one's double into the world of doubles either for the guidance and defence of the community (the magician's task) or to steal victims' *bia* (a sorcerer's task) (Cowie 2007, p. 209). It follows that if Rouch the cineaste embodies both *transe* and *bia*, and if his *ciné-transe* aesthetics makes him possessed or represents him as being possessed, then Rouch would be split from his *bia* because, as Cowie argues, Rouch hunts doubles like a sorcerer, but also as a magician 'who directs his *bia* and returns the double – the filmed images – in a process which contributes to the community' (2007, p. 209).

I take exception to Cowie's argument and contend that, if Rouch's split from his *bia* and the returning of the double do happen,[12] these would have to take place at the time the film is conceptualized, before shooting begins. Otherwise, we would not be able to differentiate between Rouch, who is not a sorcerer-thief-victimizer of Africa, on the one hand, and the likes of Griaule, 1930s French popular and visual cultures, European colonial ideology, Flaherty and *Nanook of the North* (vis-à-vis the *Inuit* people) and Vertov, on the other hand. Stated differently, without mistaking Rouch's *ciné-transe* for primitivism, *ciné-transe* should be viewed vis-à-vis each of his film projects as 'an indivisible act of creation' (Bloom 2008, p. 33); Rouch can neither be extracted totally from French culture nor be fused indiscriminately with it. Were either approach sound his 'African' possession films, such as *Tambours d'avant* and *Maîtres fous*, would not have remained compelling and/or attract sustained scholarly interest decades after their making. Village priests (*Tambours d'avant*) and a cult's priests (*Maîtres fous*) invited Rouch to film their respective possession ceremonies, film-events to which I will now turn in order to unpick Rouch's *ciné-transe* and indivisible act of creation.

Tambours d'avant shows a ceremony taking place at the *Songhay* village of Simiri (Sahel region), a place prone to scarce rainfalls, rats, locusts and other insects that destroy good crops of millet and create famines; the *Songhay* protect themselves against such adversities by staging possession ceremonies 'to make offerings to the Black Spirits, the deities of the Songhay pantheon that control soil fertility and pests' (Stoller 1992, p. 161). *Tambours d'avant* displays a clear sense of premeditated film length and camera work because Rouch had planned to shoot it in a single take of nine/ten minutes: as a *plan-séquence*.[13] Thus, Rouch's decision to end the film before the ceremony itself[14] might well be tied to technology and aesthetic choices. Yet, Rouch's opening voice-over commentary makes it plain that *Tambours d'avant* is an essay in ethnographic cinema '*à la première personne* / in the first person', and such authorial imprint justifies the film's ending and length (no text is complete, of course). Similarly, *Tambours d'avant*'s experimental status grants it a licence to challenge convention while *ciné-transe* accepts if not allows that Rouch, his camera and *Tambours d'avant* as text return, progressively, to the beginning of the film(ing), to a pre-trance state and pre-possession moment, which is also the point where Rouch and his camera had entered the space of possession or what he calls 'reality'.[15] Indeed, Rouch opens *Tambours d'avant* with:

> *Entrer dans un film c'est plonger dans la réalité, y être à la fois présent et invisible comme ce soir à quatre heures de l'après-midi quand je suivais le Zima Daouda Sito qui attendait à l'entrée de sa concession* / To enter a film is to dive into reality, to be present and invisible in it at once, like that afternoon at four O'clock when I followed *Zima* Daouda Sito who had been waiting for me at the entrance of his courtyard

and concludes the film with: '. . . *et moi, j'aurais dû continuer de filmer mais j'ai voulu faire un film pour retomber sur le début de mon histoire . . .*' / '. . . as for me, I should have continued filming but I have wanted to make a film in order to fall back on my story's beginning . . .'. Therefore, no split being, no sorcerer chasing doubles, not restoration of stolen goods or *bia*; just an indivisible act of creation. What is more, Rouch's smooth but obviously hand-held camerawork, which records the ceremony from four different angles successively as it develops, demonstrates Rouch's absent presence as empathy and spiritual union with *Tambours d'avant*'s 'reality' (i.e. the ceremony and possessed individuals). Similarly, Rouch's camerawork shows that, to the people of *Simiri*, Rouch was not 'a strange foreigner' but rather '"the one who followed the spirits", someone who had been initiated' (Stoller 1992, p. 167). This was a moment devoid of projective appropriation and ventriloquist identification during which Rouch's camera managed to unleash and accelerate possession because Rouch carried on filming the ceremony even though nothing was apparently happening. By bringing his camera close to the drummers, probably, Rouch only wished to show viewers the ancient drums *Tourou* and *Bitti*, but it so happened that the Black Spirit *Kouré* the hyena chose that precise moment to possess Sambou Albéda, Chief of a near-by village and medium to *Haousa* spirits.[16] Unsurprisingly, Rouch wrote 'The Camera and Man' after *Tambours d'avant*, although this does not necessarily make chronology a potent method for analysing his cinematic work. A thematic approach seems more effective and efficient, and is the reason why I have analysed *Tambours d'avant* before *Maîtres fous*, a film to which I will now turn.

At the beginning of *Maîtres fous*, producer Pierre Braumberger states his intentions via a written text from which I quote:

> *Mais il veut le <u>faire participer complètement à un rituel</u> et une solution particulière <u>du problème de la réadpatation, et qui montre indirectement comment certains Africains se représentent notre civilisation occidentale</u>* / But he [the producer] wants the viewer <u>to take part fully in a ritual</u>, a particular solution to <u>the problem of re-adaptation</u> that shows indirectly how some Africans represent <u>our Western civilisation</u> to themselves (<u>my emphases</u>)

Prefacing a film in which spirit-possessed black men slit a dog's throat, drink its gushing blood, and then boil and eat the meat (among other challenges to dominant society and colonial authority), Braumberger's text does more than warn viewers. In effect, since Rouch and his camera take part fully in the ritual, Braumberger's text can be seen as illustrating Rouch's *ciné-dialogue* and *ciné-transe* with the aim of extending if not representing both to Western viewers. Furthermore, not only does migration come across clearly in Braumberger's text ('the problem of re-adaptation'), ethno-fiction is unambiguously announced through 'our Western civilisation', a civilization the *Haouka*-Spirits would challenge in *Maîtres fous* by way of a prop-and-costume mockery/mimicry of British colonial authorities like Governors and army Majors. Symbols of colonial rule are imitated, ridiculed and smashed (literally) by the possessed *Haouka* in front of Rouch's participatory camera/eye: an 'electroshocking appropriation of European power – through the mimetic faculty' (Stoller 1995, p. 133). Last but not least, Braumberger's text prequels Rouch's subsequent explanatory written text which demonstrates that the so-called 'Maîtres fous'/'mad masters', or indeed 'master madmen' (Cooper 2006, p. 39), do not actually suffer from madness but impersonate Western civilization's own insanity in a 'game' Rouch believes to be only '*le reflet de notre civilisation*' / 'the mirror image of our civilisation'. In fact, as Bensmaïa points out, this game is less about mirroring than inverting:

> the essential thing is that this 'game' is obviously not gratuitous: it acts as the 'malign inversion' and the violent reversal of the 'drama' of colonisation and the submission of men to a regime which annihilates them. What is therefore exhibited here is [. . .] the 'cruelty' of the relations that links the colonised to his 'master', the coloniser. (Bensmaïa 2007, p. 77)

The visual track of *Maîtres fous* is comparable to Antonin Artaud's Theatre of Cruelty in which images push viewers beyond 'the anesthetizing influence of language' to a non-compromising clash with 'the culturally repressed dimensions of their being' (Stoller 1995, p. 6). Therefore, the *Haouka*'s openness about their new gods of power and their non-censorship of scenes from *Maîtres fous* are part of a creative process whereby Rouch's decolonized self unmasks colonization and 'compels' viewers 'if not to take a position then at least to shift around' (Bensmaïa 2007, p. 79). Again, no split being, no sorcerer chasing doubles, no restoration of stolen goods or *bia*: just an indivisible Rouchian act of creation. Thus, I would suggest in light of Bensmaïa's and Stoller's useful arguments that the Rouchian act of creation necessarily challenges portrayals in which 'neither blacks nor whites occupy a comfortable position of mastery, least of all over one another' (Cooper 2006, p. 39): *Maîtres fous* is about cruelty, violent reversal, and 'electroshocking appropriation of European power'. Maybe Rouch (film) scholars need to be cruelly and violently reminded that, unless we take Rouch's act of creation as indivisible and uncompromising, Rouch will never be perceived as 'emergent method', something long overdue.

Conclusion: Towards Rouch as 'Emergent Method'

This chapter has demonstrated that Jean Rouch's 'African' films make clear how colonial-imperial-Eurocentric philosophies and their legacies, for example, Durkheim's, are unsuitable for interpretations of 'African' spirit possession. This is because 'African' spirit possession is transgressive; through and beyond mimesis, it smashes European philosophy and symbols, Western ethnography and cinema. As we have seen, Rouch is aware of how important 'the inversion of agency' is to interpretations of spirits' performances 'as condensed ethnography or history' (film/cinema being a potent example) not least because

> In local perspective, it is certain aspects of history and ethnography becoming . . . spirits that are experienced as so strong and compelling that they carry away and take possession of their host or medium.
>
> Yet the dialectics of possession rituals allow the possessed also to become subjects in their own right again. (Behrend and Luig 1999, p. xix)

This variation in positions/roles *per se*, as well as Rouch's crucial awareness of it, supply 'the interstices of not only repeating but critically or ironically commenting on dominant historical versions as well as ethnographies' (Behrend and Luig 1999, p. xix).

In this context of shifts, inversions, and anti-static positionings, the chapter has also demonstrated that, in relation to Rouch's cinema, 'new' interpretations of spirit-possession must engage with ways in which this cinema's non-static themes form one tapestry whose threads appear in distinct film projects; to grasp Rouch's cinematic work on spirit possession means investigating how ethno-fiction, psychodrama-migration, and possession interconnect. Furthermore, I would suggest that Rouch's cinematic method/*méthode Rouch* embraces 'emergent methods':

> Emergent methods are conscious of the link between epistemology (a view on how knowledge is constructed), methodology (the theoretical question[s] that inform our research and how it is carried out), and method (the specific tools used to carry out research). . . . Research methods are often driven by new epistemologies on knowledge production, which in turn create new research questions (methodologies) that require an innovation in methods. (Hesse-Biber and Leavey 2006, pp. xii, xxx)

Indeed, like Rouch's cinematic method, emergent methods operate within and across disciplines, as well as always-already questioning their own ontology while being anti-static. Emergent methods undermine theoretical orthodoxy, rigid area/discipline-specific thinking and studies. These methods also constitute potent alternatives to projective appropriations of and ventriloquist identifications to Rouch's work threatening its foundations and legacies and, therefore, deserving much attention from (film) scholars working on Rouch. Put simply, Jean Rouch is the paradoxical liberator of ethnographic film.

Notes

1. Further references to MacDougall are drawn from this publication.
2. Further references to Anderson are drawn from this article.
3. Collaborator Safi Faye said in an interview: 'Jean Rouch? He was black and he was white' (ten Brink 2007a, p. 162).
4. The above critique of the scholarship on Rouch is centred on book-length studies. This is because the scarcity of books on Rouch in the Anglophone world gives researchers an opportunity to evaluate the field and, more importantly, to theorize new/viable entries into Rouch's cinema away from projective appropriation and ventriloquist identification. Scholars newly drawn to Rouch's

cinema are yet to take such an opportunity seriously, although Sarah Cooper's work on *Ethics and French Documentary* (2002 and 2006), if pursued, may well be an exception.

5   Despite the fact that Rouch (2003 [1973], p. 38) acknowledges other filmmakers as liberators of the camera from the tripod/immobility (Koenig and Koiter who 'opened the way for the travelling shot' in *Corral* (1954, the year Rouch made *Maîtres fous*), a technique soon refined by Michel Brault in *Bientôt Noël* (1959) where his camera follows a bank guard's revolver it is worth pointing out that Brault shot Rouch's and sociologist Edgar Morin's *Chronicle of a Summer* (1961) where he applied his handheld technique as well.

6   For an account of the controversy surrounding *Maîtres fous* from the mid-1950s onwards, including Senegalese Marxist filmmaker Ousmane Sembène's mid-1960s view that Rouch observed Africans 'like insects', see Stoller (1992, pp. 51–53).

7   MacDougall's point (1969 [1976], p. 140) that Rouch became anxious about psychodrama in his films as a result of these two episodes is accurate. However, MacDougall's 'temporarily at least [Rouch] has given up psychodrama' (p. 140) is strange for MacDougall goes on to discuss *Jaguar* outside of this psychodrama-migration framework while it is obvious that the film is a quintessential psychodrama-migration Rouch film. What is more, MacDougall's discussion foregrounds aspects of Rouch's method (use of non-actors, mixing fact and fiction) and the criticism levelled at it in the 1960s (for example, that Rouch presented his view of Africa rather than Africa itself) as if they surfaced for the first time with/as a result of *Jaguar*. In fact, both had already been in place from the late 1950s onwards, at least, with *Moi, un Noir*, a film that MacDougall should probably have focused upon.

8   Flaherty's fabrications and their consequences on Allakariallak/Nanook are summed up well in the following passage: 'Allakariallak connived at his own representation as a technical naïf (which he wasn't), living in an igloo (which he didn't) and re-enacting his father's generation's experience (when he had a contemporary Inuit lifestyle) – but his agreement to all this allowed Flaherty to take advantage of him' (Winston 2000, p. 139).

9   Imbued with an aggressive colonial mentality assuming that all informants were liars and that 'all indigenous knowledge was fair game' (Henley 2007, p. 45), Griaule's work was part of what V. Y. Mudimbe (1988, p. 67) calls 'European processes of domesticating Africa' and a discourse identifiable with 'European intellectual signs and not with African cultures'. Alongside Griaule, Africa domesticators and Eurocentric thinkers of that time included Placid Temples (*La Philosophie Bantoue/Bantu Philosophy*, 1945) and E. E. Evans-Pritchards (*Social Anthropology and Other Essays*, 1962).

10 Petrine Archer-Straw's *Negrophilia: Avant-Garde Paris and Black Culture in the 1920s* (2000) is a good introduction to visual culture, race, and the black body in 1930s France.

11 Rouch (2003 [1976], p. 44) goes on to suggest that with this type of feedback the anthropologist stops being 'a sort of entomologist observing others as if they were insects (thus putting them down) and [becomes] a stimulator of mutual awareness (hence dignity)'. Thus, Rouch clearly took seriously enough

Ousmane Sembène's mid-1960s criticism, evoked earlier in this chapter, in order to mention it in line with his cinematic method.

[12] One could argue that there is no returning of the double at all because the people Rouch films actively take part in his films' creative processes in the first place. Rouch showed his films to Western audiences too, and a split-*bia* and return-of-the-double argument/theory can hardly apply to his relation with these latter viewers.

[13] Rouch used a Bell & Howell camera.

[14] With his camera, Rouch walked backwards, away from the possession priest *Zima* Daouda Sito's courtyard as the image fades to black.

[15] Eventually the possessed villagers would also go back to a pre-possession moment, off camera.

[16] *Kouré* demands meat (lamb/goat) while Daouda Sorko, who oversees the ceremony, wants reassurances from him that the harvest will be good before an animal is sacrificed: they enter into negotiations. Old lady Tousinysé Wassi's possession by the Black Spirit *Hadjo* would lead to such a sacrifice, but this happened outside *Tambours d'avant*'s *diegesis*.

Bibliography

Ahounou, B. (2007), 'Jean Rouch and the Great Sahelian Drought: Visual Anthropology and the Wrathful Gods at Ganghel', in J. ten Brink (ed.), *Building Bridges: The Cinema of Jean Rouch*. London: Wallflower Press, pp. 59–72.

Anderson, K. T. (2003), 'Toward an anarchy of imagery: questioning the categorization of films as "Ethnographic"', *Journal of Film and Video*, 55 (2–3), 73–87.

Archer-Straw, P. (2000), *Negrophilia: Avant-Garde Paris and Black Culture in the 1920s*. London: Thames & Hudson.

Behrend, H. and Luig, U. (eds) (1999), *Spirit Possession: Modernity and Power in Africa*. Oxford James: Currey; Kampala: Fountain Publishers; Cape Town: David Philip; Madison: University of Wisconsin Press.

Bensmaïa, R. (2007), 'A Cinema of Cruelty', in J. ten Brink (ed.), *Building Bridges: The Cinema of Jean Rouch*. London: Wallflower Press, pp. 73–86.

Bloom, P. J. (2008), 'Tupi or Not Tupi: Natural Man and the Ideology of French Colonial Documentary', in P. J. Bloom (ed.), *French Colonial Documentary: Mythologies of Humanism*. Minneapolis and London: University of Minnesota Press, pp. 1–34.

Chanan, M. (2007), 'Rouch, Music, Trance', in J. ten Brink (ed.), *Building Bridges: The Cinema of Jean Rouch*. London: Wallflower Press, pp. 87–96.

Cooper, S. (2002), 'Otherwise than Becoming: Jean Rouch and the ethics of *Les Maîtres fous*', *French Studies*, 56 (4), 483–4.

Cooper, S. (2006), 'Knowing Images: Jean Rouch's Ethnography', in S. Cooper, *Selfless Cinema? Ethics and French Documentary*. London: Legenda, pp. 31–47.

Cowie, E. (2007), 'Ways of Seeing: Documentary Film and the Surreal of Reality', in J. ten Brink (ed.), *Building Bridges: The Cinema of Jean Rouch*. London: Wallflower Press, pp. 201–20.

Durkheim, É. (1912), *Elementary Forms of Religious Life*. New York: Free Press.

Gheerbrant, A. (2008 [1951]), 'L'homme du Niger', in J. Rouch, *Alors le Noir et le Blanc seront amis: Carnets de mission 1946–1951*. Paris: Mille et une nuits, pp. 9–12.

Henley, P. (2007), 'Jean Rouch and the Legacy of the "Pale Master": *The Sigui Project, 1931–2033*', in J. ten Brink (ed.), *Building Bridges: The Cinema of Jean Rouch*. London: Wallflower Press, pp. 39–58.

Hesse-Biber, S. N. and Leavey, P. L. (eds) (2006), *Emergent Methods in Social Research*. London: Sage.

MacDougall, D. (1976 [1969]), 'Prospects of the Ethnographic Film', in B. Nichols (ed.), *Movies and Methods Volume I*. Berkeley, Los Angeles and London: University of California Press, pp. 135–49.

Mudimbe, V. Y. (1988), *The Invention of Africa: Gnosis, Philosophy, and the Order of Knowledge*. Bloomington and Indianapolis: Indiana University Press.

Renov, M. (2007), 'Preface', in J. ten Brink (ed.), *Building Bridges: The Cinema of Jean Rouch*. London: Wallflower Press, pp. xiii–xv.

Rouch, J. (2003 [1973]), *Ciné-Ethnography*, ed. and trans. S. Feld. Minneapolis: University of Minnesota Press.

Stoller, P. (1992), *Cinematic Griot: The Ethnography of Jean Rouch*. Chicago: Chicago University Press.

Stoller, P. (1995), *Embodying Colonial Memories: Spirit Possession, Power and the Hauka in West Africa*. New York and London: Routledge.

Surugue, B. (2008), 'Les jalons de la vie de Jean', in J. Rouch, *Alors le Noir et le Blanc seront amis: Carnets de mission 1946–1951*. Paris: Mille et une nuits, pp. 283–94.

ten Brink, J. (2007a), 'Petit à Petit: Safi Faye' (Interview), in J. ten Brink (ed.), *Building Bridges: The Cinema of Jean Rouch*. London: Wallflower Press, pp. 155–63.

ten Brink, J. (2007b), 'Introduction', in J. ten Brink (ed.), *Building Bridges: The Cinema of Jean Rouch*. London: Wallflower Press, pp. 1–8.

Willemen, P. (1994), *Looks and Frictions: Essays in Cultural Studies and Film Theory*. London: BFI.

Winston, B. (2000), *Lies, Damn Lies and Documentary*. London: BFI.

Filmography

Nanook of the North (Flaherty, 1915).

Princesse Tam-Tam (Edmond T. Gréville, 1935 / Kino Video, 2005).

Les Maîtres fous (Rouch, 1955).

Moi, un Noir (Rouch, 1959).

Chronique d'un été (Rouch, 1961).

La Pyramide humaine (Rouch, 1961).

Jaguar (Rouch, 1967).

Petit à Petit (Rouch, 1971).

Les Tambours d'avant: Tourou et Bitti (Rouch, 1972).

Index

LIBRARY, UNIVERSITY OF CHESTER